Reforming international environmental governance

Reforming international environmental governance: From institutional limits to innovative reforms

Edited by W. Bradnee Chambers and Jessica F. Green

United Nations University Press

TOKYO · NEW YORK · PARIS

© United Nations University, 2005

The views expressed in this publication are those of the authors and do not necessarily reflect the views of the United Nations University.

United Nations University Press
United Nations University, 53-70, Jingumae 5-chome,
Shibuya-ku, Tokyo, 150-8925, Japan
Tel: +81-3-3499-2811   Fax: +81-3-3406-7345
E-mail: sales@hq.unu.edu
General enquiries: press@hq.unu.edu
http://www.unu.edu

United Nations University Office at the United Nations, New York
2 United Nations Plaza, Room DC2-2062, New York, NY 10017, USA
Tel: +1-212-963-6387   Fax: +1-212-371-9454
E-mail: unuona@ony.unu.edu

United Nations University Press is the publishing division of the United Nations University.

Cover design by Mea Rhee

Printed in the United States of America

UNUP-1111
ISBN 92-808-1111-8

Library of Congress Cataloging-in-Publication Data

Reforming international environmental governance : from institutional limits to innovative reforms / edited by W. Bradnee Chambers and Jessica F. Green.
    p.   cm.
  Includes bibliographical references and index.
  ISBN 9280811118 (pbk.)
  1. Environmental policy – International cooperation. 2. Environmental law, International. I. Chambers, W. Bradnee. II. Green, Jessica F.
GE170.R436   2004
363.7'0526—dc22   2004028731

Contents

Foreword

The European Union, the International Court of Justice and the Group of Eight (G-8) are all examples of institutions that have evolved to meet the changing realities of the world in the twenty-first century. As people have moved, political boundaries have shifted and geopolitical forces have realigned, international institutions have adapted to reflect those changes. Yet, when a similar challenge to strengthen the institutional framework of sustainable development was presented in the context of the World Summit on Sustainable Development, the outcomes fell short of the task. Just as political and economic circumstances have changed, so has the global environment. Despite an increase in our collective scientific knowledge and the institutions and instruments created to address environmental problems, the quality of the global environment continues to deteriorate. Global problems such as climate change, desertification and biodiversity loss require complex policy responses, which in turn need sophisticated institutions to deliver them.

This volume is an attempt to contribute to that discussion, and to envision what changes are needed for a more effective international environmental governance system. Before any proposals – such as the proposition to establish a World Environment Organization – can be considered, a careful analysis of the status quo is in order. That is precisely the undertaking of this volume. *Reforming International Environmental Governance: From Institutional Limits to Innovative Reforms* reviews the major institutions within the environmental arena, and then turns more broadly to a discussion of which other institutions within the multilateral system could serve to strengthen the current governance architecture. Together with *Emerging Forces in Environmental Governance*, this volume is the result of a joint project with the Kita Kyushu University and the Center for Global Partnership in Japan.

The debate about specific environmental problems will only intensify as the potential gains and losses become clear. The United Nations University Institute of Advanced Studies (UNU-IAS) is contributing to these discussions through policy-relevant research such as the work presented in this volume. As the bridge between academia and the United Nations system, UNU-IAS brings together academics, researchers and policy makers to discuss solutions to some of the world's most pressing problems. In addition, UNU-IAS training and capacity-building programmes help create the next generation of problem solvers. These activities have been at the core of the Institute since its inception, and make valuable contributions to a variety of international policy-making processes.

The need to reform international environmental governance is increasingly urgent; institutions must be able to protect environmental quality and promote sustainable development. We cannot simply promote change for change's sake. Institutional reform must remain focused on our collective goal: the protection and preservation of the environment.

A. H. Zakri
Director, UNU-IAS

Contributors

W. Bradnee Chambers is the Senior Programme Officer of the United Nations University Institute of Advanced Studies (UNU-IAS) in Tokyo, Japan. From 1996 to 2001 he was a researcher and head of its Multilateralism and Sustainable Development Programme and legal advisor to the Institute. Chambers is also a convening lead author of the Millennium Ecosystem Assessment, lectures part time at Aoyoma University (Gakuin), and is a Senior Fellow with the new Sustain Development Law Centre at McGill University, Canada. He specializes in public international law and international relations and works on environmental treaty and international economic legal issues. Chambers' current research is concentrated on finding means of improving cooperation between major multilateral environmental agreements based on an

"interlinkages" approach. He works and publishes widely on issues related to climate change, biodiversity, biotechnology policy, and trade and environment.

Steve Charnovitz practises law at Wilmer, Cutler & Pickering in Washington, D.C., USA. He was previously director of the Global Environment and Trade Study at Yale University (1995–1999) and Legislative Assistant to the Speaker of the US House of Representatives (1987–1991). He received a BA and JD from Yale University and an MPP from the Kennedy School of Government.

Jessica F. Green is the Project Manager for the Sustainable Development Governance Programme at the United Nations University Institute of Advanced Studies (UNU-IAS). She holds a Master's in Public Administration from Columbia University's School of International and Public Affairs. Her research focuses on the engagement of civil society and developing country actors in sustainable development regimes. She is a lead author of the Millennium Ecosystem Assessment. Before coming to UNU-IAS, she worked at the World Resources Institute in Washington, D.C., USA.

Lorraine Elliott, BA, MA (Hons), PhD, is a Fellow in the Department of International Relations, University of Warwick, UK. Her research focuses on global environmental politics, environmental security and the nature of contemporary human security, and she is presently engaged in a study of regional environmental governance in South East Asia. In 1997, Elliott was awarded the Australasian Political Studies Association Crisp Medal and in 1998 she was an awardee under the Vice-Chancellor's Endowment Fund for Excellence.

Sebastian Oberthür, PhD, has been working as a Senior Fellow at Ecologic, Institute for International and European Environmental Policy, in Berlin and Brussels, since 1996. Before joining Ecologic, he conducted studies in the framework of several projects, *inter alia* on behalf of the Wuppertal Institute for Climate, Environment, and Energy, the Potsdam Institute for Climate Impact Research, and the Scientific Advisory Council of the German Government on Global Environmental Change. In 1996 and 1997, he also taught international relations at the Technical University Berlin.

Joost Pauwelyn is currently a Professor of Law at Duke University School of Law, USA. He received his Bachelor's degree in law (*Cand. Jur.*), *cum laude*, from the University of Namur, Belgium; his Master's degree in law (*Lic. Jur.*), *magna cum laude*, from the Catholic University of Leuven, Belgium, his *Magister Juris*, with first class honours, from the University of Oxford, Corpus Christi College, UK, and his PhD in law from the University of Neuchâtel, Switzerland. Prior to joining the Duke Law faculty, he served as a Legal Affairs Officer for the World Trade Organization in Geneva (1996–2002), first in the Legal Affairs Division, then in the Appellate Body Secretariat.

Catherine Redgwell is a Reader in Public International Law and the Yamani Fellow in Law at St. Peter's College, Oxford, UK. She previously held lecturing positions at the universities of Manchester (1988–1990) and Nottingham (1990–1999), the latter as senior lecturer from 1994. She spent a six-month secondment to the Legal Advisers, Foreign and Commonwealth Office, London, in 1992.

Gary P. Sampson worked at UNCTAD from 1975 to 1983. From 1984 to 1986 he was Senior Fellow in Economic Policy at the Reserve Bank of Australia and Professorial Fellow at the Centre of Policy Studies at Monash University. In 1987, he was appointed Director at the GATT and, in 1995, a Director at the WTO. He holds the posts of Professor of International Environmental Governance at the

United Nations University Institute of Advanced Studies in Yokohama and Visiting Academic at the London School of Economics, UK. He teaches regularly at INSEAD in France and at the Melbourne Business School in Australia.

Richard G. Tarasofsky is the Head of the Sustainable Development Programme at the Royal Institute of International Affairs, based at Chatham House in London. From 1998 to 2003, he was an independent lawyer specializing in international sustainable development law, whose clients included think tanks, non-governmental organizations, governments and international organizations. From 1993 to 1998, Tarasofsky was a Legal Officer at the World Conservation Union Environmental Law Centre. Prior to this he was a lecturer and researcher at the Foundation for International Environmental Law and Development (FIELD), based at the University of London, UK.

Introduction: Toward an effective framework for sustainable development

W. Bradnee Chambers and Jessica F. Green

Introduction

In 1987, the oft-cited Brundtland Report challenged the international community to achieve "development that meets the needs of the present without compromising the ability of future generations to meet their own needs".[1] Though the Brundtland Report's definition of sustainable development is elegant in its simplicity, the enormous political, academic and policy debates it has spawned suggest that it is insufficient.

Since then, the world of sustainable development has grown unsustainably. New legal instruments, multilateral regimes, institutions and actors continue to appear on the policy-making scene. The research and literature of sustainable development have expanded into a vast multidisciplinary effort, recruiting academics and experts from a wide variety of areas. Even armed with new knowledge and institutions, the international community continues to struggle with the challenges presented by the Brundtland Report.

Nonetheless, progress has been made. Despite the complexity of the issues surrounding sustainable development, we have advanced our understanding of its constituent components. Achieving sustainable development requires recognizing its social, economic and environmental pillars and integrating all three considerations into policy interventions. It requires, as noted in *Agenda 21*, broad consultation with stakeholders.[2] Some would argue that sustainable development demands even larger changes.

1

To meet these challenges and implement change, international institutions have been created by the handful. Now, there is a growing awareness within the United Nations, and among governments and civil society, that these institutions must be evaluated and governance for sustainable development strengthened. Many have argued that institutions can have a profound effect on policy outcomes.[3] In the case of sustainable development governance, a growing number of studies are linking the failure to make progress to protect the environment and achieve sustainable development to the complexity, inefficiency and weaknesses of current institutions. Major declarations such as the Rio+5 review, the UN Millennium Declaration, the Malmö Ministerial Declaration and the Monterrey Consensus all point out the need to streamline and strengthen the system of international sustainable development governance, with the aim of enhancing policy coherence and implementation.

Obstacles to sustainable development

These goals, though important, will not be easy to achieve. Governance for sustainable development faces a number of obstacles. The first set of obstacles is procedural – pertaining to the institutional arrangements themselves. The international architecture for sustainable development is highly fragmented, with different institutions focused on different policy aspects. In a sense, this is logical: each of the three pillars of sustainable development has its own priorities, and institutions thus have different organizational missions and goals. Yet the unforeseen consequences of this diffusion are considerable.

The diffuse nature of the system is further fragmented by a lack of strong mechanisms for coordination across institutions. Each of the pillars has its own governing council and member states. And, although these members may and often do overlap across institutions or sectors, they tend to treat each institution separately. Consistency across institutions is highlighted as an important goal but, at the same time, there is a hierarchy of priorities within each sector. Thus, the policies of the World Trade Organization (WTO) remain focused on economic growth, while social and environmental measures often take a back seat. Similarly, the policies for sustainable development of the United Nations Environment Programme (UNEP) are environment driven, sometimes to the detriment of economic considerations. Thus, lofty intentions of consistency are overshadowed, not surprisingly, by each institution's mission. This disjuncture between desired and actual policies will persist until a mechanism is created at a level with enough legitimacy and authority to set policy priorities that can and will be adhered to by the institutions of all three pillars of sustainable development.

Lack of coordination across sustainable development institutions gives rise to further problems. Fragmentation becomes self-perpetuating, because policy makers and bureaucrats have difficulty conceptualizing the landscape of sustainable development in its entirety and understanding where individual agencies, bodies and regimes fit into that architecture. It is testimony to this tunnel vision that no in-depth examination has been undertaken of all of the structures and institutions that comprise sustainable development governance. The project that produced this volume, a three-part investigation into the prospects for international environmental governance reform, is one of the first attempts at such a survey.[4]

Fragmentation also gives rise to specialization. Because of the multitude of institutions and their associated legal instruments and processes, policy makers must become experts on one specific issue or policy. As a result, negotiations are narrowly defined and are carried out by experts. Thus, the scope of the problem is constrained by the expertise of the policy makers. Individual international agreements are often negotiated by way of "specific" regimes that are isolated from one another, by artificially decomposing the causative complexities, if only for the sake of practical manageability. Furthermore, the process of consensus-building in the context of non-cooperative game characteristics often involves log-rolling to ensure that a deal is reached. Too frequently, this bartering process obscures the interconnectedness of the goals to be shared among different, but related, regimes.

Consequently, policy-making for sustainable development remains segregated. The result is twofold. First, the proliferation of agreements and their associated activities causes unnecessary complications at the national level, as signatories struggle to meet their obligations under multiple agreements. In response to this growing complexity, some coordinating efforts, such as the Inter-agency Co-ordination Committees (IACC) and the Commission on Sustainable Development (CSD), have been established on the international level. However, it appears that these have served more as an effort to pool various bodies than to coordinate them. Second, isolation of multilateral environmental agreements (MEAs) from a larger sustainable development context has resulted in overlapping treaties and even the possibility of conflict.

Underlying these procedural problems that continue to plague sustainable development governance is the substantive complexity of the policy questions at hand. At their core, environmental processes are governed by nature, not international policy. Thus, the current approach to sustainable development governance often results in artificial divisions within ecosystem functioning for the purposes of management. These divisions are further exacerbated by several other characteristics of the interactions between science and policy. First, the scientific uncertainty that surrounds many environmental problems poses additional challenges for policy makers: What decisions can be taken in the face of uncertainty? How much risk is acceptable? What constitutes a precautionary approach? Second, effective solutions to transnational and global problems require collective responses. The incentive to free ride is high, and difficulties in measuring environmental outcomes make compliance a challenge. Finally, the scale of an ecosystem can be local, regional or global. Moreover, its well-being may be dependent on specific species or other nearby ecosystems. Institutions for sustainable development must match the scale of the system to ensure maximum effectiveness. Appropriate scales of response can be stymied by the absence of political will or by the artificial division of ecosystems for the purposes of working with units of analysis that are more manageable.

Beyond the architecture of sustainable development

We have already noted that the three pillars of sustainable development imply a multitude of policy objectives and differing priorities. The nature of sustainable development has proven problematic not only for governance within the three pillars but also for international governance as a whole. Because sustainable development is a far-reaching concept that ultimately must be integrated into many aspects of policy-making, governance needs to address a host of underlying issues, which may, at the outset, appear beyond its scope. Chapter 8 in this volume, on expanding the mandate of the UN Security Council to include environmental security, provides an apt example.

Extending beyond the governance structures of sustainable development to the international governance system at large presents yet another layer of challenges. Problems of political turf, legal jurisdiction and compatibility of overlapping structures and functions further complicate our task of identifying appropriate synergies and reforms. These issues will also be addressed in this volume.

Examining reform

The challenges of governing sustainable development have been taken up in policy circles. Issues of complexity, overlap, fragmentation and conflict have been noted, and the need for reform has been reiterated. At the World Summit on Sustainable Development (WSSD) in 2002, stakeholders assembled to examine more carefully the governance system put in place to achieve sustainable development but, as in Rio, the outcomes fell short of the degree of reform needed to improve institutional effectiveness. The continued environmental degradation that persists in the face of the rapid growth of institutions and instruments focused on sustainable development also underscores the need for reform. Finally, the increased pace of economic and population growth further highlights the need for effective governance structures at the local, national, regional and international levels to achieve balance between the three pillars of sustainable development.

Kofi Annan's 1997 report *Renewing the United Nations* was a catalyst that opened the door for other initiatives aimed at strengthening international environmental governance. These include UNEP's Malmö Declaration of the Global Ministerial Environment Forum and the International Environmental Governance process, which concluded in Cartagena with a series of recommendations for the WSSD and the General Assembly. A number of other proposals for reforms have been proffered as a panacea for the shortcomings of the international governance system. However, none of the work to date has included a careful analysis of the inherent weaknesses and gaps of the international environmental governance system. Nor does it examine what these proposals might look like substantively, once implemented, or how they would improve the overall architecture of institutions.

Unlike these previous efforts, this volume takes a systematic approach to formulating proposals for institutional changes in sustainable development governance. The volume comes out of a larger project conducted by the United Nations University Institute of Advanced Studies (UNU-IAS) to examine the gaps and flaws in international environmental governance. This study was undertaken to consider carefully alternative institutional arrangements that would address the weaknesses identified in the first part of the study. These proposals are meant to describe, as fully as possible, not only what institutional changes would be necessary but also the implications of these changes with respect to the larger context of international sustainable development governance and, indeed, the architecture of international governance as a whole. This volume casts its net widely, considering a broad range of reforms in a broad institutional context and a number of themes.

An agenda for reform: Coherence, centralization and compliance in international environmental governance

Coherence

The book begins "locally", examining three proposals for institution reform within the realm of international environmental governance (IEG).

The first three chapters examine the question of which bodies should take the lead in IEG and the ways in which their participation would increase IEG coherence.

Chapter 1 by Chambers takes a historical approach, reviewing the efforts at and institutions of coordination within international environmental governance. Beginning with the 1972 Stockholm Conference on the Human Environment and ending with the 2002 World Summit on Sustainable Development, Chambers analyses mechanisms to facilitate coordination with the international environmental governance system.

The growth in the number of MEAs has increased the breadth and depth of obligations that its Parties must satisfy. To reduce both the demands on Parties to meet their obligations as well as the human and financial resources required to administer these MEAs, some have proposed "clustering" MEAs to increase efficiency and/or effectiveness. In chapter 2, Oberthür evaluates the prospects for clustering MEAs, which, he points out, can be a risky endeavour. Thus, it is most usefully understood as an incremental process, and not as an objective at the outset. He examines two main proposals: clustering MEAs by function and by issue (or related issues). Oberthür points to a number of functions, such as scientific assessment, monitoring, implementation review or compliance that could be integrated across MEAs. Such clustering would not only potentially reduce reporting obligations by member states, but also increase both the legitimacy and the coherence of the system. Clustering MEAs by issue may be more problematic, because substantive overlap among MEAs may not be large enough to generate net gains in efficiency. Finally, Oberthür reviews the possibility of clustering regional MEAs, where a large overlap in membership is likely. In the end, the author offers "pragmatic clustering" as the best way to proceed. Such an approach would integrate only some elements of certain MEAs, either functional or substantive, on a case-by-case basis.

Unlike the creation of a new organization, such as the World Environment Organization (WEO), clustering could present political problems among MEAs. There is little incentive for MEAs to pursue clustering activities, owing to uncertain rewards and a potential loss of autonomy. Thus, clustering would require political impetus, where facilitators responsible for the process are given a clear political mandate and sufficient authority to effect changes.

Proposals for reform inevitably lead to a discussion of the role of UNEP within international environmental governance. With such a broad range of activities and environmental issues within its purview – from environmental assessment, to policy development and law, to liaising with MEA secretariats – UNEP is a likely candidate for increasing coherence within IEG. However, its broad mandate is also one of its main weaknesses.

In chapter 3, Tarasofsky proposes refining the goals of UNEP through the Global Ministerial Environment Forum (GMEF), which has been charged with ensuring policy coherence across international environmental policies.[5] With a larger role, the GMEF could potentially serve as the cornerstone of IEG, in turn enhancing the normative authority of UNEP. Such a strategy would sidestep thorny political issues about dramatic institutional changes and, instead, elaborate a legal instrument endowing the GMEF with the authority to take decisions with regard to policy coordination. The increased role of the GMEF could also enhance linkages between the international and the regional, and between MEAs, thereby promoting greater coherence within IEG.

Tarasofsky points out that insufficient and irregular funding has plagued UNEP from the outset, and is perhaps the primary obstacle to its effectiveness. Although Tarasofsky offers proposals for alleviating budgetary pressures, such as changing funding cycles or separating programme and administrative budgets, his recommendations for stepping up the role of the Global Ministerial Environment Forum are more germane to the issue of increasing coherence.

Centralization

The discussion of centralization turns first to one of the most often cited proposals for reform within international environmental governance – the call for the creation of a World Environment Organization (WEO). Although the idea of a new global-scale international environmental organization was once sidelined in the United Nations Conference on Environment and Development (UNCED) process, it regained currency several years ago in the academic literature.[6]

Many of the proposals that have been put forward may be attractive at first glance, but those seeking to probe deeper into the feasibility and utility of each are confronted with a host of complexities and challenges to assess. Charnovitz examines many of these dimensions in chapter 4 by justifying the need for a WEO, describing what it might look like and explaining how a WEO might contribute to achieving a set of specific objectives for environmental governance. The potential gains to centralization are speculative, but could include administrative savings and improvements in productivity. More importantly, given the trend in IEG for continued proliferation of governance structures, Charnovitz argues that a WEO would supply much-needed rationalization for the current IEG.

Charnovitz also stresses that any attempt to centralize the current international environmental governance system should not inadvertently stymie the strengths of the existing system of international environmental governance. It is important, he notes, that efforts to centralize do not reduce the autonomy of multilateral environmental agreements (MEAs) to the extent that the capacity for innovation is hindered.

Although reducing fragmentation within IEG is the first step toward increased effectiveness of sustainable development governance, proposals for reform must look for ways to increase coordination, centralization and compliance across international governance structures beyond the scope of the environment. In the second half of the book, the authors examine the interaction of other global institutional arrangements with IEG. Some have argued that the opposition of the WTO to governance structures of sustainable development is perhaps the most formidable obstacle to coherent governance in the age of globalization. Chapters 5–8 move beyond IEG to examine the potential of the WTO and other UN bodies to increase cooperation and synergies in international sustainable development governance.

In chapter 5, Sampson challenges the notion that trade and environment are inherently conflicting; instead, he considers incremental changes within the WTO that could enhance cooperation between the two regimes. He points out that increasing the WTO's role with respect to IEG is not the answer. Rather, changes in the focus of existing functions could serve to enhance coordination between trade and environment regimes, in a way that would not require significant changes to either set of institutions. Sampson points to the Committee on Trade and the Environment in the WTO as a viable forum for reviewing trade and environment linkages and for coordinating further discussion around them. He points out that such reorientation of existing structures is preferred to changing WTO rules, an undertaking for which there would be little political will. Instead, he proposes that standards and trade measures adopted in MEAs be adopted by WTO members in turn. This would impose some coherence across regimes and sidestep issues of rule-changing within the WTO.

Compliance

The recognition of the inherent weaknesses of the IEG structure has prompted arguments for a more integrated, coordinated and *binding* system. Thus, the last three chapters of the book examine proposals for enhancing compliance mechanisms within the international governance system as a whole or for creating new institutions for compliance within IEG.

Problems relating to compliance and dispute settlement were also highlighted through the course of UNU-IAS's project on reforming IEG. The lack of direct enforcement procedures or obligatory dispute settlement mechanisms within most MEAs has allowed serious questions to be raised about treaty implementation at the national level. Several countries have been criticized for their lack of effort, on a practical level, to implement their binding obligations under various MEAs. Proponents of greater integration in international environmental governance draw upon the WTO, with its effective compliance and dispute settlement mechanisms, as a model for IEG. Although over 20 agreements fall under the WTO umbrella, they all operate within a common and obligatory dispute settlement framework, which provides the opportunity to use economic sanctions as counter-measures or to nullify membership benefits in cases of non-compliance.

Beyond exporting WTO models to IEG, another recommendation that has attracted much attention is the creation of a World Environment Court (WEC). This proposal has gained renewed momentum because of the example set by the recent entry into force of the International Criminal Court. At a conceptual level, it is envisaged that this specialized environmental court would provide binding decisions in a more time-efficient way than the existing International Court of Justice (ICJ). A WEC could hold both states and private sector actors to account for the environmental damage they inflict while in breach of internationally binding standards. Of course, major questions remain: Who will have legal standing to sue? Who can be sued? What laws will be applicable? In chapter 6, Pauwelyn points out the need to create a compulsory dispute mechanism in international environmental law. Without it, the international community risks creating a two-class society of international norms: those that can be judicially enforced, as with the WTO; and those that cannot, as with international environmental law. Thus, the critical issue is not the institution that adjudicates non-compliance but, rather, getting states to agree to "binding and law-based dispute settlement procedures".[7] Should the WEC be deemed the appropriate institutional response to establishing such rules and procedures, Pauwelyn notes, its political feasibility would be much more likely when considered in tandem with a WEO. However, a WEC, with or without a WEO, must take care to remain integrated with the larger corpus of international law, and not become a self-contained regime.

Another suggestion made in several different forums to improve compliance involves revamping the UN Trusteeship Council, which had originally served as an international caretaker during the period of decolonization. The recommendation, made by widely recognized experts in IEG and endorsed by the UN Secretary-General, proposes that the now idle Trusteeship Council be reformed to focus on areas that do not fall under any national jurisdiction – such as the global commons. Redgwell argues in chapter 7 that such a role for the Trusteeship Council would not infringe on state sovereignty, because its purview would be restricted to those matters that are the "common concern of mankind". In this role, the Trusteeship Council would serve not as an administering authority but rather as a forum in which states would exercise their collective trusteeship. This would effectively link the Trusteeship Council to the notion of global governance.

A final proposal for enhancing compliance mechanisms within IEG is to expand the mandate of the UN Security Council to include certain environmental issues. This possibility was explicitly recognized in 1992, when the President of the Council offered a statement on behalf of members declaring that "the nonmilitary sources of instability in the economic, social, humanitarian and ecological fields have become threats to peace and security".[8] This statement was given further credence by the adoption of Security Council Resolution 1308 in 2000, which states that, if left unchecked, HIV/AIDS could pose a risk to stability and security.

In light of these discussions, extending the Security Council's mandate to include environmental threats seems a plausible proposal. At the same time, it raises questions about which environmental matters may be considered to be matters of international security, and how this new role might fit with the Council's current mandate to maintain international peace and security. In chapter 8, Elliott points out that the Security Council is already taking on additional issues, such as humanitarian emergencies and human rights abuses; thus, including environmental threats should not be considered an inappropriate addition. Certainly, environmental degradation can be linked to armed conflicts in the recent past, such as in Somalia, Liberia and Rwanda. However, more general threats to the environment in times of peace would require broadening the Security Council mandate, perhaps through a decision stating that environmental behaviours with severe negative impacts may be considered a threat to international peace and security.

Conclusion

The outcomes of the World Summit on Sustainable Development (WSSD) have reaffirmed the need for institutional reform. The "Plan of Implementation", which details the decisions taken through the course of the WSSD process, reiterates that "an effective institutional framework for sustainable development at all levels is key to the full implementation of Agenda 21 ... and meeting emerging sustainable development challenges".[9] The "Plan of Implementation" outlines 13 objectives that should govern institutional reform efforts, including integrating the three pillars of sustainable development in a balanced manner, increasing effectiveness and efficiency through limiting overlap, and strengthening international institutions. At the international level, the Plan calls for increased cooperation across regimes and institutions, and specifies new roles for the General Assembly, the Economic and Social Council and the Commission on Sustainable Development.

The WSSD confirms that institutional reform for sustainable development has reached the international stage. International policy makers have also recognized the institutional problems identified by the academic community, and have committed to take action. Issues of coherence and cooperation are especially prominent; compliance has yet to emerge as a central concern for sustainable development governance. Thus, despite criticisms that the WSSD has failed to promote change of the magnitude necessary for meaningful reform, the "Plan of Implementation" does mark the beginning of an incremental process toward effective institutional change.

Though changes in the current landscape of international governance are needed, they are not a panacea for achieving the objectives of sustainable development. The lack of coherence within the formal international institutional architecture reflects a persisting high level of disagreement about what would constitute an effective and appropriate approach to achieving sustainable development. The inability of the international community to agree upon a common approach to sustainable development governance is largely rooted in disparities between the perspectives and priorities of developed and developing countries. Reducing and overcoming these disparities remain, therefore, critical prerequisites for the creation of an effective, efficient and equitable system of sustainable development governance.

Notes

1. World Commission on Environment and Development, *Our Common Future*, Oxford: Oxford University Press, 1987, p. 8.
2. *Agenda 21* states that "one of the fundamental prerequisites for the achievement of sustainable development is broad public participation in decision-making" (United Nations, *Agenda 21: Programme of Action for Sustainable Development*, New York: United Nations Department of Public Information, 1992, p. 219).
3. See, for example, P. M. Haas, R. O. Keohane, et al., *Institutions for the Earth: Sources of Effective International Environmental Protection*, Cambridge, MA: MIT Press, 1993.
4. See D. Esty and M. Ivanova, *Global Environmental Governance: Options and Opportunities*, New Haven, CT: Yale School of Forestry and Environmental Studies, 2002.
5. United Nations General Assembly, Resolution 53/242, *Report of the Secretary-General on Environment and Human Settlements*, A/RES/53/242, 10 August 1999.
6. See G. Palmer, "New Ways to Make International Environmental Law", *American Journal of International Law*, Vol. 86, 1992, p. 259; D. Esty, *Greening the GATT*, Washington, D.C.: Institute for International Economics, 1994; F. Biermann and U. E. Simonis, *A*

World Environment and Development Organization, SEF Policy Paper 9, Bonn, Germany: Development and Peace Foundation, 1998; G. Ulfstein, "The Proposed GEO and Its Relationship to Existing MEAs", paper presented at the International Conference on Synergies and Coordination between Multilateral Environmental Agreements, UNU, 14–16 July 1999. See also the report documenting discussions at the "Strengthening Global Environmental Governance" meeting, 4–5 June 1998, organized by the Global Environmental Governance Project, Yale School of Forestry Studies, New Haven, CT; available at ⟨http://www.yale.edu/gegdialogue/docs/dialogue/jun98/jun98.doc⟩.

7. Pauwelyn, chapter 6 in this volume.
8. Statement by the Security Council President on behalf of its members, *Comprehensive Review of the Whole Question of Peace-Keeping Operations in All Their Aspects: Report of the Special Committee on Peace-Keeping Operations*, A/47/253, 4 June 1992.
9. "Plan of Implementation", in *Report of the World Summit on Sustainable Development, Johannesburg, South Africa, 26 August–4 September 2002*, A/CONF.199/20, 1 January 2002, para. 137.

1

From environmental to sustainable development governance: Thirty years of coordination within the United Nations

W. Bradnee Chambers

Introduction

In the preparations and the negotiations of the 1972 Stockholm Conference on the Human Environment (UNCHE) the question of coordination was highly controversial. Developed countries were reluctant to create more costly organizations and existing UN agencies already working on environmental issues were fearful of being rendered subservient to or redundant by a new "super-agency". A similar push for institutional coordination was evident at the United Nations Conference on Environment and Development (UNCED), which took place in Rio de Janeiro 20 years later. Yet, by this time, governments had started to lose their confidence in the ability of the United Nations Environment Programme (UNEP) to play a strong and effective coordinating role in environmental governance – ironically, a role it was created to pursue.

By the end of the 1980s, UNEP's political position was in decline. Developed countries had been alienated by Director-General Mostafa Tolba's strong support of developing country interests. Tolba's successor was equally unappealing to developing countries, which believed that UNEP was overemphasizing its efforts on the "green northern agenda" (i.e. biodiversity, climate change) instead of "brown-on-the-ground" (i.e. air pollution and clean drinking water), which were of greater concern to them. The resulting loss of confidence culminated at Rio, where developing nations looked elsewhere for coordination and follow-up to Agenda

21 and two new treaties on climate change and desertification. As a result, a new institutional personality was created, the Commission on Sustainable Development (CSD), under the United Nations Department of Economic and Social Affairs.

Kofi Annan's appointment as Secretary-General of the United Nations in 1996 marked a distinct shift in UN leadership. Annan came from within the organization and, as a UN functionary with a 20-year career, he thoroughly understood the workings of the United Nations and its administration. Most importantly, Annan understood the reality of competition between UN organizations and had specific ideas about how to improve the United Nations.

With this experience behind him, Annan launched a major reform initiative set out in his 1997 report *Renewing the United Nations.*[1] The report spurred new interest in creating greater effectiveness and efficiency and addressing criticism that the organization was overly bureaucratic and wasteful. This eventually set in motion a process within the United Nations and Specialized Agencies, non-governmental organizations, and academia to re-evaluate the international institutions associated with environment and sustainable development. This reform has continued and was evident in the 2002 World Summit on Sustainable Development process and its follow-up.

The purpose of this chapter is to recount the processes and initiatives over the course of the past three decades of environmental and then sustainable development policy-making. These efforts, focused on creating effective institutions for environmental protection and sustainable development through stronger coordination and interlinkages between UN organizations, have helped lay the foundation for understanding the current framework for environmental governance.

The first section of this chapter traces the early initiatives to create institutional coordination mechanisms, which mainly arose out of the preparations for and deliberations at the 1972 Stockholm Conference. These deliberations revolved around the creation of UNEP and the role it would play vis-à-vis other UN agencies. The chapter then turns to the Rio Earth Summit and the emergence of the concept of sustainable development, which in effect added a new layer of coordination to the environmental organization rubric by introducing the requirement for environmental policy-making to take better account of the social and economic sectors. I look in detail at the creation of the CSD, as well as other inter-agency coordination mechanisms, and at how these function in relation to existing environmental and sustainable development governance structures. The third section looks at the UNEP International Environmental Governance process launched by the UNEP Governing Council in Malmö, Norway, in 2000. I trace some of the problems that limited the opportunities for strengthening environmental governance. I also review some of the proposals put forward and the series of meetings that led up to the third preparatory meeting for the World Summit on Sustainable Development (WSSD). The final section looks at the WSSD itself and examines in detail the outcome as contained in the 2002 Johannesburg Plan of Implementation (JPOI).

The results of this historical analysis suggest that the global summits at Stockholm, Rio and Johannesburg represent missed opportunities for reform. International environmental governance, and now sustainable development governance, could have benefited greatly from strong reform efforts at these three critical meetings. The chapter concludes that coordination has now become extremely complex, and any assessments of the institutional arrangements for environment and sustainable development issues must be seen in the context of inter-sector – between social, economic and environmental organizations – and intra-sector – e.g. within the World Trade Organization (WTO), UNEP and the International Labour Organization (ILO) – cooperation, and cooperation between independent environmental organizations (e.g. UNEP, the CSD and multilateral environmental agreements), and must be distinguished according to the nature of the coordination sought.

The early days of Stockholm

In 1968, the Economic and Social Council (ECOSOC) reported to the General Assembly its concern about mounting environmental degradation.[2] This move by the Council represented the culmination of a growing movement internationally among non-governmental organizations (NGOs), conservationists and ornithologists, which had raised the alarm over the worsening state of the environment. The United Nations had no mandate on the environment, but because the impacts cut across numerous issues, such as health, culture and development, several UN organizations were already at work in the field. Economic and social issues were also viewed as a prerequisite for peace and security, the United Nations' mainstay, and thus were intrinsically linked to the environment.[3] With growing interest and activity in environmental protection, the next important question focused on the institutional structure and management within the United Nations. Would there be a new super-agency? Or would an existing agency be given additional responsibility in this new area, and, if so, which one? Or would the agencies that were already working on environmental issues simply receive an additional mandate?

Going into the Stockholm Conference, opinions were deeply divided on exactly what would be the necessary institutional arrangements for the environment. At the very beginning of the conference's planning stage, Secretary-General U Thant, the architect of Stockholm, proposed the idea of an environmental "super-agency", but this quickly became entangled in the politics within the UN headquarters in New York, institutional turf wars, financial concerns and sovereignty questions. There was, thus, a general aversion to the creation of a new UN organization.

Given these constraints, any attempts to launch a new environmental organization would have to be accompanied by assurances that this organization would not be an organization at all, but rather a non-intrusive entity to complement existing organizations. Such an organization would have to have a minimal administration and not compete legally or financially with existing organizations. This, in fact, is precisely what happened.

Two major information notes had a great deal of influence on the deliberations of the Stockholm Conference about a new environmental organization. Both quashed any idea of creating of a free-standing independent organization for the environment. The first was document A/CONF.48/12 prepared by the Administrative Coordination Committee (ACC). The ACC is composed of the heads of the various UN and Specialized Agencies, and its information document emphasized that any approach taken in Stockholm should be complementary and should give existing organizations "additional support, fresh impetus, a common outlook and direction".[4] The document outlined the argument that UN organizations have traditionally taken a vertical approach to international problem-solving, organizing themselves according to sectoral patterns in national governments. Although the ACC acknowledged that this sectoral approach "remains adequate to deal with a number of these problems", it clearly argued for a more horizontal approach given what it saw as the intersectoral, diffuse and interdisciplinary nature of environmental problems.[5] The document elaborated the actions already taken or planned by other UN organizations for the environment. Based on these existing efforts and the ACC's coordinating role, it subtly argued that the "United Nations system has institutions experience and machinery which can be adapted to new tasks and needs".[6] In other words, according to the ACC, the United Nations did not need an organization for the environment or a new mechanism for coordination.[7]

The ACC's document reflected many of the contemporary political undercurrents. Organizations such as the International Atomic Energy Agency were reluctant to lose successful environment-related programmes on radiation monitoring and were clearly prepared to defend their turf.[8] The document also played equally into the hands of both developing and developed countries, but for very different reasons. Developed countries such as the United Kingdom did not want to pay for yet another international organization and wanted the "absolute minimum" of new institutions.[9] Developing countries objected to a large new environmental organization on the grounds that regulations on the environment could be a new form of colonialism, or at the very least a restriction on their economic development.

However, the ACC position represented only half of the politics at play in New York at the time. Not to predetermine the outcome of Stockholm, and in the face of growing support for an approach of working within the existing UN system, Maurice Strong, who had been appointed to be Secretary-General of the Stockholm Conference, decided that he would hire an outside writing team to take responsibility for the preparation of Stockholm's basic information documents. This was a strategic move, because their work would serve as a counterbalance to the ACC's interests, demonstrated by its partisan information document.

Strong, an entrepreneur and self-made man, had already been responsible for the creation of the International Canadian Development Agency and International Development Research Centre, two innovative and forward-looking national organizations within the complicated political structure of the Canadian government. As an iconoclast, he had the conference secretariat prepare a document that made subtle but powerful arguments for at least some form of new institutional mechanism for the environment. Document A/CONF.48/11, which was submitted with the ACC document for consideration by the preparatory committee, acknowledged that existing organizations were already addressing environmental issues and that coordination was needed, but it argued that there were still many gaps in environmental governance, which could not be resolved within the current institutional frameworks; thus new approaches and institutional arrangements were needed.[10]

The document was the culmination of a number of meetings and consultations that Strong had held with governments and international organizations.[11] It laid out nine criteria that were said to represent the consensus reached through these meetings. In summary, these criteria affirmed that:

- any potential organization should be based on agreed need;
- no unnecessary new institutional machinery should be created;
- a network approach instead of a super-agency should be used;
- any organization should be flexible and evolutionary;
- the highest priority should be given to coordination;
- the organization should not have an operational function, so as to avoid competition;
- the organization should have a regional outlook;
- the United Nations should be the principal body to host any new organization; and

- the organization should be designed in such a way as to strengthen the overall UN system.[12]

Whether these criteria represented a true assessment of the institutional arrangements needed to address emerging environmental concerns or a savvy compromise by a Secretary-General with a knack for consensus-building remains unknown. Although the report was more realistic than the ACC proposal, it still failed to understand the difficult nature of coordination within the United Nations, and the need to empower institutions with the political clout required to get independently mandated organizations to cooperate.

Two possible locations within the United Nations for new institutional arrangements were proposed. The first was to create a subsidiary body of ECOSOC under Article 68 of the UN Charter.[13] This made sense given that environmental issues fell closer to the mandate and substantive content of the Council's deliberations. At the time, however, questions about ECOSOC were being raised, especially given that it represented nearly half the UN membership and that it could make only recommendations to the General Assembly.[14] There was also concern that, if the new organization was under ECOSOC, it might not be able to attract ministers and senior officials on a regular basis and therefore would not be capable of recommending credible decisions to the Assembly.[15]

The second choice, which was eventually accepted, was to create a subsidiary body of the General Assembly under Article 22 of the Charter. This arrangement would allow the organization to inform the Assembly "to tackle problems posed by the interconnections of development with the need to safeguard the environment and to provide policy guidance thereon".[16] It was also thought that, as a subsidiary body of the General Assembly, it would enjoy higher visibility and status and thus more political credibility than would a body under ECOSOC.

Nowhere, however, was there a proposal to create a full Specialized Agency under Article 59 of the UN Charter. Perhaps Strong believed it was a non-starter, given the political environment at the time. Yet, the absence of this choice or some other organizational arrangement politically stronger than the two put forward was a fundamental mistake. This decision put UNEP and environmental issues on a path that has made them subservient to other interests. The disadvantaged position within the larger international governance system has made it difficult to put the environment on a par with the social and economic pillars of sustainable development.

Document A/CONF.48/11 accurately sketches the terrain of needs for a future organization with regard to monitoring, reporting and information needs, but it misses the true nature of the central role of coordination. At the time, most environmental activities were conducted by well-established and well-financed Specialized Agencies such as the Food and Agriculture Organization (FAO), the International Atomic Energy Agency (IAEA), the Inter-Governmental Maritime Consultative Organization, the World Health Organization (WHO) and the World Meteorological Organization (WMO). Other activities were under way in financial institutions, such as the World Bank or the General Agreement on Tariffs and Trade (GATT), yet these organizations had other interests (such as economic development) that were counter to environmental concerns.[17] As semi-autonomous or fully autonomous organizations, coordinating efforts were difficult at best. When the heads of these agencies came together under the umbrella of the ACC, they each had their own political agenda and, more importantly, their own governance system, to which they were accountable. These agencies could not be compelled to undertake any activities not approved by their own intergovernmental council.

These competing institutional arrangements and priorities explain some of the shortcomings of the Stockholm Conference. One of the main outcomes with respect to institutional reform was the call for the creation of an Environment Coordination Board under the framework of the ACC. Yet, this body lacked the power to coordinate environmental issues and promote new agendas in a meaningful way. The institutional machinery was awkward and burdensome, and UNEP had no operational means to implement new environmental concerns on its own. UNEP was to make recommendations to the General Assembly, which would in turn recommend actions at country level or to other United Nations agencies, but it lacked any means to see them through.

Another major shortcoming of Stockholm was a misdiagnosis of the problem: what was needed in 1970 was not coordination but consolidation. A new organization needed to be on the same footing as the other Specialized Agencies, with the ability to implement programmes instead of just reviewing policy. Although environmental programmes were already under way in several agencies, there remained important issues that had not been taken up by any organization. Moreover, the way in which the programmes evolved under the mandate of different agencies was ad hoc. Consolidation under a new organization could have addressed these two problems.

In 1970, analysts were well aware of these concerns. In fact, there was discussion of some very innovative proposals for institutional arrangements, some of which are considered in this volume in their modern context. For example, an environmental council was proposed in 1972 that would have the same status as ECOSOC and thus have clear legal authority over Specialized Agencies[18] (see also Elliott, in chapter 8 in this volume). Another proposal was to reorient the Trusteeship Council towards protecting the global commons (this is still an option today – see Redgwell in chapter 7). But both of these proposals would have required (and would still require) an amendment to the UN Charter under Article 108, which raised fears that opening up the Charter to amendments could spark debates over other more sensitive areas.[19]

One of the most innovative proposals was to give the United Nations Development Programme (UNDP) the environment portfolio. This idea was based on the United Nations Fund for Population activities, which had begun a new fund to implement population programmes. Since the fund was executed by the UNDP through its country offices, it was argued that "placing environmental responsibilities within UNDP might ... help to ensure that environmental considerations are included in projects from their inceptions".[20] Turning the environment portfolio over to UNDP would also have given the United Nations the reach it needed to execute a variety of projects at the national level.

Yet, in the 1970s, many believed that the debate on institutional arrangements was premature. Instead of trying to decide on a new organization for the environment without a full understanding of the future direction of environmental governance, it was better to create a strategic unit using the existing UN machinery and with minimal investment. This feeling was reflected in the consensus cultivated by Strong: "Any action envisaged should allow for the preliminary state of knowledge and understanding of environmental problems and should be flexible and evolutionary."[21] Or, as Richard Gardner said, "any new organization established to deal with environmental problems should be capable of growth and adaptation ... Governments may be willing to make commitments for tomorrow that they may not be willing to undertake today."[22] In many ways, this was a savings clause for the future and left the possibility open to "upgrade" UNEP in the future, as circumstances warranted. However, the principle came without mechanisms to implement it, and it would be 20 years before governments had another chance to think about implementation and creating the appropriate institutional arrangements. By that time, however, the principles of sustainable development would have to be considered in tandem with environmental governance.

Rio and institutional coordination deliberations

Just as the representatives to Stockholm wrestled with the seemingly competing issues of environment and development,[23] so did the policy makers at the United Nations Conference on Environment and Development (UNCED) in Rio in 1992. In the 20 years between the two summits, the trade/development debate did not wane, but rather intensified. This growing tension warranted further exploration of institutional remedies. Thus, it became apparent that any future world conference would have to treat environment and development issues simultaneously, and that coordination rather than reconciliation of these two issues would be the challenge. Yet, just as in Stockholm, politics trumped policy at UNCED, and the institutional outcomes proved to be suboptimal. Although the Rio summit did produce some outcomes to enhance coordination with other sectors beyond environment, its decisions created greater coordination problems within the environment sector.

Several outcomes of the Rio summit went to the heart of coordination between the areas of development and environment. At the conceptual level, the appropriation of the concept of sustainable development as proposed by the Brundtland Commission Report was an attempt to reconcile these two areas, which had previously been considered separately.[24]

If sustainable development formed the basis for the deliberations of the institutional arrangements, *Agenda 21* became the blueprint of how this goal should be achieved. Chapter 38 of *Agenda 21* set out various layers of coordination. First, it called on all relevant agencies of the UN system to "adopt concrete programmes for the implementation of Agenda 21" and to publish regular reports and reviews of these activities.[25] It also set up three new bodies: a high-level inter-agency coordination mechanism under the ACC, a high-level advisory body to provide guidance to the Secretary-General, and a high-level commission under ECOSOC to follow up on the implementation of *Agenda 21*. The most significant of these was the last, the Commission on Sustainable Development (CSD).

The CSD was created to monitor the implementation of *Agenda 21* and to promote the integration of the three pillars of sustainable development. It was formally established by ECOSOC Decision 1993/207.[26] Accordingly, the Commission was to report to ECOSOC and, through it, to the Second Committee of the General Assembly. The CSD also was given the role of coordinating the Rio follow-up within the UN system, through the Inter-Agency Committee on Sustainable Development (IACSD).[27]

Although the CSD was created to follow up on *Agenda 21*, it in fact displaced and overlapped with UNEP. UNEP was already playing a major role in sectoral issues outlined in *Agenda 21* such as oceans and seas, fresh water, land management, forests, biodiversity, chemicals, hazardous waste and air pollution. UNEP either acted as a catalyst, by identifying emerging issues and threats, or worked with other agencies to address these issues.

The cross-sectoral issues taken up in *Agenda 21* also caused difficulties in coordinating work between UNEP and the CSD. The CSD was responsible for considering cross-sectoral issues such as education, the role of major groups and financial resources.[28] Yet it is widely agreed that the CSD was not effective in addressing these cross-sectoral issues. Much of the CSD's work has become more environment rather than development oriented, and its successes are more focused on environmental policies, such as the Forestry Principles, or work on energy and fresh water. In the 10 years since Rio, issue areas such as education, technology transfer, capacity-building or strengthening coordination with the Bretton Woods institutions and the WTO, where clearly the CSD should have played a role, have garnered little success. The CSD has been credited with putting new issues on the international agenda, such as energy, tourism and transport, but, according to some analysts, this work on emerging issues clearly fell under UNEP's mandate.[29]

What was needed, but never came to pass, was a clearer division of labour between UNEP and the CSD. UNEP was already well placed in a number of sectoral issues and could have continued its work in these areas, with *Agenda 21* and the renewed commitment by Rio to strengthen its mandate. The CSD, by contrast, was better suited to work on integrated policies and substance between the issues as well as the clearly identified cross-sectoral issues such as the nexus of the three pillars of sustainable development, education, the role of major groups, and financial matters. The establishment of the CSD created an often unnecessary layer of bureaucracy, which not only was detrimental to the division of labour with UNEP, but caused larger coordination problems with environmental governance more generally. As mentioned earlier, there was considerable overlap between the CSD and UNEP, as well as with other intergovernmental bodies. Thus, the CSD had little to offer that was not presented, discussed or decided elsewhere. Critics have also argued that the CSD created a "decoy effect" by considering sectoral issues that have been dealt with in more specialist forums for many years, thereby drawing attention away from, or potentially conflicting with, other international decisions.

The recent reform of the CSD, following the decision of the World Summit on Sustainable Development to "place more emphasis on actions that enable implementation at all levels", is part of the attempt to address some of these criticisms.[30] The first meeting of the CSD after its structure and focus were reformed took place in April–May 2004, when the emphasis was on exchange of information rather than negotiating a formal decision. Although it is too early to know what the effects of these reforms will be, they have certainly served to restructure the CSD's work around more focused issues on a bi-annual basis.

The CSD is true to the outcomes of Rio in the sense that it views sustainable development as a cross-cutting concept – much like environment was regarded when UNEP was created. However, although the CSD was intended to provide the coordination to implement *Agenda 21*, it did not strengthen UNEP or enhance its implementation capability. Thus, environmental governance was renamed sustainable development governance, yet, as with the creation of UNEP, the corresponding institutional infrastructure was lacking. Nowhere is this more evident than in the contrasting multilateral institutional apparatus for economic development, social development and environmental protection. Economic institutions (such as the WTO, the World Bank, the International Monetary Fund, the United Nations Industrial Development Organization and the United Nations Conference on Trade and Development) are numerous and well developed, and, in the case of the WTO, even have a compliance mechanism. Institutions for social development (such as the ILO, WHO, FAO and the Human Rights Commission) are similarly strong. In comparison, the corresponding environmental institutions are quite weak.

UN reform and the Malmö process: UNEP's comeback?

The loss of confidence in UNEP in the late 1980s and early 1990s was replaced by a renewed confidence in UNEP's potential by Kofi Annan shortly after he became Secretary-General in 1996. Annan put the question of improving the coordination and effectiveness of international environmental institutions on the international political agenda with the release of his 1997 programme for reform *Renewing the United Nations*. In the report, Annan makes strong statements concerning the performance of environmental institutions and the "need for a more integrated systematic approach to policies and programmes".[31] The Secretary-General prepared the report in response to the growing criticism that the United Nations had become a wasteful, self-serving organization where there was a lot of talk but very little action. These sentiments were shared by a number of countries including the United States, which refused to pay its arrears to the United Nations of over US$1 billion until the United Nations initiated reforms. Conscious of the pressures to improve the United Nations' efficiency, Annan knew that the most important task when he took office would have to be the creation of a comprehensive reform strategy, which would necessarily involve addressing environment and sustainable development issues. For UNEP, this was the chance to reassert its importance in the international community, and, with Maurice Strong's understanding of the situation and power to work behind the scenes, it began a process that has led to a strengthening of UNEP's institutional foundations.

On 14 July 1997, only four months after taking office, Annan transmitted a letter to the President of the General Assembly, officially submitting his report to the General Assembly and outlining the motivation behind it. In the letter, Annan states that the objective of the report was "nothing less than to transform the leadership and management structure of the Organization, enabling it to act with greater unity of purpose, coherence of efforts, and agility in responding to the many challenges it faces".[32] The report was not only aimed at the internal management and administration of the UN system but also "intended to renew the confidence of Member States in the relevance and effectiveness of the Organization and revitalize the spirit and commitment of its staff".[33]

This renewal included UNEP. As was noted earlier, the creation of the Commission on Sustainable Development and the emergence of the concept of sustainable development shifted policy conversations away from traditional environmental issues towards the notion of balancing environmental with economic and social priorities. The CSD appeared to be in competition with UNEP, which left UNEP searching to define its role in implementing *Agenda 21*. As the UN Office of Internal Oversight Services (the auditors of UN activities) observed, "the basic issue facing UNEP concerns its role following the United Nations Conference on Environment and Development. It is not clear to staff or to stakeholders what that role should be".[34]

Until this point, UNEP had been mandated to act as coordinator and focal point for environmental action within the UN system. Though sustainable development was not entirely within the scope of the environmental sector, it served to anchor environmental discussions leading up to the Rio summit. Two of the major treaties that emerged from Rio, the Climate Change and Desertification Conventions had been initiated by UNEP but were mandated under the UN Secretariat instead of UNEP. Annan's predecessor, Boutros Ghali, had sent a strong signal of non-confidence when he created the new internal coordination structure for the UN system on sustainable development without a major role for UNEP. In addition, in a report to the General Assembly following Rio, Boutros Ghali recommended the creation of a new department for implementing *Agenda 21*. The Department of Policy Coordination and Sustainable Development would be headed by an Under-Secretary-General, to whom UNEP would report via the newly established Commission on Sustainable Development. In addition to this, two further layers of structure were created. A High-level Advisory Board made up of 15–25 eminent persons from around the world was to advise the Secretary-General of the follow-up to UNCED; the Board did not include the executive director of UNEP. Boutros Ghali also created the Inter-Agency Committee on Sustainable Development, which placed coordination of environmental issues outside the leadership of UNEP.[35] This last move transferred the authority for inter-agency coordination from UNEP to UN Headquarters, leaving UNEP at the periphery.

In 1973, following the adoption of the Resolution that created UNEP, the General Assembly also created an internal mechanism by which UNEP could coordinate the rest of the United Nations on environmental issues. The Environment Coordinating Board (ECB) was set up under the auspices of the Administrative Committee on Coordination. But, within only five years of its creation, the board had "failed to live up to expectations and was abolished" by the General Assembly through Resolution 32/197 of 10 December 1977. Its tasks then reverted to the ACC. UNEP then attempted to produce a "system-wide medium-term environment programme" through lower-level meetings of Designated Officials for Environment Matters (DOEM). This system worked fairly well and became the backbone for organizing the inputs into Rio. This mechanism was replaced in 1995 by the Inter-Agency Environment Coordination Group (IAECG).

Though the IAECG functioned up until 1999, it was perceived by many as ineffective and unable to establish the necessary authority and vision for coordination.[36] The primary problem, however, was that it was overshadowed by the Inter-Agency Committee on Sustainable Development (IACSD), which was created to assist the ACC in identifying issues to follow up on UNCED.[37] The IACSD was crafted in the likeness of the DOEM, so it used a system of focal points between agencies, so-called task managers, with one manager per chapter of *Agenda 21*. The IAECG was composed of executive heads from each relevant agency and thus was top heavy and less functional in contrast to the IACSD. Also given that *Agenda 21* was a comprehensive plan covering almost every environmental issue, including cross-cutting and emerging issues identified at Rio, it left little room for the UNEP to work and added to the ineffectiveness of the IAECG.

The Secretary-General's report marked the first step towards changing all this and renewing confidence in UNEP. The report, written by Maurice Strong, the chairman of the Stockholm and the Rio conferences and the first executive director of UNEP, paid explicit attention to ensuring that UNEP was recognized as the "environmental voice" of the United Nations and the "environmental agency of the world community".[38] The report called for UNEP to be given the status, strength and access to resources it required to function effectively. This support was also in accordance with the Nairobi Declaration made that same year by the UNEP Governing Council, in which it affirmed the continued relevance of UNEP and the importance of its mandate. The report briefly touched on the past rivalry between the new Rio institutions and UNEP when it stated that the IACSD should not "preclude or inhibit" UNEP's role, because both the IACSD and UNEP report to the General Assembly through the Economic and Social Council.[39]

Later that year, the General Assembly undertook a five-year review of the outcome of the Earth Summit[40] and adopted the *Programme for the Further Implementation of Agenda 21*.[41] The Programme emphasized that, given the increasing number of decision-making bodies concerned with various aspects of sustainable development, including international conventions, there was an ever greater need for better policy coordination at the intergovernmental level, as well as for continued and more concerted efforts to enhance collaboration among the secretariats of those decision-making bodies. At the review, governments stated that "the conference of the parties to conventions signed at the United Nations Conference on Environment and Development or as a result of it, as well as other conventions related to sustainable development, should cooperate in exploring ways and means of collaborating in their work to advance the effective implementation of the conventions to continue to pursue sustainable development objectives".[42]

As part of the *Programme of Reform*, the UN Secretary-General, in consultation with the executive directors of UNEP and of UN Habitat, made certain recommendations for strengthening and restructuring the Organization to the 53rd Session of the General Assembly. To initiate the process, the Secretary-General decided to create a Task Force on Environment and Human Settlements, to work under the following terms of reference:

To review existing structures and arrangements through which environment and environment-related activities are carried out within the United Nations, with particular reference to departments, funds and programmes that report to the Secretary-General but also taking into account the relevant programmes and activities of the specialized agencies;
In this respect, to focus particularly on the distinctive functions of policy, development of norms and standards, programme development and implementation, and financing, as well as relationships among those functions;
To evaluate the efficacy and effectiveness of existing structures and arrangements, and make recommendations for such changes and improvements as will optimize the work and effectiveness of United Nations environmental work at the global level and of UNEP as the leading environmental organization or "authority", as well as the role of UNEP as the principal source of environmental input into the work of the Commission on Sustainable Development;
To prepare proposals for consideration by the Secretary-General and subsequent submission to the General Assembly on reforming and strengthening United Nations activities in the area of environment and human settlements.[43]

This Task Force concluded that substantial overlaps and unrecognized linkages and gaps characterized current UN activities and that these flaws were "basic and pervasive".[44]

The Task Force made a number of important recommendations to the Secretary-General that the General Assembly later adopted. Of particular significance were Recommendation One, to establish an Environmental Management Group (EMG) and abolish the ineffective Inter-Agency Environmental Coordination Group (IAECG), and Recommendation Thirteen, which suggested the establishment of "an annual ministerial level, global forum in which ministers can gather to review and revise the environmental agenda of the United Nations in the context of sustainable development".[45] The rationale behind these recommendations was simple. The IAECG had been in place since 1995 as a successor of the DOEM and had had two formal meetings but, according to the Task Force, the need for coordination tended toward substance and not administration. It foresaw a stronger role based on an "issue management" approach, whereby once inter-agency cooperation identified a problem it would have the capability to mobilize the right agencies and resources to the tackle problem. In this regard, there was a need to create collaboration among members but also to link with other organizations and financial institutions outside the UN system. The IAECG was too rigid for this purpose, being operationalized not towards action but rather to review and information-sharing.

The proposal to create a high-level ministers' forum, which later became the Global Ministerial Environment Forum (GMEF), was directed at re-establishing the importance of UNEP and attracting ministers back to UNEP decision-making. The Task Force also considered the possibility of universalizing participation in UNEP's Governing Council (beyond the then 58 members). In order to do this without undermining the existing credibility of the Council, established over 30 years earlier, it was recommended that the ministerial meeting have universal membership and convene every year, but that in alternate years it would be in the form of the UNEP Governing Council. However, this proposal eventually became controversial, and, although the Final Report adopted by the GMEF on the International Environmental Governance (IEG) process recommended universal membership,[46] the Johannesburg Plan of Implementation (2002) deferred the decision to the 57th Session of the General Assembly. The General Assembly in turn decided the issue was a complex one and required further examination by the UNEP Governing Council and other relevant bodies of the United Nations system, and that it would revisit the issue at its 60th session.[47]

The Task Force nonetheless set in motion a major review of UNEP's role and how to strengthen environmental governance. At the first meeting of the GMEF, which took place in Sweden from 29 to 31 May 2000, over 100 ministers adopted the Malmö Declaration, which requested the WSSD to "review the requirements for a greatly strengthened institutional structure for international environmental governance based on an assessment of future needs for an institutional architecture that has the capacity to effectively address wide-ranging environmental threats in a globalizing world. UNEP's role in this regard should be strengthened and its financial base broadened and made more predictable."[48] This clause of the Declaration was operationalized by UNEP Governing Council Decision 21/21 on international environmental governance, which called for an Open-ended Intergovernmental Group of Ministers or Their Representatives on International Environmental Governance (hereafter the IEG Working Group) "to undertake a comprehensive policy-oriented assessment of existing institutional weaknesses as well as future needs and options for strengthened international environmental governance".[49]

With this mandate, the IEG Working Group set to work on a number of recommendations for the GMEF to be fed into the World Summit on Sustainable Development. In total, six sessions took place between April 2001 and the final meeting in Cartagena in February 2002. The level of documentation was impressive and the Working Group considered many possible reforms – including the upgrading of UNEP to a Specialized Agency, the clustering of multilateral environmental agreements, and a means of stabilizing UNEP's financial base.[50] From early in the process, however, ministers and representatives agreed that the "process of strengthening international environmental governance should be evolutionary in nature" and based on an incremental approach.[51]

The final recommendations reflected this cautious approach to institutional change. Clearly, countries placed a great deal of confidence in the newly established GMEF as a means to improve coherence. The basic premise behind the Forum was to attract decision makers at a high enough level that they might have a significant impact on policy guidance and coordination with other UN entities.[52] However, the balance of the CSD and the GMEF has been an issue; some analysts are concerned that the "work of the Environment Forum does not become undermined and/ or paralysed by the unconstructive political dynamics, which have impaired the work of the CSD, and which have dominated many recent international environmental negotiations".[53] In the context of how the GMEF reports its work on sustainable development to the CSD in New York, this concern is an important one, especially since the CSD has been criticized for renegotiating existing commitments and could have the potential to water down the GMEF's high-level inputs.

The greatest potential for progress in coordinating environmental governance in the late 1990s was at the level of multilateral environmental agreements (MEAs). It was also the area in which the results from the IEG process were far too cautious. Several years before the IEG process, there had been a great deal of research conducted on MEA coordination,[54] and MEA secretariats had responded strongly to strengthening their synergies and interlinkages. The documents prepared by the UNEP secretariat clearly demonstrated the potential for collaboration in the areas of technology transfer, finance, scientific assessment, indicators, education, awareness-raising and capacity-building.[55] Despite the evidence and richness of the inputs, the recommendations by the IEG Working Group called only for a soft approach, for example the "initiation of pilot projects",[56] the promotion of collaboration, and more coordination in the periodicity and scheduling of meetings for MEAs. The problem that the Working Group faced was the question of how far they could go in suggesting reforms, given that most MEAs had autonomous decision-making authority. The recommendations did, however, call for UNEP to provide periodic reviews of the effectiveness of MEAs.[57] It is to be hoped that future UNEP Governing Council meetings will be able to follow up on this mandate and provide a system for evaluation, which would include assessing the degree of collaboration between MEAs. This type of analysis is crucial for decision makers in strengthening individual MEAs as well as realizing a more systematic legal framework between MEAs in the future.

On 25 March 2002, the executive director of UNEP, on behalf of the Secretary-General, transmitted the recommendations of the IEG Working Group and the Governing Council to the Third Preparatory Meeting (Prepcom III) of the CSD, which was acting as the preparatory committee for the World Summit on Sustainable Development (WSSD) in Johannesburg.

The Johannesburg Plan of Implementation

Preparations for the Johannesburg summit began in 2000 with a series of preparatory committee meetings (prepcoms) carried out by the UN regional economic and social commissions and a preliminary international prepcom in New York that laid out the objectives and processes of the summit. Institutional issues were first categorized under the title of "Sustainable Development Governance", later changed to "Institutional Framework for Sustainable Development", and taken up by Working Group IV. Since UNEP's Governing Council had planned to conclude its discussions on international environmental governance later in 2002, it was decided that the Working Group would not deliberate until Prepcom III – after UNEP's discussions had concluded.

Until this point, there was widespread expectation that the WSSD would produce significant institutional reforms. The in-depth assessment by UNEP and the ministerial-level contributions to the IEG process, coupled with the considerable criticism of overlap between UNEP and the CSD and the calls for an international organization for environment and sustainable development, led many to be optimistic. In addition, it was well known that many European countries such as France and Germany were pushing quietly for UNEP to be upgraded to a Specialized Agency.

Despite the forces pushing for institutional reform, pressure from development agencies and from countries not wishing to allow the United Nations to gain control over bodies such as the WTO played a considerable part in blocking progress toward reform. The first volley against changes to the status quo came from Nitin Desai, Secretary-General of the summit and head of the CSD, in his opening speech to Prepcom III. His job was to advise the governments on the priority areas and the organization of work for the meeting, but his comments went much further. In introducing the agenda item on sustainable development governance, Desai frankly stated that the CSD had been the "centerpiece" for sustainable development governance over the past decade. He further asserted that it was largely an "innovative organization", which had had significant achievements such as attracting non-environment ministers to its deliberations, engaging "a high level of interest from capitals", attracting many stakeholders through its dialogues, and developing a "strong inter-agency process [to] guid[e] it". He conceded that the CSD had weaknesses, such as not generating "sufficient pressure for effective implementation", but he stated that the Type II Partnerships – voluntary initiatives between public and private actors to promote sustainable development – launched by the Johannesburg preparatory committee would likely address this shortcoming. He also mentioned the need to connect better to the regional level, which he believed that CSD could achieve by working with regional organizations to create stronger regional processes.[58]

These observations, though perhaps accurate, presumed that the CSD should continue its role of coordinating sustainable development governance. Nowhere in the discussion was there an independent review of the institutional effectiveness of the CSD, or a formal information paper for governments on how it might be strengthened. This was a glaring omission, given that the CSD was created as a result of the previous summit 10 years earlier, and that governments were about to be asked to deliberate again on institutional questions concerning sustainable development governance. It is unclear if this lack of independent analysis was an intentional omission, or rather the result of international organizations trying to protect themselves during a time of scrutiny and potential criticism. At Stockholm 30 years earlier, Maurice Strong avoided any conflict of interest by using an independent secretariat. Perhaps this is an approach to reconsider for future summits.

The discussion paper by the co-chairs of Working Group IV placed the existing organizations (CSD, ECOSOC and the General Assembly) at the heart of the framework for sustainable development governance and any deliberations of the Working Group.[59] This arrangement stuck, and it informed the general structure of the final section within the Johannesburg Plan of Implementation (JPOI). The discussion paper considered three main dimensions of coordination, which were based on the Secretary-General's *Report on Implementing Agenda 21*, prior discussions at Prepcom II and informal discussions held in New York. The first dimension concerned potential new roles for the CSD, ECOSOC and the General Assembly in strengthening sustainable development governance,[60] the second related to the coordination of regional institutions, and the third (and by far the most controversial) was how to "provide for effective policy formulation, coordination, implementation and review" as well as "coherence and consistency"[61] between the economic, environmental and social sectors.

Though these goals raise the right kinds of questions, the JPOI itself is disappointing. It offers very few changes from the status quo and certainly nothing imaginative in terms of a future vision of effective institutional arrangements.[62] Earlier drafts of the JPOI had sought to address coordination between the pillars. In particular, the Bali draft circulated at Prepcom IV held in Bali, Indonesia, proposed the creation of a new "high-level inter-agency co-ordinating body on sustainable development which would include the principal UN agencies and institutions dealing with sustainable development, the international financial institutions, the OECD and the WTO, which will report to the CSD".[63] The references to coordination with the WTO, however, became a sticking point in the negotiations. The final language of the JPOI is intentionally ambiguous, and leaves unresolved the questions of the relationship of the WTO to the follow-up to *Agenda 21* and achieving the goal of sustainable development.[64]

The objectives for strengthening governance laid out in the JPOI include "strengthening coherence, coordination and monitoring"; "increasing effectiveness and efficiency through limiting overlap and duplication of activities of international organizations"; and integrating "the economic, social and environmental dimensions of sustainable development in a balanced manner".[65] These are all important priorities, but the Plan proposes no concrete new actions. It places the future of sustainable development governance in the hands of the existing institutional framework. At the top of the hierarchy in the JPOI is the General Assembly, which is to be the overarching key element for achieving sustainable development and provide the political direction for implementing *Agenda 21*. This was nothing new as it already had this mandate, and it was known that it was well placed to perform these tasks. The question has always been rather about the consistency of its commitment and priority to sustainable development in the face of an ever-growing political agenda that it must deal with:

The ECOSOC will continue to be the key coordination mechanism of the UN system, but it should strengthen its oversight for integrating the three pillars of sustainable development, "make full use of its high-level coordination" abilities, promote greater coordination, provide closer links to the follow up of WSSD to the Monterrey Process, and explore ways to develop arrangements for meeting with the Bretton Woods Institutions and WTO.[66]

Nowhere does the JPOI explain how ECOSOC should go about achieving these goals. As early as 1970, ECOSOC had been criticized for its lack of coordination in other fields of the UN.[67] In 1992, Chapter 38 of *Agenda 21* had already clearly designated ECOSOC to "undertake the task of directing system-wide coordination and integration of environmental and developmental aspects of United Nations policies and programmes", making full use of its high-level and coordination segments.[68] Given its failure to fulfil this function over the past 30 years, and since it has not been provided with any further power to operationalize these provisions, there is no reason to believe that ECOSOC will ever realize these goals.

In order to achieve the above objectives, the JPOI places most emphasis on what it terms an "enhanced" CSD. According to the JPOI, the CSD should continue to play its role as a "high-level commission for sustainable development within the United Nations system and serve as a forum for consideration of issues related to integration of the three dimensions of sustainable development". But an enhanced CSD needs to amend its approach to include "reviewing and monitoring progress in the implementation of Agenda 21", which is already part of its mandate, as well as "fostering coherence of implementation, initiatives and partnerships", which is a new role given to the Type II Partnerships coming out of WSSD. In addition, the JPOI states that the CSD should place more emphasis on action and implementation with "governments, international organizations and relevant stakeholders". In terms of coordination, it will *inter alia*:

Focus on the cross-sectoral aspects of specific sectoral issues and provide a forum for better integration of policies, including through interaction among Ministers dealing with the various dimensions and sectors of sustainable development through the high-level segments;

Focus on actions related to implementation of Agenda 21, limiting negotiations in the sessions of the Commission to every two years;

Limit the number of themes addressed in each session;

Take into account significant legal developments in the field of sustainable development, with due regard to the role of relevant intergovernmental bodies in promoting the implementation of Agenda 21 relating to international legal instruments and mechanisms.[69]

At the eleventh session of the CSD (CSD-11), 28 April–9 May 2003, the details of the implementation of these new components were negotiated. The result was the creation of a new two-year work cycle, which will include an "implementation" session and a "policy" session. Delegates will negotiate only in the second year of the cycle. After a long and divisive debate, a 15-year programme was agreed upon. The first session (2004–2005), the first meeting of which took place in April 2004, focused on water, sanitation and human settlements; this will be followed by energy, industrial development, air pollution and climate change (2006–2007). An overall appraisal of *Agenda 21* will be undertaken in 2016–2017.[70] It was agreed that cross-cutting issues should be considered in every work cycle, using most of the JPOI-agreed sections of poverty, unsustainable consumption and production patterns, protecting and managing the natural resource base, etc. The Type II Partnerships were to be followed up with a voluntary reporting system as well as annual events at the CSD – the Learning Center and the Partnerships Fair – which were created to promote the exchange of lessons learned in projects promoting sustainable development and to disseminate successful cases of public/private collaboration.

Although these reforms were expected to shift the CSD away from its old habits of acting as a "talking shop" towards focusing on implementation and bringing more cross-cutting issues into the negotiations, CSD-11, the first session after the Johannesburg summit, was not a promising start. Discussion continued to focus on environmental issues rather than development, but observers have argued that this may have been owing to the fact that representation was "overwhelmingly from Environment Departments, and officials from development or planning ministries (particularly from European countries)" were not so present or engaged.[71] Observers also remarked that negotiations at CSD-11, which would set the stage for the next decade of the CSD, failed to include provisions for building coherence on sustainable development issues, WTO-related issues that were controversial in Johannesburg, corporate accountability (an obvious omission given its prominence in WSSD), and "strengthening the national reporting process to allow voluntary 'peer review' to develop between interested countries".[72]

However, CSD-11 occurred very soon after Johannesburg, so the session may have been suffering from conference fatigue. Indeed, the session in 2004, which was the first under the newly "enhanced" system and based on recommendations in the JPOI, was in many ways very promising. Before the session began, the chairman, Børge Brende, spent significant time encouraging support from governments in various sectors, and as a result over "100 ministers representing sectors as diverse as water, housing, environment, development, finance and agriculture" were present.[73] The meeting discussed the links between the Millennium Development Goals (MDGs) and the JPOI, and discussed in particular how the CSD could assist in achieving poverty reduction.[74]

Nevertheless, because only the second year of each CSD thematic session will be a negotiated session, it remains to be seen whether the CSD can produce substantive outcomes from these new components. The first test will be in 2005, when the Secretary-General is due to report to the General Assembly on the implementation of the MDGs for its review.[75] It is to be hoped that the CSD will provide a clear assessment of the current status of some of the links between ecosystems and human well-being in the context of social and economic development. The future effectiveness of the CSD clearly depends on its ability to add value to the international institutional arrangements for sustainable development by dealing with the substance of the links between the environment and economic and social development. If it can make these connections and produce results, then the confidence that countries placed in it at the Johannesburg summit will not be lost.

Conclusion: Addressing the nature of today's institutional needs

The historical analysis presented here suggests that the coordination and institutional needs for environment and sustainable development issues have changed according to the three periods demarcated by the Stockholm, Rio and Johannesburg summits. Despite the shortcomings of the current institutional framework for sustainable development and the opportunities missed at each of these summits, these changes indicate that states have recognized political and environmental changes and have tried – with some measure of success – to adapt to them. However, the institutional landscape today has become so complex that it is no longer sufficient to think of addressing coordination and institutional arrangements through a singular approach, such as creating a World Environment Organization. Yet, heeding the cautionary words of the Stockholm, Rio and Johannesburg summits and favouring an incremental approach over major reforms have also produced far too few results.

Future improvements to sustainable development governance must focus on a number of institutions and varying levels of coordination. First and foremost, institutions within the environmental sector must be strengthened. The environment pillar of sustainable development is clearly the weakest. Despite the rhetoric and the sticking plaster solutions, there is still too much overlap between the CSD and UNEP. The CSD must clearly forget the sectoral elements that it has clung to for the past 10 years and focus on cross-cutting issues such as poverty, trade, health, education, finance and capacity-building. If strengthened, UNEP could be adequately equipped to bring its sectoral elements to CSD's forum, as do the economic and social institutions. Then, the CSD could become the forum on sustainable development that was originally intended.

Within the environment sector, UNEP also has many opportunities to strengthen cooperation between MEAs. Though not originally mandated to be the legal umbrella for MEAs, UNEP has evolved into this role and in fact has performed it very well.[76] Now it must progress to the next stage and, like the GATT, think of creating a closer network for the MEAs to regularize cooperation, strengthen dispute settlement, and codify principles. The modest suggestion by the JPOI concerning clustering could be augmented into an overarching institutional structure if the political will existed.

Intersectoral coordination for sustainable development governance is by far the greatest institutional challenge. There has been a consistent reluctance on the part of certain developed countries to bringing organizations outside the United Nations, such as the WTO, into the sustainable development fold. It is obvious that ECOSOC cannot rise to this task. Its ineffectiveness was notorious long before Stockholm yet, because it is a principal organ of the United Nations, there is strong resistance to amending the UN Charter, and so this piece of the institutional framework remains a problem. It is equally obvious from the Rio and Johannesburg summits that the most powerful countries will never allow the Bretton Woods institutions and the WTO to be controlled by the United Nations. Some middle ground solution must be found, where countries would be willing to discuss coordination.

Finally, the implementation of intersectoral projects presents real coordination challenges. Environment and sustainable development issues have both been relegated to makeshift, ad hoc institutional arrangements because of their cross-cutting, multidisciplinary nature. Thus, neither UNEP nor CSD has an implementation arm at the national level.

Rather they must rely on institutions that are working on issues with an environmental or sustainable development dimension to carry out projects and activities.

To provide a truly effective sustainable development regime, UNEP, the CSD and other institutions must be endowed with genuine implementation capacity, as well as compatibility at the national and regional levels. This can be achieved only through deeper reforms than those undertaken to date in global summits. The remainder of this book looks at what some of these reforms might perhaps look like in the event that one day the political will to create an effective sustainable development regime will materialize.

Notes

1. See *Report of the Secretary-General: Renewing the United Nations, A Programme for Reform*, A/51/950, 14 July 1997.
2. See United Nations Economic and Social Council, Resolution 1346 (XLV), 30 July 1968.
3. See, for example, the 1975 Helsinki Final Act, *International Legal Materials*, Vol. 14, p. 1292, which states "that their efforts to develop cooperation in the fields of trade, industry, science and technology, the environment and other areas of economic activity contribute to the reinforcement of peace and security in Europe and in the world as a whole".
4. Administrative Coordination Committee, *The United Nations System and the Human Environment*, A/CONF.48/12, 17 December 1971, p. 4.
5. Ibid., p. 5.
6. Ibid., p. 73.
7. Peter B. Stone, *Did We Save the Earth at Stockholm: The People and Politics in the Conference on the Human Environment*, London: Earth Island, 1973.
8. This was demonstrated by an account by Peter Stone in his book on the Stockholm Conference of a telegram sent to the US, Swedish and other delegations, but leaked to ECO, that was intended to weaken any potential organization arising from the conference. See Stone, *Did We Save the Earth at Stockholm*, p. 56.
9. Ibid., p. 33.
10. *International Organizational Implications of Action Proposals*, A/CONF.48/11, 10 January 1972, para. 5.
11. A. O. Adede (in *Renewing International Environmental Governance: Issues for Consideration by African Countries*, ACTS, at ⟨http://www.acts.or.ke/Renewing.pdf⟩, accessed 1 June 2004) cites the plethora of meetings convened on this issue, including International Organization and the Human Environment, co-sponsored by the Institute on Man and Science and the Aspen Institute for Humanistic Studies, held at Rensselaerville, New York, 21–23 May 1971; The Crisis of the Human Environment and International Action, sponsored by the International Studies Program, University of Toronto, held at Toronto, Canada, 25–27 May 1971; the Sixth Conference on the United Nations of the Next Decade, sponsored by the Stanley Foundation, held at Sinaia, Romania, 20–26 June 1971; the First International Environmental Workshop, co-sponsored by the International Institute for Environmental Affairs and the Aspen Institute for Humanistic Studies, held at Aspen, Colorado, 20 June–6 August 1971; the Panel of Experts on

International Organizational Implications, convened by the Secretary-General of the United Nations Conference on the Human Environment, held at Geneva, Switzerland, 8–9 July 1971; International Legal and Institutional Responses to the Problems of the Global Environment, co-sponsored by the Carnegie Endowment for International Peace and the American Society of International Law, held at Harriman, New York, 25 September–1 October 1971; and the UN System and the Human Environment, sponsored by the Institute for the Study of International Organization, University of Sussex, held at Brighton, England, 1–4 November 1971.

12. *International Organizational Implications of Action Proposals*, A/CONF.48/11, para. 7.
13. Ibid., para. 57.
14. R. Gardner, "The Role of the UN in Environmental Problems", *International Organization*, Vol. 26, 1972, pp. 237, 248.
15. Ibid.
16. *International Organizational Implications of Action Proposals*, A/CONF.48/11, para. 60.
17. In fact, the only UN-based agencies having activities that were principally environmental were the Department of Economic and Social Affairs, which had activities on transport and on housing, population and planning; and UNESCO, which had a number of activities on atmospheric pollution, conservation of land and marine environments, and water and pollutants. For an overview of UN-related activities in 1970 see appendix 1 in B. Johnson, "The United Nations Institutional Response to Stockholm: A Case Study in the International Politics of Institutional Change", *International Organization*, Vol. 25, 1972, p. 289.
18. See Johnson, "The United Nations Institutional Response to Stockholm", p. 272. Also see UN Charter Article 63, which allows ECOSOC to coordinate the activities of the Specialized Agencies through consultation and recommendations.
19. See Johnson, "The United Nations Institutional Response to Stockholm", p. 273.
20. Ibid., p. 274.
21. *International Organizational Implications of Action Proposals*, A/CONF.48/11, para. 7(d).
22. See Gardner, "The Role of the UN in Environmental Problems", p. 245.
23. See *Report of the Deliberation of the Second Committee on Natural Resource Management and Development Chapters X*, A/CONF.48/14/Rev.1, 1973, paras. 170–259. Also see preparatory meeting reports such as *Environment and Development*, Fournex, Switzerland, 4–12 June 1971.
24. For a definition of sustainable development, see World Commission on Environment and Development, *Our Common Future*, Oxford: Oxford University Press, 1987. See also UN General Assembly, *Report of the Brundtland Commission*, A/42/427.
25. See *Agenda 21, Report of the United Nations Conference on Environment and Development*, A/CONF.151/26 (vol. III), 1992, Chapter 38, para. 38.8 and para. 38.4, respectively.
26. *Establishment of the Commission on Sustainable Development*, E/1993/207, 12 February 1993; available at ⟨http://www.un.org/documents/ecosoc/res/1993/eres1993-207.htm⟩.
27. The IACSD is a subsidiary body of the Administrative Coordinating Committee (ACC), which in turn acts as a kind of "cabinet" for the Secretary-General. The IACSD is made up of senior-level officials from nine core members of the ACC: the FAO, IAEA, ILO, UNDP, UNEP, UNESCO, WHO, World Bank and WMO. Officials from other UN bodies and intergovernmental agencies and representatives from major groups are able to attend by invitation.
28. For an overview of problems of CSD from 1994 to 1996 and from 1997 to 2001, see Felix Dodds, Rosalie Gardiner et al., "Paper #9 Post Johannesburg: The Future of the UNU Commission on Sustainable Development", *Stakeholder Forum*, Vol. 5, 2002.
29. Pamela Chasek, "The United Nations Commission on Sustainable Development: The

First Five Years", paper for The United Nations University Conference on the Global Environment in the 21st Century: From Common Challenges to Shared Responsibilities, UNU, 1997.

30. World Summit on Sustainable Development, *Report of WSSD and Plan of Action, Reissued Text*, A/CON.99/20, available at ⟨http://www.johannesburgsummit.org/html/documents/summit_docs/131302_wssd_report⟩, 4 September 2002, para. 146.

31. *Report of the Secretary-General: Renewing the United Nations.*

32. *Letter of Transmittal to President of General Assembly*, 14 July 1997.

33. Ibid.

34. Daniel J. Shepard, "Linkages between Environment Development and UN Reform", *Linkages Journal*, Vol. 3, 1998, pp. 1–2.

35. United Nations General Assembly, *Institutional Arrangements to Follow up the United Nations Conference on Environment and Development*, A/CONF.47/191, 29 January 1993.

36. United Nations Environment Programme, *Inter-Agency Coordination Group and System-wide Strategy in the Field of the Environment*, UNEP/GC.20/7, 1999.

37. The ACC and the IACSD were replaced after the review of the ACC in October 2001 established the UN Chief Executives Board (CEB) for Coordination.

38. See *Report of the Secretary-General: Renewing the United Nations*, para. 176.

39. Ibid., para. 175.

40. *Rio+5 General Assembly Special Session*, A/S-19/29, 27 June 1997.

41. *Programme for the Further Implementation of Agenda 21*, A/RES/S-19/2, 28 June 1997.

42. *Rio+5 General Assembly Special Session*, para. 118.

43. See *The Report of the United Nations Task Force on Environment and Human Settlements to the Secretary-General*, 1998, annexed in the *Report of the Secretary-General: United Nations Reform – Measures and Proposals – Environment and Human Settlements*, A/53/463, 6 October 1998.

44. Ibid.

45. The United Nations General Assembly supported this recommendation through a Resolution passed on 10 August 1999.

46. UNEP Governing Council, *International Environmental Governance*, Appendix SS.VII/1, 2001, para. 11(a).

47. United Nations General Assembly, *Report of the Governing Council of the United Nations Environment Programme on Its Seventh Special Session*, A/RES/57/251, 21 February 2003, agenda item 87, para. 4.

48. Malmö Ministerial Declaration, Adopted by the Global Ministerial Environment Forum – Sixth Special Session of the Governing Council of the United Nations Environment Programme, Fifth Plenary Meeting, Malmö, Sweden, 31 May 2000.

49. UNEP Governing Council, Decision 21/21, 2001.

50. For more on clustering, see Oberthür in chapter 2 in this volume.

51. United Nations General Assembly, *International Environmental Governance: Note by Secretary General*, A/CONF.199/PC/3, 22 March 2002, p. 5.

52. See chapter 3, where Richard Tarasofsky provides a more in-depth examination of the permanent role of the GMEF and its work to date.

53. Johannah Bernstein, "Paper #2 Analysis of UNEP Executive Director's Report on International Environmental Governance (UNEP/IGM/1/2)", *Stakeholder Forum*, Vol. 4, May 2001.

54. See, for example, United Nations University Interlinkages Initiative at ⟨http://www.unu.edu/inter-linkages/⟩; Daniel C. Esty and Maria H. Ivanova, "Revitalizing International Environmental Governance: A Function-Driven Approach", in Daniel C. Esty and Maria H. Ivanova, eds, *Global Environmental Governance: Options and Opportunities*,

New Haven, CT: Yale School of Forestry and Environmental Studies, 2002, pp. 181, 193–194, accessed at ⟨http://www.yale.edu/environment/publications⟩; Joy Hyvarinen and Duncan Brack, *Global Environmental Institutions: Arguments for Reform*, London: Royal Institute of International Affairs, 2003.

55. See, for example, UNEP, *Implementing the Clustering Strategy for Multilateral Environmental Agreements*, UNEP/IGM/4/4, 16 November 2001.

56. United Nations General Assembly, *Report of the Governing Council of the United Nations Environment Programme on Its Seventh Special Session*, para. 27.

57. Ibid., para. 28.

58. Opening Remarks, Mr. Nitin Desai, Secretary-General for World Summit on Sustainable Development, Third Preparatory Committee for the World Summit on Sustainable Development, 25 March 2002.

59. "Sustainable Development Governance at the International, Regional and National Levels: Discussion Paper Prepared by the Vice-Chairs Mr. Ositadinma Anaedu and Mr. Lars-Goran Engfeldt for consideration at Third Session of the Preparatory Committee for WSSD", Prepcom III, 25 March 2002, paras. 11, 12 and 18.

60. Ibid., para. 1.

61. Ibid., para. 3.

62. Nicolas A. Robinson, "Befogged Vision: International Environmental Governance a Decade after Rio", *William and Mary Environmental Law and Policy Review*, Vol. 27, 2002, p. 339.

63. "Prepcom IV to WSSD, Sustainable Development Governance Working Group, Compilation text", 15 May 2002.

64. See coordination provisions referring to the WTO in *Report of WSSD and Plan of Action, Reissued Text*, para. 97(c).

65. Ibid., para. 137.

66. Ibid., para. 144.

67. See the Stanley Foundation, "Sixth Conference of the United Nations of the Next Decade", Sinaia, Romania, 20–26 June 1971, p. 20.

68. *Agenda 21*, Chapter 38, para. 10.

69. *Report of WSSD and Plan of Action, Reissued Text*, para. 147.

70. Tom Bigg, "The World Summit on Sustainable Development: An Assessment", accessed at ⟨http://www.wssd-and-civil-society.org/docs/WSSD%20%20an%20assessment.pdf⟩, p. 15.

71. Ibid., p. 14.

72. Ibid., p. 15.

73. International Institute of Sustainable Development, *Earth Negotiations Bulletin*, Vol. 211, 3 May 2004, p. 13.

74. Ibid.

75. *Implementation of the United Nations Millennium Declaration: Report of Secretary General*, A/58/323, September 2003, para. 99.

76. See Adede, *Renewing International Environmental Governance*.

2

Clustering of multilateral environmental agreements: Potentials and limitations

Sebastian Oberthür

Introduction

International discussions on a restructuring and reform of international environmental governance (IEG) have acquired new momentum with the advent of the Johannesburg process leading to the World Summit on Sustainable Development (WSSD) in South Africa in August–September 2002. In particular, in February 2001 the Governing Council of the United Nations Environment Programme (UNEP) established an "open-ended intergovernmental group of ministers or their representatives on international environmental governance".[1] In February 2002, the Seventh Special Session of the UNEP Governing Council also meeting as the Global Ministerial Environment Forum (GMEF) adopted the report of the intergovernmental group and decided to review the implementation of the recommendations contained therein at its next, twenty-second, session.[2] Subsequently, the WSSD Plan of Implementation resolved that this decision should be fully implemented.[3]

The concept of "clustering" multilateral environmental agreements (MEAs) acquired particular prominence in the discussions of the UNEP Working Group on IEG.[4] Generally speaking, "clustering" has been defined as "grouping a number of international environmental regimes together so as to make them more efficient and effective".[5] The report of the intergovernmental group on IEG adopted by the UNEP Governing Council/GMEF contains the statement that "the clustering approach to multilateral environmental agreements holds some promise" and has a whole section on "improved coordination among and effectiveness of [MEAs]".[6]

Although various concepts for reforming IEG have been discussed in the literature for several years,[7] clustering of MEAs has been introduced only relatively recently.[8] Generally, clustering of MEAs is meant to provide a means for addressing the fragmentation of the IEG system. Accordingly, the large and increasing number of MEAs, which already number more than 200, has been identified as endangering the efficient and effective functioning of the system. In particular, an increasing potential for duplicated work and conflict between different MEAs, a growing demand for coordination, and the greater resources required for effective participation in the system from governments and other actors such as intergovernmental and non-governmental organizations have been identified as problems.[9]

The notion of a growing potential for conflict and calls for a more centralized coordination of MEAs have met with criticism. It has been pointed out, for example, that conflict has hardly ever arisen, so the demand for coordination is overestimated (though, for a discussion of conflicts between trade and environmental law, see Sampson in chapter 5 in this volume). Where such demand has occurred, suitable responses have been developed within the current system. Furthermore, any attempt at centralized coordination would prove ineffective at best given the decentralized nature of international environmental law.[10] Eventually, this decentralized nature reflects the differentiated problem structure of the policy area of environmental policy.[11] Clustering appears to go some way to taking into account and responding to such criticism since it does not call for a centralized or hierarchical approach to coordination (see below).

Rather than discussing the usefulness of coordination and integration in international environmental policy and law at a general level, this chapter employs a bottom–up approach to evaluating the potentials and limitations of clustering MEAs as a tool to increase the consistency of the system and enhance synergy. To this end, I proceed in three steps. First, I attempt to decompose what has been proposed to be "clustered" into its elements and assess the merits and potential drawbacks of clustering these elements. In particular, I introduce a distinction between the organizational/administrative components of MEAs and their various functional elements. I then present some approaches to building clusters of MEAs that have been put forward in the international discussion (in particular, clustering by issue, function or region) and assess them against the background of the distinction between organizational and functional elements. Thirdly, I provide an overall assessment of the clustering of

MEAs by comparing its potentials with the major challenges faced in international environmental policy. The chapter ends with a summary of the main conclusions.

Elements of clustering

What is proposed in the debate about clustering MEAs? Would parts of MEAs be clustered or full MEAs be merged? To the extent that we are talking about integrating parts of MEAs, which parts could be clustered in which way and what would be the prospects of doing so? To approach these questions, a distinction between the organizational/administrative elements and the various functions of MEAs is introduced in the following discussion. Clustering of any of these aspects of MEAs would not, a priori, exclude clustering of another aspect at the same time. In addition to identifying the major organizational elements and functions of MEAs, the following subsections assess the advantages and disadvantages of their clustering.

Clustering of the organizational elements of MEAs

Most MEAs share a number of organizational characteristics, which have also been referred to as "autonomous institutional arrangements".[12] As a general rule, a Conference or Meeting of the Parties (COP, MOP) to an agreement serves as the supreme decision-making body. As such, it may set up subsidiary bodies, adopt new obligations for parties, review implementation and compliance, respond to cases of non-compliance, liaise with other international institutions and agreements, etc. In most cases, the COP meets once a year, although longer intervals between sessions occur in some instances.[13]

Decisions by the COP are commonly prepared by open-ended subsidiary bodies. The number and legal status of such subsidiary bodies can vary between MEAs. For example, the Meeting of the Parties to the 1987 Montreal Protocol on Substances that Deplete the Ozone Layer established an open-ended working group of parties on an ad hoc basis by a MOP decision.[14] In contrast, the United Nations Framework Convention on Climate Change (UNFCCC) and its 1997 Kyoto Protocol, as well as the Convention on Biological Diversity (CBD), establish two standing subsidiary bodies for, respectively, scientific and technical/technological advice and implementation. In addition, the COP of the UNFCCC has established various ad hoc working groups with a more limited mandate.[15] Parties to the 1974 Convention on International Trade in Endan-

gered Species of Wild Fauna and Flora (CITES) set up several committees by means of simple COP decision-making.[16]

Furthermore, various specialized, functional subsidiary bodies,[17] dealing, for example, with the transfer of financial and technological resources, compliance, and scientific and technological advice, have been
created in the context of many MEAs. These functional subsidiary bodies
frequently have a more limited membership. For example, the Implementation Committee of the Montreal Protocol comprises 10 members
and the Executive Committee of its Multilateral Fund has 14 members,
each elected by the MOP.[18] Also, other compliance bodies usually are
not open-ended.[19] The Global Environment Facility (GEF), which operates the financial mechanisms of both the UNFCCC and the CBD, is
governed by a Council composed of 32 member states.[20] Members of
the Technology and Economic Assessment Panel under the Montreal
Protocol need to possess relevant expertise to qualify, and a certain geographical balance of the overall membership is to be achieved.[21] In contrast, membership of the Intergovernmental Panel on Climate Change
(IPCC), which provides scientific advice to parties to the UNFCCC, is
open-ended.[22]

MEAs also commonly possess secretariats to help arrange meetings,
collect and disseminate information, and provide the communicative infrastructure. MEA secretariats may, *inter alia*, conduct studies, facilitate
liaison with other international organizations and agreements, issue invi-
tations to meetings, and prepare agendas and reports. They usually operate within the framework of an existing international organization, such
as the United Nations, UNEP or the International Maritime Organization (IMO).[23] Irrespective of their organizational home, MEA secretariats are located around the world with a certain concentration in some
cities. For example, Bonn hosts the secretariats of the UNFCCC, the
1994 UN Convention to Combat Desertification (UNCCD) and the 1979
Convention on the Conservation of Migratory Species of Wild Animals
(CMS); Montreal hosts those of the CBD and the Montreal Protocol's
Multilateral Fund; the secretariat of the Montreal Protocol itself is located at UNEP in Nairobi; the IMO in London is the institutional home
of the International Convention for the Prevention of Pollution from
Ships[24] and the 1990 International Convention on Oil Pollution Pre-
paredness, Response and Co-operation and provides secretariat services
for the parties to the 1972 London Dumping Convention. Even where
secretariats have their seat in the same city, they may not be co-located
in the strict sense. The CMS secretariat in Bonn, which is operated by
UNEP, has a different address from the UNFCCC and UNCCD secretariats (which are located together). The same is true for the CBD secretar-

iat and the secretariat of the Montreal Protocol's Multilateral Fund in Montreal.

COPs usually do not take place at a permanent location; their location changes from session to session. The same generally holds for subsidiary bodies of all kinds (including various working groups). However, a certain concentration may occur, commonly at the location of the seat of the secretariat, in particular with respect to working sessions that attract less political attention. For example, sessions of the subsidiary bodies to the UNFCCC that are not held in conjunction with a COP usually take place in Bonn, the seat of the UNFCCC secretariat. As a consequence of these arrangements, a host of international meetings related to MEAs take place every year in various locations all over the world.[25]

Proposals for clustering the organizational elements of MEAs range from creating a permanent location for a number of COPs and their subsidiary bodies to arranging meetings "back to back" (i.e. one following the other sequentially in the same location). With respect to secretariats, it has been proposed to co-locate MEA secretariats. Since COPs usually have the authority to determine the dates and places of their meetings (including meetings of their subsidiary bodies) and the location of the secretariat, changing the current practice would primarily require related COP decisions.[26]

Holding combined meetings of MEA bodies and co-locating MEA secretariats have in particular a potential to lead to efficiency gains. Less administrative effort might be required for organizing any combined meetings, and common infrastructure could in principle be shared by several meetings. If a significant overlap of government representatives exists, combined meetings could reduce their travel costs (and related burdens). Further, the transaction costs of governments and others might be reduced if secretariats were concentrated in one or a few locations because it would be easier to identify where to turn to in matters relating to MEAs. Similarly, co-located MEA secretariats could share facilities and personnel and integrate administrative procedures. Co-location might also facilitate coordination between MEA secretariats. The success of such coordination, however, depends on proper procedures such as joint meetings and the establishment of clear communication channels, which might be installed even without co-location.[27]

These advantages primarily relate to reducing costs and making the overall organizational and administrative system of MEAs leaner and more efficient. It does not necessarily follow that the effectiveness of IEG would increase as a result, i.e. that better environmental protection would be achieved (see also the final section of the chapter). In some cases, coordinated decision-making could be facilitated by co-locating meetings if appropriate arrangements for enhancing learning and cross-fertilization are devised. Obviously, such a potential exists only where there are issues of common concern. In the case of MEAs that operate in closely related issue areas, this might occur regularly (for example, in biodiversity-related MEAs). In other cases, such issues may occur only ad hoc and sporadically (if at all).

Abandoning the current system of rotating meeting locations would, however, also lose the advantage that arranging for separate meetings limits the overall administrative and organizational burden on host countries. This especially facilitates the hosting of international environmental meetings by developing countries. Hosting COPs of the UNFCCC and the CBD, which have each become a major international meeting extending to two weeks, either concurrently or consecutively would overstrain even many industrialized country hosts. Rotating meeting places also serves the purpose of heightening awareness of the particular environmental problems in the host country/region, and spreading and strengthening this awareness throughout the world. If meetings were combined or held at a permanent location, one environmental issue might dominate and MEA meetings would no longer serve as focal points for raising public awareness in host countries. With respect to co-locating MEA secretariats, the fierce competition between host countries makes this a politically daunting task.[28] This competition may be why the UNEP Governing Council/GMEF in February 2002 encouraged the "co-location of *future* [MEA] secretariats".[29]

Clustering the functions of MEAs

In addition to their organizational elements, MEAs fulfil a number of common functions that could be subject to clustering. I shall first elaborate on these common functions, and then assess the potential advantages and drawbacks of integrating such functions across MEAs.

Common functions of MEAs

MEAs commonly perform a number of similar functions. These functions can be divided into three areas: the preparation and taking of collective decisions, implementation review and compliance (including dispute settlement), and implementation support and other supporting activities. I discuss the common functions of MEAs in that order below.

First of all, *scientific and technological assessments* (including monitoring and assessment of the state of the environment) are an indispensable part of any decision-making within MEAs and are a crucial precondition for effective decision-taking.[30] Various arrangements exist in different MEAs to ensure proper scientific input into the decision-making process. The most prominent example is provided by the IPCC, which provides advice to the UNFCCC although it is institutionally independent of the UNFCCC.[31] Under the Montreal Protocol, regular scientific, technological and economic assessments are conducted by special assessment panels established within the framework of the Protocol itself.[32] In other cases, MEAs make use of existing scientific institutions for scientific input.[33]

Transparency of and participation in decision-making are another common theme in all MEAs. Core aspects include accreditation to MEA bodies, access to meetings and documents, and the ability to participate actively in and contribute to discussions. MEA rules on these issues diverge to some extent and are frequently rudimentary. Much depends on practice, which has been comparatively liberal in most MEAs.[34]

Another crucial element of the decision-making process in MEAs is their *decision-making rules*. Decision-making in international environmental governance is generally based on the consensus principle, which has been relaxed only on rare occasions (e.g. the Montreal Protocol and the Global Environment Facility).[35] Trying to define another standard for certain clusters of MEAs would be doomed to failure, since voting rules belong to the politically most sensitive features of international regimes in general. This aspect is therefore not further investigated in the following sections. Implementation review and response in the framework of MEAs are regularly based on national self-reporting by member states. MEAs provide for the relevant *reporting obligations* in this respect. As a result of the proliferation of MEAs over recent decades, the reporting burden for member states has increased dramatically, creating problems in particular, although by no means exclusively, for developing countries with limited institutional capacities.[36]

Arrangements for the ensuing *implementation review*, usually undertaken within the framework of MEAs, vary significantly. A number of MEAs, for example the Montreal Protocol, rely solely or mainly on a review by the COP or its subsidiary bodies, which may be based on a synthesis of available country reports by the secretariat.[37] In some MEAs, such as the UNFCCC and its Kyoto Protocol, procedures for the independent review of countries' self-reports by experts, including the possibility of country visits, have been put in place.[38] As is the case in CITES, the review may at times even take into account information other than that reported by countries.[39] It is not just the concrete arrangements for implementation review but also the dates and frequency of such reviews (and the underlying reporting) that vary widely among MEAs, depending on the specific needs and conditions of each regime.[40]

Various MEAs also have *arrangements for responding to cases of non-compliance with commitments*. In particular, specific non-compliance procedures have been elaborated for a number of MEAs since the early 1990s, including the establishment of specialized committees – the most prominent example being the Montreal Protocol's non-compliance procedure.[41] In other cases, non-compliance is responded to directly by the COP or an open-ended subsidiary body under it.[42] Even where particular non-compliance procedures are established and share certain characteristics, their design can display marked differences due to varying functional requirements. For example, the newly devised compliance system under the Kyoto Protocol differs qualitatively from any of the existing non-compliance procedures under other MEAs, owing in particular to the specificity of the procedural regulations and the far-reaching sanctions.[43]

Most MEAs also contain provisions on *dispute resolution*. Dispute settlement procedures in MEAs fulfil a substantially different function from similar procedures in, for example, the World Trade Organization (WTO). Because of the structure of mutual obligations, bilateral dispute settlement provides a prime tool for responding to non-compliance with international trade rules and for enforcing them. Any restriction of international trade in contravention of WTO rules results directly in an economic disadvantage and loss for the trading partners of the country introducing such a restriction. These trading partners therefore have a direct interest in remedying the situation via use of the WTO dispute settlement procedure (for further discussion, see Sampson in chapter 5 in this volume). In contrast, states' non-compliance with MEAs regularly affects the common good that is to be protected rather than the immediate economic stakes of other member states. Since the latter may at best have an indirect interest in seeking remedies bilaterally (and can hardly retaliate), coordinated multilateral responses by the community of actors as a whole – with or without specialized compliance systems – have become the primary tool for ensuring effective implementation of MEAs. It is therefore hardly surprising that states have rarely, if ever, used the dispute settlement provisions of MEAs.[44]

Many MEAs include mechanisms to support implementation by providing for a *transfer of financial resources and technology* and assisting in *capacity-building*.[45] The GEF is often a focal point for global MEAs, operating the financial mechanisms of both the CBD and the UNFCCC. It will also operate the new funds created under the UNFCCC and its Kyoto Protocol in 2001[46] and is set to operate the financial mechanisms of the 2001 Stockholm Convention on Persistent Organic Pollutants (Article 14). Other MEAs operate separate trust funds or financial mechanisms, the most prominent being the Multilateral Fund for the Implementation of the Montreal Protocol.[47]

Furthermore, MEAs are involved in a number of *supporting activities* (sometimes financed by the above financial mechanisms). Such activities include assistance in building institutional capacities at the national level (e.g. setting up units within ministries responsible for an environmental issue), drafting national laws, training (workshops) and awareness-raising campaigns. Information dissemination and the communication strategies of MEAs are also part of these supporting activities. In particular, virtually all MEAs now have a presence on the World Wide Web, as well as using standard communication channels (mail, telephone, fax, email).

Finally, diverse issues not explicitly foreseen in the treaty can emerge during the operation of MEAs. At times, such an *ad hoc issue* may occur in the context of several MEAs. For example, states draw on customs codes determined by the World Customs Organization in order to control imports and exports as required to ensure compliance with several trade-related MEAs, including the Montreal Protocol, CITES, the 1989 Basel Convention on the Control of Transboundary Movements of Hazardous Wastes and Their Disposal, and the Stockholm Convention. Such trade-related MEAs thus are all to some extent linked to and have sought cooperation with the World Customs Organization, including adaptation of its system of customs codes.[48]

Clustering of MEA functions: Promises and pitfalls

As in the case of the clustering of organizational elements, the clustering of MEA functions in many cases could be implemented by means of simple decision-making by the governing bodies of MEAs. For example, most rules on transparency and participation are regularly contained in the rules of procedure adopted by the COP. Furthermore, several MEAs mandate their COPs to elaborate the details of the functional arrangements described in the previous subsection, which may also allow integration across MEAs. This far-reaching authority of the COPs has been crucial for MEAs' flexibility, which is one of their particular strengths.[49]

However, several MEAs diverge from the general rule in that the treaty itself makes certain determinations. In such cases, treaty amendments would be required, which would hinder clustering. For example, the due date for the reporting of data under the Montreal Protocol is set by the Protocol itself. As a result, efforts to harmonize data-reporting under the Protocol itself with that of the Protocol's Multilateral Fund have been doomed, because the Fund needs data for its proper functioning earlier than they are due under the Protocol.[50] Similarly, CITES provides for different accreditation requirements for international and national NGOs, whereas more modern MEAs do not make this distinction. Harmonizing this aspect, which promises limited benefits, again would require a treaty amendment.[51] A number of similar cases exist; identifying all of them would require a case-by-case assessment that is beyond the scope of this chapter.

Substantively, proposals for clustering MEA functions have aimed either at the harmonization of rules or at a consolidation of functions and procedures. For example, clustering in the area of transparency and participation in decision-making would mean defining common rules. Likewise, clustering in the area of non-compliance procedures could mean the promotion of common (minimum) standards, as is already done by UNEP, which has elaborated guidelines on compliance with and enforcement of MEAs (for more on UNEP's role in promoting clustering, see Tarasofsky in chapter 3 in this volume).[52] Such efforts would aim to enhance the coherence of existing rules while maintaining the current decentralized system of MEAs. In contrast, proposals that amount to a consolidation of existing structures include creating an overarching structure responsible for providing scientific advice to various MEAs (either as a separate entity or under an existing institution such as UNEP); further combining the financial mechanisms of MEAs (e.g. within the GEF); introducing a country-specific implementation review of several/ all MEAs instead of the existing MEA-specific reviews; consolidating or merging existing non-compliance procedures as well as mechanisms for dispute resolution; and cooperating more closely in supporting activities such as dissemination of information, communication, training and capacity-building.[53]

The potential benefits of such harmonization and consolidation can primarily be seen in increased efficiency as a result of cost reductions and enhanced coherence. The latter is the logical consequence of both harmonization and consolidation because both reduce the potential for divergence between MEAs and their functional elements. Increased coherence may translate into efficiency gains, because parties to MEAs may have to expend less effort and thus incur lower costs in managing these MEAs at the national level (for example, with respect to reporting). Likewise, the mentioned consolidation may in particular be expected to lead to cost reductions at the international level (e.g. resulting from fewer scientific assessments, compliance committees and financial mechanisms or from combined training activities). Further benefits in terms of increases in legitimacy and effectiveness are less certain.

In some cases, however, the expected benefits might be minimal, or even non-existent. For example, integrating the dispute settlement provisions of MEAs may in many instances not present insurmountable problems. Indeed, the Permanent Court of Arbitration has already elaborated common rules for the arbitration of environmental disputes, which may provide a basis for such integration.[54] However, given the very limited significance of dispute settlement for MEAs, the impact of any such measure is likely to be small.[55]

A centralization and harmonization of MEA functions might also provide an opportunity to realize some substantive reforms as side-benefits.

For example, concern has been raised that environmental monitoring and scientific assessments are insufficient with respect to many environmental issues, especially those that are not particularly high on the political agenda, such as climate change.[56] Establishing a centralized structure for providing scientific advice thus creates the opportunity for some central planning and a more equal treatment of various environmental issues.[57] Similarly, a harmonization of rules on transparency and participation in decision-making might help to codify and extend progressive practice. However, such attempts risk overburdening the reform agenda by trying to take two steps at once, which could reinforce political opposition and eventually backfire. In general, attempts to weave substantive policy changes into the reform of institutional structures need to take into account that there is frequently a political and sometimes a functional rationale for the policies pursued in MEAs so far. In any event, there is little reason to assume that opposition to such substantive changes might be more easily overcome in the course of clustering.

There are also potential drawbacks. In particular, there is the danger that a clustering of MEA functions might result in dysfunctionalities that hamper the effectiveness of the MEAs involved. For example, undertaking one scientific assessment for all MEAs could lead to less flexibility for single MEAs to receive scientific input according to their own needs. Given the varying functional needs of implementation review systems and non-compliance procedures in MEAs, successful combination of these elements would require substantial similarities in existing systems and their functional needs. Otherwise, clustering might at best create an overall general scientific assessment,[58] implementation review or non-compliance procedure that is additional to the existing specific ones – which would mean more than undoing the expected efficiency gains.

In some cases and to some extent, reaping the aforementioned benefits will also require some additional investment. With respect to the various supporting activities (training, awareness-raising, presence on the World Wide Web, etc.), exchange of information is required between the administrative units concerned, as well as resources for coordination. Addressing ad hoc issues through flexible "issue management" – i.e. coordination for the purpose of managing a particular issue, including the termination of such coordination upon resolution of the issue[59] – also requires sufficient resources to enable the secretariats of MEAs in particular to participate flexibly in such issue-specific cooperation.

It follows from the above that the clustering of MEA functions requires careful analysis of whether functional needs and the pre-existing structures are compatible in each case. Such a step-by-step process is already pursued in several fields to some extent. For example, some scientific advisory bodies such as the International Council for the Exploration of the Sea (ICES) or the joint Group of Experts on the Scientific Aspects of Marine Environmental Protection (GESAMP) provide advice to more than one agreement. The creation of the GEF and the ongoing activities to extend its areas of activity can be understood as an attempt to economize on financial mechanisms in IEG.[60] Initiatives to integrate reporting obligations are, *inter alia*, pursued by several biodiversity-related MEAs.[61] As mentioned, in the area of non-compliance and enforcement, UNEP has elaborated guidelines in order to increase coherence. The experience gained in these and other contexts has confirmed the existence of a number of obstacles, originating in particular from diverging functions but also from political interests, that require detailed examination in order to avoid negative repercussions and devise workable and acceptable arrangements.[62]

Approaches to clustering

A number of different approaches to clustering have been put forward in the policy debate. In particular, various ways of clustering MEAs by issue/sector, function, and/or region have been proposed. In the following, I first introduce these approaches, then I assess their merits and limitations against the backdrop of the discussion in the preceding section. I conclude by pointing to the need to base any clustering on a systematic analysis taking into account a number of factors.

Proposed types of clustering

Three main approaches to clustering MEAs have been put forward in the international policy discussions: clustering by issue, by region and by function.

Clustering by issue refers to the grouping of MEAs according to certain thematic areas or sectors. Accordingly, thematic areas would be defined and each MEA subsequently assigned to one (or more) of them. In principle, different options for designing and defining thematic clusters exist. Konrad von Moltke, for example, has proposed the following groupings: conservation, global atmosphere, hazardous substances, marine environment, and extractive resources.[63] In contrast, UNEP has, in the framework of its IEG process, suggested four thematic clusters: sustainable development conventions; biodiversity-related conventions; chemicals and hazardous wastes conventions; and regional seas conventions and related agreements.[64] Difficulties can arise with respect to the allocation of specific MEAs to these clusters. For example, the CBD would qualify for both the sustainable development and the biodiversity-related conventions. In such cases, one cluster can be selected pragmatically or (as was done in the example) the MEA can be allocated to both clusters.

Clustering by region refers to the integration, combination or grouping of MEAs according to the geographical region to which they belong.[65] At the heart of clustering by region appears to be the overlap of memberships that comes with the overlap in regional scope of the MEAs grouped together. The UN Economic Commission for Europe (UN-ECE), which provides the organizational home for a number of regional environmental (and other) conventions, is an example that is yet to be copied in other regions.[66]

Clustering of functions generally refers to the integration or combination of the same functions of two or more MEAs, as outlined above.[67] It thus operates at a different level from clustering by issue or by region. When MEAs are grouped together by issue or by region, the MEA is looked at as one entity. Clustering of functions, in contrast, generally refers to sub-units of MEAs and therefore splits up the MEA. As a consequence, no lists of MEAs belonging to functional clusters have been put forward. The composition of the groups of MEAs displaying similarities of functional arrangements is likely to change depending on the function. For example, transparency and participation in decision-making appear to be a common theme for all MEAs, so that common rules might in principle be developed in an integrated manner for all of them (and building upon regional or other clusters may serve as a step in the process towards such encompassing rules). In contrast, integration of reporting obligations may have to start from MEAs with a large overlap of the respective issue areas and regulatory approaches. The composition of MEA clusters would thus vary from function to function.

Whereas the international debate has focused on the above approaches to clustering MEAs, other criteria have occasionally been suggested, including clustering on the basis of the source of environmental harm, the ecosystem or scientific research. Thus, it might be possible to group MEAs together where industry or certain parts of industry represent the source of the environmental problem addressed; or to combine those MEAs that have a significant impact on a specific ecosystem or type of ecosystem.[68]

Merits and limitations

Both clustering by issue and clustering by region appear to be particularly suitable starting points for thinking about integrating the organizational elements of MEAs. Holding combined meetings of convention bodies should be particularly promising if the MEAs involved are closely related thematically and a large overlap in membership exists, as may be the case with MEAs from the same region. For example, the potential for learning may be particularly high in the case of MEAs that deal with similar issues, such as the CBD and the 1971 Ramsar Convention on Wetlands, where a significant overlap of government delegates may also be expected (compared with MEAs addressing largely unrelated issues, such as the UNCCD and the Basel Convention). Where membership of regional MEAs overlaps, meetings of convention bodies may be arranged far more easily jointly or sequentially at the same location. In the case of MEAs belonging to an issue-specific cluster, secretariats are more likely to have to deal with similar topics and might therefore most usefully co-operate, be co-located or even be merged. Secretariats of MEAs with a similar regional scope might be more easily combined, since disputes over the sharing of administrative costs are less likely to occur than in the case of largely different memberships.

However, neither thematic closeness nor a regional/membership overlap is a sufficient condition for successful integration of the organizational elements of MEAs. Even where the issues addressed by MEAs are similar, the overlap of COP meeting agendas may be very limited and the potential benefit of combining such meetings might not justify the costs involved. For example, the agendas of the Agreement on the Conservation of Bats in Europe and the Agreement on the Conservation of Seals in the Wadden Sea display little overlap. Consequently, they hold separate COPs, even though they both operate under the umbrella of the CMS. Furthermore, besides the fact that the membership of MEAs can diverge significantly even within regions, membership is not the only factor that needs to be considered when thinking about combining the organizational elements of MEAs. For example, even though both the UNFCCC and the CBD largely overlap in their membership, it would be impracticable to combine their COPs.

Thematic closeness and common membership are of even less importance when it comes to integrating the functional elements of MEAs. For example, the various functions performed by MEAs can take very different forms and/or respond to divergent needs irrespective of the issue they address and their membership. Combining the implementation review under the CBD with either that of the UNFCCC/Kyoto Protocol (common membership) or that of CITES (in a conservation cluster) offers little prospect for synergy, and in fact may appear dysfunctional. This is not to say that overlap in thematic areas and membership could not be important for functional clustering. For example, reporting of data may be expected to display certain overlaps and potentials for creating synergy within thematic clusters, as evidenced by attempts to economize on reporting to biodiversity-related conventions. Overall, however, additional factors such as the similarities of the functions performed need to be taken into account in pursuing clustering of MEA functions.

For such clustering of MEA functions, the commonality of these functions across various MEAs offers a promising starting point (whereas such partial functional overlaps provide a weak basis for combining meetings of COP bodies or integrating secretariats). As indicated before, functional integration may involve different sets of MEAs depending on the specific function in question. The relevant functions and the potential benefits and disadvantages resulting from clustering them have already been discussed and do not need to be repeated here.

Overall, integration both of the organizational/administrative elements and of the functions of MEAs requires a careful analysis of the compatibility of the elements to be combined in each case. Whereas the main types of clustering proposed emphasize one factor each (issue/sector, regional scope/membership, function), the success of any attempt to integrate parts of MEAs is dependent on a range of factors. Factors that need to be taken into account with respect to the clustering of organizational elements include the actual overlap of issues and membership of the MEAs involved and the practical feasibility and manageability. The clustering of MEA functions requires detailed analysis of the specific needs and structures of each MEA involved with respect to the function in question, the degree of similarity of the issues addressed by the functional sub-unit, the overlap of membership, and so on. In either case, legal requirements and obstacles must be considered (is a treaty amendment required or only a COP decision?). It is in this type of detailed analysis that factors highlighted by other proposed approaches to clustering – such as the source of environmental harm, the ecosystem or scientific research – can gain relevance.

Clustering of MEAs: Putting it straight

One of the established principles of environmental policy is that solutions have to fit the problems they are meant to address.[69] This principle is applicable not only to specific environmental policies but also to international environmental governance. Consequently, a possible clustering of MEAs has to take into account the full range of factors that might influence its prospects, while preserving the effectiveness of the MEAs concerned. In this respect, the diversity of approaches and the flexibility of single MEAs and of the system of MEAs have been major strengths of IEG to date, because they have allowed experimentation and "innovation in niches" as well as rapid adaptation to evolving scientific and technological knowledge and economic and political conditions.[70]

Any clustering of MEAs has to reflect this multidimensional structure of the challenge. In contrast to the main proposals reviewed above, eventually a matrix of criteria rather than one factor will need to be considered when thinking about the integration of MEAs. Different factors may be weighted differently, depending on whether clustering of organizational elements or of functions is considered. The degree and type of overlap and the differences uncovered in such an effort will determine whether and to what extent a clustering of organizational elements and/or functions of MEAs appears promising. Careful consideration of all important factors will allow the possibilities for enhanced coordination and the existing constraints to be identified. The greater the similarities in the relevant features, the better the chances for successful clustering (and the fewer the constraints).

On this basis, a full merger of two MEAs is likely to remain the exception rather than the rule, since it would require far-reaching overlap. The only case in IEG concerned the 1972 Oslo Convention for the Prevention of Marine Pollution by Dumping from Ships and Aircraft and the 1974 Paris Convention for the Prevention of Marine Pollution from Land-Based Sources. These two conventions were merged into the 1992 OSPAR Convention, the Convention for the Protection of the Marine Environment of the North-East Atlantic. This case was very special and may not easily be repeated because the Paris and Oslo Conventions related to the same region/membership, their subjects were closely related and complementary, and their institutional structures were very similar and closely related even before the merger.[71]

By building upon a careful analysis of the similarities and differences of various MEAs, clustering does not constitute the objective of the reform process but can best be understood as a tool for pursuing this reform process bottom–up.[72] It provides a framework for establishing, elaborating, strengthening and/or diversifying arrangements for coordination between MEAs. Such coordination may take the form of joint meetings of convention bodies and secretariats, memoranda of understanding, joint implementation of common activities, the development of communication networks, routines and structures, and so on (as appropriate and feasible). As such cooperative arrangements evolve over time, the development of more formal structures for clustering MEAs may become possible in the future.

Such a process-oriented approach towards clustering would assist in limiting the potential costs and problems that might arise from an integration of MEAs as discussed above. It allows such costs and problems to be anticipated and weighed against the expected benefits of clustering. Although not all problems and dangers (or benefits) can necessarily be anticipated, a process-oriented approach would also facilitate later corrections and adaptations in a process of "trial and error".

Even such a process-oriented approach to clustering is likely to face serious opposition. Some actors would have to change their accustomed routines, others would feel that coordination would lead to their losing control, and still others would have little incentive to pursue clustering activities proactively because of the uncertainty of any rewards. Clustering may thus require political impetus and adapting to political realities. Relocation of existing secretariats, for example, is known to face serious political resistance and is therefore unlikely to succeed. Consequently, the UNEP Governing Council/GMEF in February 2002 envisaged co-location only of new secretariats.

Clustering and the challenges of international environmental policy

The assessment in the previous section mainly examined the absolute potential of clustering for improving IEG. To get a fuller picture, we also have to assess its potential contribution in relation to the major challenges of international environmental policy.

Three main challenges in the field of international environmental policy have been identified in relevant assessments.[73] First, decision-making in IEG remains predominantly based on the consensus principle. As a result, decision-making is usually relatively slow and laggards can regularly extract considerable concessions ("lowest common denominator rule"). Second, actual progress in implementation "on the ground" tends to be slow and of limited effectiveness owing to a lack of "carrots and sticks", i.e. sanctions in the case of non-compliance and financial or other assistance in the case of inability to implement effectively. Third, a potential for inter-institutional conflicts and inconsistencies between MEAs or between an MEA and another agreement has increasingly been found. Examples are the role of the Kyoto Protocol in providing an incentive for forestry activities that maximize carbon sequestration but could compromise the objectives of the CBD,[74] as well as the relationship between the WTO and various MEAs.[75] Significant improvements have been achieved in all these areas during recent decades, but cannot be discussed in detail here. In any event, given the state of the global environment, significant progress has still to be made.[76]

Relative to these major challenges of international environmental policy, the contribution that can be made by clustering MEAs necessarily appears small. As pointed out earlier, the potential benefits of combining and integrating MEAs consist primarily in efficiency gains and an increased coherence of the governance system. No direct link exists between these effects and the way in which decisions are made and implemented. The effectiveness of international environmental policy may thus be supported only indirectly and in a longer-term perspective. Enhanced coherence – in particular if resulting in fewer and shorter international meetings – may contribute to increased transparency and economies in IEG. This would facilitate the effective participation of governments and other stakeholders, especially from developing countries. Ultimately, the legitimacy of the governance system may thereby be enhanced, with positive repercussions on both decision-making and implementation. Whether and to what extent such indirect effects materialize and can contribute to solving the underlying challenges remains uncertain, however.

The potential effects on the availability of resources to promote implementation can also be assessed as limited and indirect. Clustering generally holds out the promise of increasing the efficiency of the use of available resources and enhancing synergies in implementation. However, efficiency gains realized mainly by streamlining the operation of MEAs are unlikely to free significant financial resources for financing sustainable development. For example, the programme budget of the UNFCCC and its secretariat for 2002 was of the order of US$16 million.[77] Any reduction in this budget achieved by means of clustering would be a drop in the ocean compared with the financial demands for financing climate protection, which is counted in billions of dollars.[78] The willingness of donors to allocate more funds for this purpose may at best be influenced very indirectly, in the longer term, and to the extent that the efficient use of resources may enhance their willingness to pay.

With respect to inter-institutional coordination, clustering of MEAs (e.g. joint meetings, coordination of secretariats) might facilitate an intensified exchange of information and thus improve the conditions for policy learning across institutional borders. Clustering might also increase the visibility of environmental issues vis-à-vis non-environmental policy areas such as international trade governed by the WTO. However, where inter-institutional issues are rooted in differences of objectives and interest, a solution requires political decision-making by the parties to the agreements concerned. In such circumstances, the exchange of information and policy learning might have a facilitative and supportive role, but would not suffice.[79]

There is also little empirical evidence from areas where efforts at integration have already borne fruit to rebut this overall assessment. Thus, despite the partial clustering of financial mechanisms in the GEF, criticism of the inadequacy of resources has continued.[80] Furthermore, no outstanding improvements with regard to decision-making, implementation or inter-institutional coordination have been reported where scientific advisory bodies serve several MEAs or where secretariat services have been pooled (as in the case of IMO) or co-located (e.g. the secretariats of the UNCCD and the UNFCCC in Bonn). The same holds with respect to the one case of a full merger of two MEAs in the OSPAR Convention. Nevertheless, it is worth mentioning that these integrative arrangements have rarely been criticized for harming the effectiveness of the MEAs involved, and have in fact been commented upon rather favourably.

In summary, a clustering of MEAs can hardly be expected to contribute directly to resolving the main challenges of international environmental policy. Its prime potentials – increased efficiency and enhanced coherence of the system of MEAs – may eventually also have a positive impact on the effectiveness of MEAs. Such effects will be only indirect and remain uncertain, but on balance they appear to be positive rather than negative, if clustering is properly designed.

Conclusion

The concept of clustering has been introduced into the debate about reforming the IEG system early in the twenty-first century. Broadly speaking, clustering refers to the combination, grouping, consolidation, integration or merging of MEAs or parts thereof in order to improve international environmental governance. Despite its relatively recent emergence, the concept has found its way into the IEG process led by UNEP, the results of which were agreed to be implemented in the preparations for the World Summit on Sustainable Development in Johannesburg in August/September 2002.

Elements of the clustering of MEAs thus understood already exist and have been strengthened over the years. The establishment of the GEF as the central financial institution with respect to global environmental challenges and the merger of the Oslo and Paris Conventions into the OSPAR Convention constitute only two of the most visible examples. In addition, a number of other relevant initiatives, such as the co-location of some MEA secretariats (e.g. the UNFCCC and UNCCD secretariats in Bonn) or efforts to integrate reporting obligations under biodiversity-related MEAs, that are less obvious to the observer have been pursued.

The clustering of MEAs as discussed at the beginning of the twenty-first century is about advancing this process of integration more systematically. In doing so, it is important to distinguish between the organizational/administrative elements (secretariats, MEA bodies) and the functions of MEAs (such as responding to non-compliance, implementation review, financial assistance), which differ with respect to both the preconditions and the potential effects of integrating them. In particular, consolidating MEA functions carries the danger of creating dysfunctionalities that will hamper the effective operation of the agreements concerned. Thus, clustering MEA functions requires careful consideration of the various functional requirements, and overlap of issues and membership as well as practical feasibility rank particularly high when it comes to the integration of organizational elements.

Proposals put forward in the international debate thus far have focused on one major factor that would guide the clustering efforts (issue/sector, regional scope/membership, function). However, such a unidimensional approach does not sufficiently reflect the multidimensional structure of the challenge. A number of factors must be taken into account in any effort to integrate MEAs, including overlap of membership and issues, practical feasibility, legal obstacles and functional requirements. The aforementioned proposals have helped identify some of these factors. Eventually, however, a systematic and comprehensive framework for analysing and designing further steps in the clustering process will be required. Each step will need to be based on a careful case-by-case analysis because of the particular attributes of each MEA and the functional elements that may be considered for clustering.

The clustering of MEAs thus understood constitutes a framework for a reform process rather than a recipe for a fundamental restructuring of IEG. Even such a moderate approach faces serious (political) opposition and impediments. Political impetus may thus be needed to make progress and, because of the process character of the effort, would likely extend discussions into a continuing process. One possibility to promote clustering might be to give a clear political mandate for pursuing the clustering process to one or several coordinators or facilitators.[81] In addition, regular political review and guidance may be required; this could be conducted by the GMEF, which provided the first impetus in 2002.[82]

The potential benefits of clustering MEAs consist primarily of efficiency gains and increased coherence of the governance system. The direct contribution to mastering the major substantive challenges of international environmental policy – namely, reaching agreement on measures, implementing them, and preventing inter-institutional conflict – is rather limited. Clustering may contribute to better environmental protection only indirectly and over the longer term. In particular, increased coherence and efficiency of the system of MEAs may lead to greater transparency and legitimacy of international environmental governance, which should enhance its capacity to address these challenges. However, it is still uncertain whether and to what extent these indirect effects might materialize.

Nevertheless, the clustering of MEAs has a notable potential to contribute to rationalizing and economizing on the IEG system in a step-by-step process that might eventually also be felt with respect to the more fundamental underpinnings. Realization of its potentials, however, cannot be taken for granted. It requires careful design and analysis on a case-by-case basis. If done the wrong way, the clustering of MEAs might well fail to improve the situation, and could even worsen it. Approached properly, a systematic effort to extend and deepen the integration of MEAs could constitute a valuable building block in the process of enhancing international environmental governance.

Notes

The article on which this chapter is based was previously published in *International Environmental Agreements: Politics, Law and Economics*, Vol. 2, No. 4, 2002, pp. 317–340. The current version has been slightly updated. I would like to thank Kluwer for permission to reprint the article. The contents of the article remain the sole responsibility of the author.

1. UNEP Governing Council, Decision 21/21, *International Environmental Governance*, para. 2, available at ⟨http://www.unep.org/IEG/Background.asp⟩.
2. UNEP, *Report of the Governing Council Seventh Special Session*, Decision SS.VII/1, UN General Assembly A/57/25, New York: United Nations, 2002, p. 21.
3. World Summit on Sustainable Development, *Plan of Implementation of the World Summit on Sustainable Development*, A/CONF.199/20, New York: United Nations, 2002, para. 140(d), available at ⟨http://www.johannesburgsummit.org/html/documents/summit_docs/131302_wssd_report_reissued.pdf⟩.
4. See the reports at ⟨http://www.unep.org/IEG/Meetings.asp⟩.
5. Konrad von Moltke, *On Clustering International Environmental Agreements*, Winnipeg: International Institute for Sustainable Development, 2001, p. 3, available at ⟨http://www.iisd.ca/pdf/trade_clustering_meas.pdf⟩.
6. UNEP, *Report of the Governing Council Seventh Special Session*, Decision SS.VII/1, pp. 24, 29–30.
7. See, for example, Joy Hyvarinen and Duncan Brack, *Global Environmental Institutions: Analysis and Options for Change*, London: Royal Institute of International Affairs, 2000; WBGU (German Advisory Council on Global Change), *World in Transition: New Structures for Global Environmental Policy*, London: Earthscan, 2001; and Jacob Werksman, "Consolidating Governance of the Global Commons: Insights from the Global Environment Facility", *Yearbook of International Environmental Law*, Vol. 6, 1996, pp. 27–63.
8. For early contributions to the debate, see von Moltke, *On Clustering International Environmental Agreements*; and Konrad von Moltke, *Whither MEAs? The Role of International Environmental Management in the Trade and Environment Agenda*, Winnipeg: International Institute for Sustainable Development, 2001.
9. See, for example, United Nations University, *Inter-Linkages: Synergies and Coordination between Multilateral Environmental Agreements*, Tokyo: UNU Institute of Advanced Studies and Global Environment Information Centre, 1999; Frank Biermann, "The Case for a World Environment Organisation", *Environment*, Vol. 42, No. 9, 2000, pp. 22–31; WBGU, *World in Transition*; von Moltke, *On Clustering International Environmental Agreements*; and von Moltke, *Whither MEAs?*
10. David G. Victor, "The Market for International Environmental Protection Services

and the Perils of Coordination", paper prepared for the International Conference on Synergies and Coordination between Multilateral Environmental Agreements, United Nations University, Tokyo, 14–16 July 1999, available at ⟨http://www.geic.or.jp/interlinkages/docs/online-docs.html⟩. The full range of views is reflected in the reports of the *Earth Negotiations Bulletin* on the UNEP IEG process available at ⟨http://www.iisd.ca/linkages/vol16/⟩.

11. Von Moltke, *On Clustering International Environmental Agreements*; Thomas Gehring and Sebastian Oberthür, "Was bringt eine Weltumweltorganisation? Kooperationstheoretische Anmerkungen zur institutionellen Neuordnung der internationalen Umweltpolitik", *Zeitschrift für Internationale Beziehungen*, Vol. 7, No. 1, 2000, pp. 185–211.

12. Robin R. Churchill and Geir Ulfstein, "Autonomous Institutional Arrangements in Multilateral Environmental Agreements: A Little-Noticed Phenomenon in International Law", *American Journal of International Law*, Vol. 94, 2000, pp. 623–659.

13. Ibid., p. 626.

14. Decision I/5, UNEP, *Handbook for the International Treaties for the Protection of the Ozone Layer*, 5th edn, Nairobi: UNEP, 2000.

15. Sebastian Oberthür and Hermann E. Ott (in collaboration with Richard G. Tarasofsky), *The Kyoto Protocol: International Climate Policy for the 21st Century*, Berlin: Springer, 1999.

16. Peter H. Sand, "Commodity or Taboo? International Regulation of Trade in Endangered Species", *Green Globe Yearbook of International Co-operation on Environment and Development*, 1997, pp. 19–36.

17. Please note that this paragraph addresses only the organizational aspects of functional subsidiary bodies; clustering of their functions is discussed below.

18. UNEP, *Handbook for the International Treaties for the Protection of the Ozone Layer*.

19. Markus Ehrmann, *Erfüllungskontrolle im Umweltvölkerrecht – Verfahren der Erfüllungskontrolle in der umweltvölkerrechtlichen Vertragspraxis*, Baden-Baden: Nomos, 2000; Sebastian Oberthür and Simon Marr, "Das System der Erfüllungskontrolle des Kyoto-Protokolls: Ein Schritt zur wirksamen Durchsetzung im Umweltvölkerrecht", *Zeitschrift für Umweltrecht*, Vol. 13, No. 2, pp. 81–89.

20. David Fairman, "The Global Environment Facility: Haunted by the Shadow of the Future", in Robert O. Keohane and Marc A. Levy, eds, *Institutions for Environmental Aid: Pitfalls and Promise*, Cambridge, MA: MIT Press, 1996, pp. 55–87.

21. UNEP, *Handbook for the International Treaties for the Protection of the Ozone Layer*.

22. On the IPCC, see Shardul Agrawala, "Structural and Process History of the Intergovernmental Panel on Climate Change", *Climatic Change*, Vol. 39, No. 4, 1998, pp. 621–642.

23. Churchill and Ulfstein. "Autonomous Institutional Arrangements in Multilateral Environmental Agreements", p. 627.

24. Known as MARPOL 1973/78.

25. See Calendar of Events at ⟨http://sdgateway.net/events⟩.

26. In some cases, the secretariat function has been designated in the MEA itself. See also Churchill and Ulfstein, "Autonomous Institutional Arrangements in Multilateral Environmental Agreements", p. 627. For example, Article 12, para. 1, of CITES determines that the executive director of UNEP shall provide a secretariat. Even in this case, however, the location is not specified, and a decision of the COP would presumably suffice to give effective guidance to UNEP's executive director in this respect.

27. On employing modern communications technology, see von Moltke, *On Clustering International Environmental Agreements*, pp. 7–8.

28. See also von Moltke, *On Clustering International Environmental Agreements*, pp. 7–8.

29. UNEP, *Report of the Governing Council Seventh Special Session*, Decision SS.VII/1, p. 30, emphasis added.
30. On the relationship between science and politics in international environmental policy, see e.g. Stellar Andersen, Toa Skodvin, Arild Underdal and Jørgen Wettestad, *Science and Politics in International Environmental Regimes: Between Integrity and Involvement*, Manchester: Manchester University Press, 2000.
31. Oberthür and Ott (in collaboration with Tarasofsky), *The Kyoto Protocol*, chap. 1.
32. Edward A. Parson, "Protecting the Ozone Layer", in Peter M. Haas, Robert O. Keohane and Marc A. Levy, eds, *Institutions for the Earth: Sources of Effective International Environmental Protection*, Cambridge, MA: MIT Press, 1993, pp. 27–73.
33. For example, the International Council for the Exploration of the Sea (ICES) provides advice to a number of regional management regimes in the North-East Atlantic. Also, the joint Group of Experts on the Scientific Aspects of Marine Environmental Protection (GESAMP) provides input to a number of international agreements related to the marine environment; see their respective websites at ⟨http://www.ices.dk⟩ and ⟨http://gesamp.imo.org⟩.
34. See, in general, Farhana Yamin, "NGOs and International Environmental Law: A Critical Evaluation of Their Roles and Responsibilities", *Review of European Community and International Environmental Law*, Vol. 10, No. 2, 2001, pp. 149–162; Sebastian Oberthür, Matthias Buck, Sebastian Müller, Alice Palmer, Stefanie Pfahl, Richard G. Tarasofsky and Jacob Werksman, *Participation of Non-Governmental Organisations in International Environmental Governance: Legal Basis and Practical Experience*, Berlin: Ecologic, 2002, available at ⟨http://www.ecologic.de⟩.
35. Churchill and Ulfstein, "Autonomous Institutional Arrangements in Multilateral Environmental Agreements", p. 643.
36. See United Nations University, *Inter-Linkages*; UNEP, *Implementing the Clustering Strategy for Multilateral Environmental Agreements: A Framework, Background Paper by the Secretariat*, UNEP/IGM/4/4, Open-Ended Intergovernmental Group of Ministers or Their Representatives on International Environmental Governance, 16 November 2001, pp. 20–21.
37. For the Montreal Protocol, see Owen Greene, "The System for Implementation Review in the Ozone Regime", in David G. Victor, Kal Raustiala and Eugene B. Skolnikoff, eds, *The Implementation and Effectiveness of International Environmental Commitments: Theory and Practice*, Cambridge, MA: MIT Press, 1998, pp. 89–136; in general, Jesse H. Ausubel and David. G. Victor, "Verification of International Environmental Agreements", *Annual Review of Energy and the Environment*, Vol. 17, 1992, pp. 1–43.
38. See Oberthür and Ott (in collaboration with Tarasofsky), *The Kyoto Protocol*, pp. 209–212; Molly Anderson, Trevor Findlay and Clare Tenner, "The Kyoto Protocol: Verification Falls into Place", in Trevor Findlay and Oliver Meier, eds, *Verification Yearbook 2001*, London: VERTIC, 2001, pp. 119–135.
39. See Rosalind Reeve, "Verification Mechanisms in CITES", in Findlay and Meier, eds, *Verification Yearbook 2001*, pp. 137–156; Oliver Meier and Clare Tenner, "Non-Governmental Monitoring of International Agreements", in Findlay and Meier, eds, *Verification Yearbook 2001*, pp. 207–227.
40. See, in general, Victor, Raustiala and Skolnikoff, eds, *The Implementation and Effectiveness of International Environmental Commitments*.
41. Currently, non-compliance procedures are under development or consideration, *inter alia*, under the Basel Convention, the 2000 Cartagena Protocol on Biosafety to the CBD, the 1998 Rotterdam Convention on the Prior Informed Consent Procedure for Certain Hazardous Chemicals and Pesticides in International Trade, and the 2001

Stockholm Convention on Persistent Organic Pollutants, and in the negotiations on a Protocol on Pollutant Release and Transfer Registers (PRTR) to the 1998 Aarhus Convention on Access to Information, Public Participation in Decision-Making and Access to Justice in Environmental Matters.

42. On the example of CITES, see Sand, "Commodity or Taboo?", pp. 21–22.

43. See Oberthür and Marr, "Das System der Erfüllungskontrolle des Kyoto-Protokolls"; see also, in general, Victor, Raustiala and Skolnikoff, eds, *The Implementation and Effectiveness of International Environmental Commitments*.

44. See Patrick Szell, "The Development of Multilateral Mechanisms for Monitoring Compliance", in Winfried Lang, ed., *Sustainable Development and International Law*, London: Kluwer Law International, 1995, pp. 97–109. See also Churchill and Ulfstein, "Autonomous Institutional Arrangements in Multilateral Environmental Agreements", p. 644.

45. See, in general, Peter H. Sand, *Trusts for the Earth: New Financial Mechanisms for International Environmental Protection*, Hull: University of Hull, 1994; and Keohane and Levy, eds, *Institutions for Environmental Aid*.

46. Karsten Sach and Moritz Reese, "Das Kyoto Protokoll nach Bonn und Marrakesch", *Zeitschrift für Umweltrecht*, Vol. 13, No. 2, 2002, p. 71.

47. Elizabeth R. DeSombre and Joanne Kauffman, "The Montreal Protocol Multilateral Fund: Partial Success", in Keohane and Levy, eds, *Institutions for Environmental Aid*, pp. 89–126.

48. See Sebastian Oberthür, "Linkages between the Montreal and Kyoto Protocols: Enhancing Synergies between Protecting the Ozone Layer and the Global Climate", *International Environmental Agreements: Politics, Law and Economics*, Vol. 1, No. 3, 2000, pp. 357–377.

49. See Churchill and Ulfstein, "Autonomous Institutional Arrangements in Multilateral Environmental Agreements", pp. 623–659; Hermann E. Ott, *Umweltregime im Völkerrecht. Eine Untersuchung über neue Formen internationalisierter Kooperation am Beispiel der Verträge zum Schutz der Ozonschicht und zur Kontrolle grenzüberschreitender Abfallverbringung*, Baden-Baden: Nomos, 1998; Thomas Gehring, *Dynamic International Regimes: Institutions for International Environmental Governance*, Frankfurt/Main: Peter Lang, 1994.

50. See Sebastian Oberthür, *Production and Consumption of Ozone Depleting Substances 1986–1999: The Data Reporting System under the Montreal Protocol*, Eschborn: GTZ, 2001, pp. 28–31.

51. Oberthür et al., *Participation of Non-Governmental Organisations in International Environmental Governance*, chap. 3.2.

52. See ⟨http://www.unep.org/DEPI/Implementationlaw.asp⟩.

53. For discussion of some such proposals, see von Moltke, *On Clustering International Environmental Agreements*, pp. 19–22; see also the reports at ⟨http://www.unep.org/IEG/Meetings.asp⟩ and the related *Earth Negotiations Bulletins* at ⟨http://www.iisd.ca/linkages/vol16/⟩. Such proposals do not amount to a centralization of decision-making authority, which has been criticized as being ineffective and incompatible with the decentralized IEG system. Clustering of reporting would have features of both harmonization and consolidation because a harmonization of rules might eventually result in fewer reports (ultimately, one report) being submitted. In some areas, such as non-compliance procedures, both harmonization of rules and consolidation might constitute options, whereas in others only one of these approaches appears promising. For example, centralization regarding transparency and participation in decision-making is not feasible given the large number of formally independent MEAs. Conversely, harmonizing the rules applying to financial mechanisms or to training activities holds little promise, since

it is exactly the consolidation of such functions that is hoped to deliver the benefits expected by those proposing a clustering in these areas.

54. Permanent Court of Arbitration, *Optional Rules for Arbitration of Disputes Relating to Natural Resources and/or the Environment*, The Hague, 19 June 2001, The Secretary-General and the International Bureau of the Permanent Court of Arbitration, available at ⟨http://pca-cpa.org/BD/⟩.

55. See also, von Moltke, *On Clustering International Environmental Agreements*, pp. 22–24.

56. See, e.g., WBGU, *World in Transition*; UNEP, *Implementing the Clustering Strategy for Multilateral Environmental Agreements*, p. 14.

57. Von Moltke, *On Clustering International Environmental Agreements*, pp. 19–20.

58. Discussions on scientific assessments in the framework of the UNEP IEG process led to the decision that the establishment of an "intergovernmental panel on global environmental change" that would be additional to existing assessment panels should be considered; see UNEP, *Report of the Governing Council Seventh Special Session*, Decision SS.VII/1, p. 26.

59. See United Nations University, *Inter-Linkages*; Bret Orlando, "Issue Management", paper prepared for the International Conference on Synergies and Coordination between Multilateral Environmental Agreements, United Nations University, Tokyo, 14–16 July 1999, available at ⟨http://www.geic.or.jp/interlinkages/docs/online-docs.html⟩.

60. Werksman, "Consolidating Governance of the Global Commons".

61. See information available at ⟨http://www.biodiv.org/world/reports.asp⟩.

62. On problems encountered in the development of the GEF, see Werksman, "Consolidating Governance of the Global Commons", p. 60. Political obstacles were, for example, decisive when some industrialized countries tried unsuccessfully to integrate the Montreal Protocol's Multilateral Fund into the GEF in 1992. See Ian H. Rowlands, "The Fourth Meeting of the Parties to the Montreal Protocol: Report and Reflection", *Environment*, Vol. 35, No. 6, pp. 25–34.

63. Complemented by regional clusters; see von Moltke, *On Clustering International Environmental Agreements*, pp. 12–18.

64. UNEP Governing Council, Decision 21/21, *International Environmental Governance*, para. 2.

65. UNEP (*Implementing the Clustering Strategy for Multilateral Environmental Agreements*) has applied regional clustering in a different sense by suggesting the combination of regional seas conventions and related agreements *from different regions*. This approach is not considered here as clustering by region because it seems to be based on a common issue (regional seas) rather than a common regional focus. See also von Moltke, *On Clustering International Environmental Agreements*, p. 18.

66. See ⟨http://www.unece.org/env/welcome.html⟩.

67. See also UNEP, *Implementing the Clustering Strategy for Multilateral Environmental Agreements*, p. 8.

68. See "Summary of the Expert Consultations on International Environmental Governance, 28–29 May 2001", *Sustainable Developments*, Vol. 53, No. 1, 7 June 2001, p. 4.

69. See also Oran R. Young, *The Institutional Dimensions of Environmental Change: Fit, Interplay, and Scale*, Cambridge, MA: MIT Press, 2002.

70. See Gehring, *Dynamic International Regimes*; Ott, *Umweltregime im Völkerrecht*.

71. See ⟨http://www.ospar.org/eng/html/welcome.html⟩.

72. See also, von Moltke, *On Clustering International Environmental Agreements*, p. 5.

73. See, e.g., WBGU, *World in Transition*; Peter H. Sand, *Lessons Learned in Global Environmental Governance*, Washington, D.C.: World Resources Institute, 1990.

74. See, e.g., Maria Concetta Pontecorvo, "Interdependence between Global Environmen-

tal Regimes: The Kyoto Protocol on Climate Change and Forest Protection", *Zeitschrift für ausländisches öffentliches Recht und Völkerrecht*, Vol. 59, No. 3, 1999, pp. 709–749.

75. See, e.g., Richard G. Tarasofsky, "Ensuring Compatibility between Multilateral Environmental Agreements and GATT/WTO", *Yearbook of International Environmental Law*, Vol. 7, 1997, pp. 52–74.

76. UNEP, *Global Environment Outlook 2000*, Nairobi: UNEP, 1999.

77. See ⟨http://unfccc.int/secret/secretariat.html⟩.

78. With a GEF contribution of about US$1 billion, co-financing of GEF climate change projects has reached US$5 billion; see *Summary of Negotiations on the Third Replenishment of the GEF Trust Fund*, 5 November 2002, p. 16, available at ⟨http://www.gefweb. org/Replenishment/Summary_of_negotiations_ENGLISH_Revised_11-5.doc⟩. However, clustering can hardly be expected to lead to significant savings in this regard.

79. The point that inter-institutional coordination requires decision-making by parties was also made in the UNEP IEG process; see *Final Report of MEA Meeting on Governance*, New York: UN Headquarters, 18 April 2001, p. 7, available at ⟨www1.unep.org/meas/ finalreportmeasgovernancemtgny18april2001.doc⟩.

80. See the diverse reports that have been produced in the context of the UNEP IEG process available at ⟨http://www.unep.org/IEG/WorkingDocuments.asp⟩.

81. See also von Moltke, *On Clustering International Environmental Agreements*, p. 10.

82. UNEP, *Report of the Governing Council Seventh Special Session*, Decision SS.VII/1.

3

Strengthening international environmental governance by strengthening UNEP

Richard G. Tarasofsky

Introduction

This chapter examines the prospects for strengthening the United Nations Environment Programme (UNEP) without changing its legal status. Other chapters in this volume will examine other possibilities for institutional reform, both within the current UN system and in the creation of a new organization. Therefore, this chapter is limited to exploring the possibilities for enhancing the role and contribution of UNEP (basically, as it is now constituted) within an improved regime of international environmental governance.

The first section of this chapter will present UNEP as it is now, and the second section will explain why reform of UNEP is necessary and what changes took place prior to the recent initiative on international environmental governance. I shall then examine in detail the options that have emerged in recent discussions on enhancing UNEP, including those relating to the Global Ministerial Environment Forum and the Environmental Management Group. Finally, some general conclusions will be drawn.

UNEP's approach, structure and achievements

The United Nations Environment Programme (UNEP) was established following the 1972 United Nations Conference on the Human Environment. Its constituent document is UN General Assembly (UNGA) Resolution 2997 (XXVII). UNGA Resolution 53/242 of 28 July 1999, as well as other instruments, continue to affirm UNEP's role as the leading global environmental authority that sets the global environmental agenda and promotes the integration of the environmental aspects of sustainable development in the work of the United Nations system.

Mission and approach

UNEP's mission is:

To provide leadership and encourage partnership in caring for the environment by inspiring, informing, and enabling nations and peoples to improve their quality of life without compromising that of future generations.

This mission statement reveals that UNEP's role is a catalytic one, in the sense of leveraging and enabling others to act in the protection of the environment. In other words, UNEP is not an implementing agency – and has never had the capacity to be one – unlike UN bodies such as the United Nations Development Programme (UNDP) and the Food and Agriculture Organization (FAO).

Rather, UNEP seeks to achieve improvement through the actions of nations and peoples. Achieving this requires at least three elements: strategic partnerships with governmental and non-governmental actors involved in policy-setting and implementation, the credibility to provide leadership and set the agenda, and the resources to motivate its partners to carry out implementing actions.

Governing bodies

Governing Council

UNGA Resolution 2997 (XXVII) established a Governing Council (GC) as the governing body of UNEP, composed of 58 members selected by the General Assembly for three-year terms. The seats on the Governing Council are allocated specifically according to region. The main functions and responsibilities of the Governing Council are to:
- promote international cooperation in the field of the environment and to recommend policies to this end;
- provide general policy guidance for the protection and coordination of environmental programmes within the United Nations system;
- keep under review the world environmental situation in order to ensure that emerging environmental problems of wide international significance receive consideration by governments;

- promote contributions from scientific and other professional communities to the acquisition, assessment and exchange of environmental knowledge and information and the formulation and implementation of environmental programmes within the United Nations system; and
- maintain under continuing review the impact of national and international environmental policies and measures on developing countries, and ensure that such programmes and projects are compatible with the development plans of those countries.

UNGA Resolution 53/242 of 28 July 1999 agreed to the creation of a Global Ministerial Environment Forum (GMEF), to act as the Governing Council. At present, the GMEF is to meet in alternate years, when the GC is not meeting, and is to be a special session of the GC.

Committee of Permanent Representatives

The Committee of Permanent Representatives (CPR) is a subsidiary organ of the Governing Council. The CPR consists of representatives of all UN member states and members of its Specialized Agencies, and the European Community accredited to UNEP. The CPR meets four times a year, but there have been suggestions to increase this to six, because of the heavy workload. The CPR establishes subsidiary bodies, subcommittees and working groups on specific subjects, which meet inter-sessionally. Decision 19/32 elaborated the following mandate for the CPR:

- to review, monitor and assess implementation of Council decisions on administrative, budgetary and programme matters;
- to review the draft programme of work and budget during their preparation by the secretariat;
- to review reports requested of the secretariat by the Governing Council on the effectiveness, efficiency and transparency of the functions and work of the secretariat, and to make recommendations thereon to the Governing Council;
- to prepare draft decisions for consideration by the Governing Council based on inputs and the secretariat and the results of the functions specified above.[1]

Accordingly, the CPR provides a useful "reality check" of the work of the secretariat, and acts as a bridge between UNEP and its member states.

Secretariat

A small secretariat in Nairobi was established by UNGA Resolution 2997 (XXVII) "to serve as a focal point for environmental action and coordination within the United Nations system in such a way as to ensure a high degree of effective management". The responsibilities of the secretariat include:

- coordinating environmental programmes within the United Nations system, keeping their implementation under review and assessing their effectiveness;
- advising intergovernmental bodies of the United Nations system on the formulation and implementation of environmental programmes;
- securing the effective cooperation of, and contribution from, the relevant scientific and other professional communities in all parts of the world;
- providing, on request, advisory services for the promotion of international cooperation in the field of the environment.

The cost of servicing the Governing Council and providing the secretariat are to be borne by the regular budget of the United Nations. The programming and administrative costs are to be borne by the Environment Fund, also established by the Resolution.

The initial focus of UNEP was sectoral and largely linked to pollution issues. Since then, as the environmental agenda has grown in breadth and complexity, UNEP has become increasingly cross-sectoral. These developments, although necessary, have had some undesirable effects, such as increased competition among UN bodies, as well as duplication of functions.[2]

UNEP's secretariat structure has evolved over its lifetime, and reflects the growing complexity of its mandate and programme. It can no longer be considered a "small" secretariat, although by UN standards it is still relatively modest. UNEP now has six regional offices, covering every area of the world, as well as a number of offices relating to science and technology and a host of environmental treaty secretariats.

UNEP's achievements

UNEP has a record of important environmental achievements. UNEP was at the forefront of developing environmental law at national, regional and global levels. At the global level, major treaties such as the Montreal Protocol on the Protection of the Ozone Layer, the Basel Convention on the Control of Transboundary Movements of Hazardous Wastes and Their Disposal and the Convention on Biological Diversity were the result of UNEP initiatives. UNEP was also a key promoter of regional seas treaties, e.g. the Barcelona Convention, and has an extensive programme to assist developing countries in developing national environmental law.

UNEP has also built tremendous credibility as an institution that provides policy-relevant scientific information about the environment. The best example of this is the *Global Environment Outlook* (GEO). GEO-2000 was an important achievement in reviewing the state of the world's environment. The process leading up to GEO-2000 was both participatory and cross-sectoral, and based largely on the work of a coordinated network of Collaborating Centres that prepared most regional inputs. The result was an integrated assessment combined with bottom–up environmental reporting. Usefully, GEO-2000 not only identified the environmental challenges and priorities in each of the earth's regions, but also provided guidance on real-life alternative policy responses to address the issues raised. This highlights UNEP's strong potential to link credible scientific assessment with policy advice. GEO-2003 builds on this experience by reviewing the environmental policy choices made over the past 30 years and considering various scenarios for the coming 30 years.

Finally, UNEP has succeeded in raising the importance of environmental issues throughout the UN system. Since 1972, a large number of UN agencies have developed environmental programmes,[3] and the importance of the environmental agenda within the UN is now unquestioned.

The UNEP reform process

Despite these impressive achievements, there has been consensus for a number of years that UNEP was not fulfilling its full potential and that steps needed to be taken to strengthen it.

Why reform of UNEP is necessary

Reforming UNEP is necessary for a number of reasons:
- UNEP's budget is insufficient for UNEP to carry out its mandate; contributions fluctuate from year to year, and the level of contributions is unpredictable;
- UNEP's role and focus have been under increasing question since the United Nations Conference on Environment and Development (UNCED) in 1992;
- there is a perceived need for a more forceful and authoritative global environmental institution;
- there is an increasing sense of policy incoherence among the different international bodies dealing with environmental issues, with UNEP lacking the authority to play a coordinating role.

The year of UNCED proved to be fateful for UNEP, and in many ways a turning point. UNEP's role during the UNCED process was unclear. Certainly, it did not play a leadership role. UNCED itself created several new institutions, but two key ones – the UN Commission on Sustainable Development (CSD) and the UN Framework Convention on Climate Change – were not linked directly to UNEP. Indeed, the CSD's mandate appeared to overlap somewhat with that of UNEP, again creating confusion about what exactly UNEP's role was in the UN system. Adding to the confusion is that both UNEP and the CSD report to the Economic and Social Council (ECOSOC), sometimes on overlapping issues – although in the case of UNEP, it reports to the UN General Assembly through ECOSOC.

Notwithstanding the importance that *Agenda 21* assigned to UNEP, 1992 was also the high point in government financial contributions to UNEP. Gradual discontent among donors led to a financial crisis in 1996 and 1997, when some donor governments froze their contributions. In 1998, 73 countries contributed to the Environment Fund, whereas in 2000 only 56 countries contributed.[4]

Previous initiatives

Although the official discussion on reforming UNEP – and international environmental governance – is relatively recent, there have been several milestones that have impacted on UNEP's work.

A key milestone was UNCED, which established a new set of norms and institutions that UNEP needed to fit into. Chapter 38 of *Agenda 21* includes a set of 14 priority areas, on which UNEP was meant to concentrate.[5] In 1997, the Governing Council adopted the Nairobi Declaration on the Role and Mandate of the United Nations Environment Programme. This Declaration emphasized that UNEP was and should continue to be the principal UN body in the field of the environment. According to this Declaration, UNEP is to be the leading global environmental authority that sets the global environmental agenda, promotes the coherent implementation of the environmental dimension of sustainable development within the UN system, and serves as an authoritative advocate for the global environment. The Declaration went on to elaborate a mandate for UNEP that focused on the following areas:

- to analyse the state of the global environment and assess global and regional environmental trends, to provide policy advice, to provide early warning information on environmental threats, and to catalyse and promote international cooperation and action, based on the best scientific and technical capabilities available;
- to further the development of international environmental law aimed at sustainable development, including the development of coherent interlinkages among existing international environmental conventions;
- to advance the implementation of agreed international norms and policies, to monitor and foster compliance with environmental principles

and international agreements, and to stimulate cooperative action to respond to emerging environmental challenges;
- to strengthen its role in the coordination of environmental activities in the UN system in the field of environment, as well as its role as an implementing agency of the Global Environment Facility, based on its comparative advantage and scientific and technical expertise;
- to promote greater awareness and facilitate effective cooperation among all sectors of society and actors involved in the implementation of the international environmental agenda, and to serve as an effective link between the scientific community and policy makers at the national and international levels;
- to provide policy and advisory services in key areas of institution-building to governments and other relevant institutions.[6]

In 1998, the UN Task Force on Environment and Human Settlements was established at the initiative of the UNEP executive director. It made a number of recommendations on improving the effectiveness of UNEP. This led to UNGA Resolution 53/242 of 28 July 1999, which paved the way for a more focused UNEP mandate concentrated on the following priority areas:
- environmental information, assessment and research, including environmental emergency response capacity and strengthening of the early warning and assessment functions of UNEP;
- enhanced coordination of environmental conventions and development of environmental policy instruments;
- technology transfer and industry;
- support to Africa.[7]

This latest refocusing of the mandate seems useful. Given the limited financial resources and the complexity of the challenge of providing global leadership, it is not possible for an intergovernmental institution such as UNEP to be very diffuse in its scope while at the same time trying to be effective in all areas. A limited focus should facilitate priority-setting and lead to more effective and targeted outputs.

From 2000 to 2002, UNEP anchored an expert process on international environmental governance (IEG). This did not lead to major innovations,[8] although a number of interesting ideas were proposed, several of which are discussed in the next section.

Current proposals to strengthen UNEP

In the context of the current discussions on international environmental governance, a number of proposals have been made to strengthen UNEP without changing its legal status.

The Global Ministerial Environment Forum (GMEF)

The GMEF is at the heart of a revitalized UNEP. The extent to which UNEP will be strengthened in coming years will depend on the success of the GMEF in providing environmental leadership and leveraging concrete results.

Role and functions

The Nairobi Declaration stated that UNEP should serve as the world forum for the ministers and the highest-level government officials in charge of environmental matters in the policy and decision-making processes of UNEP.[9] Following this, UNGA Resolution 53/242 established the GMEF as an annual ministerial-level forum. The UNEP Governing Council constitutes the forum in the years that it meets in regular session, and in alternate years the GMEF takes on the form of a special session of the Governing Council. Participants are to:

gather to review important and emerging policy issues in the field of the environment, with due consideration for the need to ensure the effective and efficient functioning of the governance mechanisms of the United Nations Environment Programme, as well as possible financial implications, and the need to maintain the role of the Commission on Sustainable Development as the main forum for high-level policy debate on Sustainable Development.[10]

The UN Legal Counsel has clarified that, because the GMEF is merely a forum for discussions and dialogue, it does not have its own independent legal standing or status.[11] Therefore, an affirmative decision, reflected in an instrument, will have to be taken in order to change this status, which should address both the GMEF and the GC.

To date, five meetings of the GMEF have taken place, with the last one in March 2004 in Jeju, South Korea. These meetings have been successful in raising the profile of the environmental agenda,[12] but more thought needs to be given to defining the role and structure of the GMEF. The Committee of Permanent Representatives to UNEP asserted in 2001 that the GC/GMEF should be:

placed as the cornerstone of the international institutional structure of International Environmental Governance. It should provide general policy guidance to and promote coordination with the other relevant organizations in the environment field, while respecting the legal independence of the MEAs. GC/GMEF should become the central forum for Ministerial policy discussions along the lines of a refined "Malmö model", i.e. a well focused and well structured forum for its extensive discussions to define priorities and address problems and needs – institutional, operational and financial – in the global environmental field.[13]

The CPR argues that the GC/GMEF could usefully be guided by the development of objectives, principles, provisions, rights and obligations. This would help strengthen the normative authority of UNEP. It would clarify the links between UNEP and existing instruments, such as MEAs. It would also clarify the role of UNEP in contributing to the wider sustainable development agenda. Similarly, the G-77 proposed that the GMEF be remodelled by encouraging it to "provide general policy guidance to, and promote coordination with, the other relevant organizations in the environmental field".[14]

The President of the UNEP Governing Council has proposed that the GMEF consider grouping issues relating to environmental assessment and monitoring, early warning, and emerging issues.[15] It was further suggested that the GMEF consider addressing the environmental aspects of one or two selected sectoral issues on an annual basis. The President also recommended having the UNEP CPR continue to play its mandated role in monitoring the implementation of GC/GMEF decisions, as well as in preparation for the sessions. All of these suggestions would appear likely to enhance the impact and effectiveness of the GMEF and have the potential to link usefully with UNEP's current focused mandate.

The relationship between the GMEF and the GC is complex and remains to be clarified. In some ways, the GMEF is very different from the traditional UNEP Governing Council. The GMEF addresses issues that are beyond UNEP's programme and it operates in a different manner from the GC. However, since UNEP's role in supporting the GMEF and the implementation of its recommendations is pivotal, it may be appropriate to link the GMEF closely to the Governing Council – for example by deeming GMEF meetings to be a special session of the Governing Council. Indeed, the functions of the Governing Council under UNGA Resolution 2997 are sufficiently broad to allow it to capture most of the functions of the GMEF. Indeed, UNEP's CPR provides a useful basis for supporting the GMEF. The specific functions of the GMEF need to be better clarified so that the distinction from a normal GC meeting becomes more apparent – and to ensure that the participants in a GMEF meeting are fully unencumbered in addressing issues that are beyond the current UNEP programme. A fuller examination of the functions and membership needs to take place, based on the experience with the GMEF.[16] In addition, the size of the bureau and the Rules of Procedure may need to be altered. Ultimately, a new UNGA resolution may be necessary.

In order for the GMEF to have the proper authority to take decisions regarding coordination, a legal instrument will need to be elaborated. The European Union has called for the elaboration of a "general agreement", without specifying its form. Such an instrument could take the form of a memorandum of understanding between the relevant organizations or even a statute adopted by member states. A UNGA resolution would also be possible, but that would bind only UN institutions.

A reformed GMEF should also be credible to civil society. Structured mechanisms to ensure a meaningful civil society input will be discussed further in subsequent sections of this chapter. Civil society input will be particularly important because the intent of the GMEF is to be a different type of forum from other intergovernmental bodies, in the sense of promoting "actual debate, more in-depth discussions, more interaction with major groups to produce innovative strategies that can meet tomorrow's challenges".[17] It has been suggested that the GMEF adopt "CSD-style approaches" to interactive discussion between states and observers.

The results of GMEF deliberations should be fed through the UNEP process, as well as throughout the Environmental Management Group (EMG), which was created to improve coordination throughout the United Nations on work related to environment and human settlements. G-77 recommends that it report to the Commission on Sustainable Development. It is an open question whether the GMEF should report to ECOSOC or directly to the UN General Assembly. Having it report to both might be appropriate, since ECOSOC would be able to link the results more closely to the work of the CSD, which also reports to it. The President of UNEP has suggested that environmental policy and financing issues would be better linked by having the GMEF play a stronger role in providing policy advice to multilateral financial institutions and the Global Environment Facility (GEF), including through regular dialogues with the heads of these institutions. This could also lead to increased and coordinated funding of GMEF outputs.

It is important that the work of the GMEF does not become undermined or paralysed by the political dynamics that have had an adverse impact on the effectiveness of the CSD. Much will depend on the political will of the GMEF members, but also on the clarity of the mandate and programmes of the GMEF, as well as its structure.[18] A clear division between the GMEF and the CSD must be made, although the two agendas might also usefully be linked for particular items. In principle, the starting point should be that the GMEF addresses environmental issues, with a view to achieving sustainable development, whereas the CSD seeks to create appropriate balances between all three pillars of sustainable development – environmental protection and economic and social development.

Membership

A key issue on which consensus has yet to emerge is whether membership in the GMEF should be universal. So far, the format has been to limit formal membership to members of the Governing Council, while allowing any other state to attend as an observer. The UN Legal Counsel has argued that, to fulfil the mandate of the GMEF, it is necessary for it to have universal membership, as has the President of the UNEP Governing Council.[19] The European Union has also indicated that it favours universal membership. Indeed, universal membership would seem to be in accordance with the leadership role and coordinating functions that the GMEF should have.

The G-77 is open to considering the expansion of the membership of the GMEF so as to be universal, although it considers the present arrangement to be adequate. If the membership were to be expanded, the G-77 would not oppose this as long as it does not impact negatively on UNEP, does not consume additional financial resources, and does not jeopardize the present position of the Commission on Sustainable Development as "the main forum for high-level policy debate on sustainable development".[20] The issue of universal membership remains unresolved, but the report of the International Environmental Governance process endorsed the need for universal "participation" in the GMEF.[21]

In order to ensure that the GMEF can address all environmental issues, it is necessary to ensure that participation is not limited to environment ministers.[22] Other ministries (such as fisheries and forests) that traditionally deal with some environmental issues should also be encouraged to participate in the GMEF, as appropriate. But in principle this should be in coordination with, and under the leadership of, the environment ministries. This would be another argument for not limiting membership in the GMEF to UNEP members, since UNEP members tend to be represented at UNEP through their environment ministries.

Another issue is the participation of representatives of other international institutions that have an impact on the environment. In principle, their participation should be encouraged – perhaps by convening meetings of the EMG adjacent to meetings of the GMEF. Depending on the membership of the EMG, it would also be useful to allow the GMEF the right to invite representatives from agencies on an ad hoc basis, depending on the particular agenda items. The institutions invited might also come from outside the UN family (for example, the WTO, the World Bank and the International Monetary Fund).

The role of scientific assessments and raising awareness

In order for the GMEF to be able to lead in setting the environmental agenda, it will need to be serviced with credible scientific information. The GEOs have been useful but are not well suited to the needs of decision makers. Both the Committee of Permanent Representatives to

UNEP and Norway proposed enhancing UNEP's function of providing scientific assessments and raising awareness by establishing an Intergovernmental Panel for Assessing Global Environmental Change.[23] So far the decision to establish this has not been taken. The envisaged Intergovernmental Panel would be a subsidiary body of the GC/GMEF; it would be based on the experience of the Intergovernmental Panel on Climate Change and supported by UNEP's programme. According to the Committee of Permanent Representatives:

The Panel would respond to and fuel the environmental agenda with cutting edge science on environmental change and its consequences for social and economic development. It would synthesize knowledge and interlinkages, inter alia, based on existing initiatives. The pyramidal outputs ranging from in-depth reports, outlooks (GEO), and ICT-products to summaries would enjoy both political ownership and scientific credibility.[24]

The CPR also proposed reviewing the modalities of an independent and impartial system that could receive, gather and present information on solutions to new and emerging environmental concerns. This system should be based on UNEP's ongoing activities.

This proposal is a welcome one, so long as it has functional linkages with the work of other UNEP bodies and regional networks catalysed through regional ministerial environmental forums. According to the Norwegian proposal, "the Global Environmental Outlook could become a point of departure for defining the scope of the assessment and become an integral part of the outputs generated".[25]

Linking the global and regional agendas

To provide relevant leadership on the most pressing environmental issues, the GMEF will need to have links to what actually happens on the ground. UNEP has both a global and a regional structure, with the potential to ensure that the global and regional levels are linked in such a way that the GMEF can provide global leadership that takes account of regional priorities. However, to fulfil this potential, clear linkages will have to be made to regional environmental forums (which suggests that regional programmes develop the capacity and structure to feed into the GMEF process). The importance of linking the GMEF to regional ministerial environmental forums was noted in GC Resolution 21/20 of 9 February 2001 on Governance of the United Nations Environment Programme and Implementation of General Assembly Resolution 53/242.

Regional ministerial environmental forums do not yet exist in every region. However, the Forum of Ministers of the Environment of Latin

America and the Caribbean, formed in the 1980s, provides an instructive experience of their potential. That Forum of Ministers established an Inter-Sessional Committee, which is charged with reviewing progress in the implementation of agreements, making proposals for future work and identifying themes for future consideration by the forum. In addition, an Inter-Agency Technical Committee was established to develop and implement projects and activities based on the decisions and priorities of the Forum of Ministers. The members of the Inter-Agency Technical Committee currently include UNEP (the coordinator), the Inter-American Development Bank, the UNDP, the United Nations Economic Commission for Latin America and the Caribbean, and the World Bank.

As an illustration of the types of decision taken at the Forum of Ministers of the Environment of Latin America and the Caribbean, the Thirteenth Meeting decided, *inter alia*:[26]

- to approve the Regional Strategic Action Plan 2002–2005;
- to recommend the ratification of various multilateral environmental agreements;
- to develop a strategy for countries of Latin America and the Caribbean to adopt sustainability indicators;
- to request UNEP to continue providing leadership in the preparation of integrated environmental assessments at the regional level, and to provide support to countries in preparing national assessments within the framework of the Global Environment Outlook process and methodology;
- to request UNEP to continue developing sectoral and targeted assessments within the GEO methodology;
- to request UNEP to continue developing environmental databases and indicators;
- to request the Inter-Agency Technical Committee to cooperate in designing and coordinating project proposals to the GEF.

This experience suggests that it is possible to develop positive linkages between the global and regional agendas. However, to become more meaningful, the regional level will need to be endowed with sufficient capacity and programmatic basis to ensure that the global agenda is effectively implemented in the most appropriate fashion at the regional level. Regional ministerial environmental forums, similarly to the GMEF, should seek close relations with other regional institutions, including those established by regional environmental treaties (as called for by the World Summit on Sustainable Development Plan of Implementation in 2002[27]). The optimal scenario would be a legal instrument between relevant institutions that would clearly articulate the policy and programmatic role of regional ministerial environmental forums. Certain obstacles will need to be overcome, such as the reality that many regional environmental treaties are not UN based. However, the importance of achieving synergies at the regional level suggests that modalities for enhanced cooperation ought to be found. Beyond the adoption of a legal instrument, participating governments will need to be politically committed to effective implementation of the results of these forums.

UNEP's role in enhancing synergies among MEAs

There is a need to ensure coordination of the programming and further development of MEAs, to avoid unnecessary duplication, as well as to maximize synergies (for a discussion of clustering of MEAs, see chapter 2 in this volume). There is consensus on the need for coherence between MEAs, coordination, compliance, and capacity-building for implementation.[28] The UN Task Force on Environment and Human Settlements made the following recommendations:

UNEP's substantive support to global and regional conventions should be founded on its capacities for information, monitoring and assessment, which need to be strengthened substantially and urgently. UNEP should build its capacity and its networks of support in order to ensure the scientific underpinning of conventions, to respond to their requests for specialized analysis and technological assessments, and to facilitate their implementation.[29]

To achieve this, action is needed at both the secretariat and policy-making levels. UNEP is well placed to make this happen by:
• linking MEA actions with GMEF and EMG recommendations;
• providing technical support in the development and implementation of cross-cutting themes (e.g. compliance and dispute resolution); and
• establishing a mechanism for monitoring the decisions of MEA bodies to identify inconsistencies and then bring such inconsistencies to the appropriate MEA bodies.

The International Environmental Governance process also recommended having the GC/GMEF review progress through MEA Conferences of the Parties (COPs).[30] The GMEF could usefully make normative and organizational recommendations directed at MEAs. Normative recommendations could include clarifying the main principles to be incorporated into MEAs with a view to harmonizing their implementation; organizational recommendations might include the clustering of MEAs.

Some formal issues need to be considered here. For example, not all MEAs are affiliated with UNEP, and not all MEAs have the same membership. However, UNEP has already been active in enhancing coordination for a number of years, and so far these obstacles have not proved to be insurmountable. It might also be useful to distinguish between the challenges of achieving policy synergy and programmatic synergy, because the choice of instruments would be different.

One of the proposals currently being considered is to enhance coordination between MEAs through annual meetings of the bureaus of the MEA COPs.[31] It is proposed that these meetings should consider the priorities of their work programmes and linkages to other MEAs and intergovernmental organizations in an integrated manner. This could entail:

- promotion of cooperation and complementarity at the policy level;
- joint efforts to respond to basic human needs, such as poverty alleviation, food security, access to clean water and technology;
- building synergies at the programmatic, scientific and technical levels;
- avoiding potential inconsistencies among decisions adopted by Conferences of Parties;
- monitoring the implementation of COP decisions.

The GMEF could take a central role in developing a work programme for these meetings. It also has been suggested that such meetings of the bureaus could be dovetailed with GMEF meetings. Furthermore, since synergy and coordination between MEAs are vital at the implementation level, UNEP, in collaboration with MEA secretariats and possibly the UNDP, the FAO and the World Bank, could facilitate the establishment of national coordination mechanisms and provide advice on these issues.[32]

One example of how UNEP can support synergy between MEAs was the proposal for the 2002 meeting of the GMEF that a set of guidelines on enforcement and compliance with MEAs be adopted.[33] The guidelines, adopted in 2002,[34] include a set aimed at enhancing compliance with MEAs and a set aimed at national enforcement and international cooperation to combat violations of laws implementing MEAs. The success of these guidelines will partly depend on the extent to which UNEP can support effective implementation – for example through information exchange and capacity-building – and can define linkages and feedback loops between the two sets of guidelines.

UNEP's role in the coordination of environmental activities within the UN system

UN General Assembly Resolution 53/242 of 28 July 1999 expressed support for the creation of an Environmental Management Group (EMG), with a view to enhancing inter-agency coordination in the field of environment and human settlements. At present, the executive director of UNEP chairs the EMG. At the second meeting, held on 15 June 2001, 27 organizations were represented, including UNEP.[35] A secretariat has recently been established for the EMG, based in Geneva.

According to the executive director of UNEP:

[the EMG is to be a] problem-solving, results-oriented mechanism to foster coordinated action on specific environmental issues. It is envisaged that an important goal of the Environmental Management Group will be to achieve effective coordination and joint action to identify, address and resolve collectively specific problems and concrete environmental issues. It will provide a forum for an early discussion and the sharing of information on such issues. It is expected that the Environment Management Group will facilitate the mandate of UNEP to integrate the environmental dimension of sustainable development into United Nations programmes, as emphasized by the Governing Council in its Decision 20/12.[36]

The G-77 had expressed the view that the reporting relationship of the EMG should be not only to the GMEF but also to the CSD.[37] However, this may not be necessary if the GMEF interacts effectively with the CSD. Since the focus of the EMG is on the environmental pillar of sustainable development, it should have a direct relationship with the GMEF rather than with the CSD, whose focus is on all three pillars of sustainable development. This would allow the EMG to respond most effectively to any policy guidance from the GMEF.

The EMG has developed criteria for selecting priority themes. In addition to selecting themes of common concern to the Group, the EMG works on issues that are prominent on the international agenda; can be concretely addressed in 6–12 months, producing deliverable outcomes; and are not being taken up in other parts of the United Nations.[38] Currently, the EMG has established three Issue Management Groups: Harmonization of National Reporting for Biodiversity Related Conventions; Environment Related Capacity Building; and Intergovernmental Strategic Plan for Capacity Building and Technology Support. In October 2001, the Issue Management Group on the Harmonization of Information Management and Reporting for Biodiversity-Related Treaties proposed that an action plan for a more proactive approach to harmonization be developed, partly on the basis of pilot projects, which would identify lead roles, participation and available resources.[39] The issue management approach is useful and should produce concrete results. Once the GMEF begins to address coordination issues, the EMG could also be more active in facilitating the coordination of priority implementation issues.

Civil society inputs into UNEP

UNEP's authority and credibility can be enhanced if it takes civil society inputs on board in a meaningful way. According to the Malmö Declaration, civil society "provides a powerful agent for promoting shared environmental purpose and values. Civil society plays an important role in bringing emerging environmental issues to the attention of policy makers, raising public awareness, promoting innovative ideas and approaches, and promoting transparency as well as non-corrupt activities in environmental decision making."[40]

There is a need to ensure that civil society has an input into the policy, programme and implementation components. At the same time, capacity-building is necessary to ensure meaningful public participation in developing countries. Achieving this will entail some formalization.

The Nairobi Declaration called for the establishment of a "cost-effective and politically influential inter-sessional mechanism" whereby the participation of major groups would be increased.[41] Partly in response, UNEP established a Civil Society and Non-Governmental Organizations Unit within the secretariat. In addition, the GMEF was initially established with the idea of attracting civil society input.

UNEP Governing Council Decision 21/19 of 9 February 2001 called for the development of a strategy on enhancing the engagement of civil society in the work of UNEP. This strategy was presented at two meetings of the GMEF in February 2002 in Cartagena, Colombia, and in February 2003 in Nairobi, Kenya.[42] The strategy calls for a more institutionalized relationship between civil society, the GC/GMEF and the secretariat through a Global Civil Society Forum, composed of stakeholder representatives. It was intended that this multi-stakeholder body would meet prior to the GC/GMEF meetings "to reflect on issues of major concern of the global environment, and to make recommendations on these matters to be considered by these meetings. Such a body shall not have any decision-making role, but modalities for the development of the forum will be agreed with the CPR."[43]

The strategy implies that certain legislative changes might be necessary to strengthen the input of civil society. Rule 69 of the Governing Council Rules of Procedure currently limits participation to international non-governmental organizations (NGOs). The strategy suggests that this restriction is outmoded and that the categories of group to be allowed observer status should include international NGOs, representatives of civil society networks (including national-level designated representatives), national/local NGO members of global multi-stakeholder networks dealing with environmental policy, national NGOs with documented contributions to global environmental policy processes, and NGOs accredited to the CSD or an MEA. This would need to be worked on further, so as to define "NGO" more precisely, particularly as regards the private sector.

The strategy has evolved over time in part out of recognition that significant additional financial resources are not likely to become available to support the engagement of civil society. Thus, the current version refrains from proposing major new activities for which financial resources would be unavailable.

These proposals, if fully implemented, would considerably enhance the participation of civil society in the setting of global environmental policy, as well as in the activities of UNEP. The strategy is therefore to be welcomed. However, one element is questionable. In the strategy, the executive director is to select the members of the Civil Society Advisory Group to the Executive Director. This group might be more credible if the NGO community determined the membership. There is a strong tradition of "self-selection" by NGOs in various international environmental forums, and there is every reason to believe that the NGOs would be able to self-select in this instance.

Improving the financing of UNEP

Regular finances

The lack of sufficient and predictable funding for the UNEP programme has been a significant – perhaps the most significant – handicap since the beginning. At present, UNEP is funded by voluntary contributions to the Environment Fund, counterpart contributions earmarked in support of selected project activities, trust funds, and the UN regular budget. Its budget is generally in the area of US$60 million per year, which is far less than the budget of most environmental ministries in developed countries, and even of some international NGOs. The Governing Council decided that the programme and support budget for the 2002–2003 biennium would be US$119.88 million.

The executive director has identified several problems associated with the funding of UNEP:

- the apportionment of the UN regular budget has decreased over the years to a very low level;
- contributions to the Environment Fund are on a voluntary basis;
- the limited number of countries contributing to the Environment Fund;
- the decrease in the number of countries contributing to the fund;
- increasingly, contributions are made in earmarked form.[44]

The result is that the funding is both inadequate and unpredictable. Both of these factors significantly impede effective programming.

The CPR examined several options for funding UNEP.[45] In its view, mandatory assessments using the UN scale of assessments were not politically feasible and would be opposed by both donor and developing countries. Thus, the only feasible options were variants of the current

system, which is based on voluntary contributions. These options included: (1) negotiated and agreed assessed contributions on a voluntary basis, with a multi-year perspective; (2) voluntary contributions on the basis of the UN assessed scale, with a multi-year perspective; and (3) increased voluntary contributions on an agreed basis, with a multi-year perspective, in support of "operational" costs by developed countries, and enhanced financing of "administrative" costs from the UN regular budget. In particular, the idea of a voluntary indicative scale of contributions was endorsed by the IEG process.[46] Although the options examined by the CPR were considered to have the advantages of flexibility and stability, several potential disadvantages were also identified:
- a system of periodic negotiations may be a time-consuming and cumbersome process;
- a new mechanism for such negotiations has to be developed;
- it still may be difficult to reach a consensus on the adequate level of payments;
- late payments could affect cash flow.

Given these conditions, it cannot realistically be expected that the financing of UNEP will become fully adequate and stable in the near future. Other solutions must also be pursued.

One possibility, which has already been raised, is to distinguish between programming and administrative budgets. It would then be envisaged that the UN regular budget would cover the administrative costs, whereas the Environment Fund would cover the programming costs. This separation was envisaged by UNGA Resolution 2997 but has not been fully implemented. Although this approach seems sensible, it may not be realistic to expect any significant increase in the allocation from the UN regular budget, given the overall budgetary constraints and deficits in the UN system.

Another possibility is to examine whether the programming and funding cycle is adequate. Although planning on a biennial basis is probably more suitable than an annual basis, it might be too short a cycle for UNEP to act strategically. If indeed UNEP is to be programmatically led by the Global Ministerial Environment Forum, and if multi-year contributions are indeed the more feasible option for funding UNEP, it might make more sense for the programming to cover the same time period. That way, the budgetary needs for the full contribution period might be clearer, and, at the same time, donors might be more attracted to funding a programme that is more strategically oriented.

Linkages between UNEP and the Global Environment Facility

The idea of UNEP and the Global Environment Facility (GEF) having a more intensified relationship has been on the agenda for years.[47] The

1998 Task Force on Environment and Human Settlements recommended the following:

Consistent with the GEF instrument, UNEP's role in providing environmental advocacy, analysis and advice in shaping GEF priorities and programme should be strengthened, building on UNEP's current responsibility for ensuring the scientific underpinning of GEF activities. UNEP should act as a catalyst and advocate for new directions and should take the lead among the three GEF implementing agencies in providing environmental advice.[48]

The GEF was launched formally in 1994, following a three-year pilot phase. Its implementing agencies are the World Bank, the UNDP and UNEP. Membership in the GEF is open to any state member of the United Nations or its Specialized Agencies.[49] Its mandate, structure and functions are described in the Instrument for the Establishment of a Restructured GEF (1994).[50] It was intended to be a mechanism for international cooperation providing new and additional grants and concessions on funding to meet the "agreed incremental costs of measures to achieve agreed global environmental benefits" in four focal areas: climate change, biodiversity, international waters, and ozone depletion (Article 2). In addition, the agreed incremental costs of activities concerning land degradation as they relate to the four focal areas are eligible for funding (Article 3).

The GEF is also the financial mechanism for the implementation of the UN Framework Convention on Climate Change (FCCC) and the Convention on Biological Diversity (CBD). As such, it is to function under the guidance of, and be accountable to, the Conferences of the Parties of these conventions, which have the authority to decide on policies, programme priorities and eligibility criteria for the purposes of the conventions (Articles 6 and 26). The GEF has been called upon to be the financial mechanism on an interim basis for the Convention on Persistent Organic Pollutants and a new focal area on land degradation will support the implementation of the Convention to Combat Desertification.

UNEP's primary role is defined as catalysing the development of scientific and technical analysis and advancing environmental management in GEF-financed activities. It is to provide guidance on relating GEF-financed activities to global, regional and national environmental assessments, policy frameworks and plans, and international environmental agreements (Article 11(b) of Annex D). UNEP is also to establish and provide the secretariat for the Scientific and Technical Advisory Panel (STAP), which is an advisory body to the GEF (Article 24).

STAP is intended to provide objective, strategic scientific and technical advice on GEF policies, operational strategies and programmes; to conduct selective reviews of projects; and to maintain a roster of experts. STAP's activities are to be integrated with those of the GEF secretariat and the implementing agencies. STAP is to be complementary to other scientific and technical bodies, especially those under the CBD, the FCCC and the Convention to Combat Desertification. For areas in which the GEF is not a financial mechanism for a convention, STAP is to advise on the development of scientific and technical criteria and provide scientific and technical advice on priorities for GEF funding.

STAP's role in providing strategic advice to the GEF includes the following:

- advising on the state of scientific, technical and technological knowledge relating to each focal area, and highlighting policy and operational implications for the GEF;
- advising on the scientific and technical aspects of specific strategic matters, such as cross-cutting issues, scientific coherence and integration of national and global benefits;
- advising on research that would improve the design and implementation of GEF projects and reviewing the research work of the implementing agencies and the GEF secretariat;
- participating in the editorial review board for GEF scientific and technical publications.

In the first 10 years of its existence, the Global Environment Facility allocated US\$3 billion to project activities. During 1999–2000, the overall UNEP–GEF-funded project portfolio amounted to an accumulated total of US\$286 million. This level of funding, although representing an increase over previous years, indicates that UNEP does not account for a very significant proportion of overall GEF expenditure.

It has been proposed that the GEF become a more integrated funder of UNEP activities, but there are limits to the extent to which this can happen. First, the two institutions have different objectives: whereas the GEF is limited to funding the "incremental costs", UNEP's mandate is far broader than just the incremental benefits of global environmental action. Secondly, the GEF is meant to work with all three implementing agencies, each of which has a different approach and constituency, as well as with the Conferences of the Parties of the conventions for which it is the financial mechanism. Enhancing UNEP's role and financial share would therefore be complex and might encounter institutional resistance.

Although there are limits to the extent to which the GEF can be used to support UNEP, a number of steps could be taken to strengthen the operational partnership between the two. Indeed, UNGA Resolution 53/242 of 28 July 1999 called for the enhancement of the role of UNEP as the implementing agency of the GEF.[51] Much could be done to enhance collaboration between UNEP and the GEF, as well as with the other implementing agencies, through business planning and country coordination, and through reviewing and modifying the GEF operational programmes. The latter, in particular, would seem timely, since most of the operational programmes were adopted in 1996, well before the MEA COPs could provide much guidance. Moreover, the Strategic Partnership between UNEP and the GEF, agreed in 1999, forms a useful basis upon which to deepen cooperation. The initial phase of that Partnership covered three areas: assessment, global environmental knowledge management, and global environmental outreach. The CEO/chairman of the GEF proposed that the GEF should fund UNEP's mutually agreed activities of relevance to the global environment and the GEF, including: assessment; scientific information; best practice and policy analysis; capacity-building and training; and country-level coordination for sustainable development.[52]

Coordination between the three implementing agencies could be improved. An institutionalized high-level forum consisting of the heads of the implementing agencies is intended to focus on strategic operational issues, a common direction and broad guidance, and should meet not less than once a year.[53] Article 22 of the GEF Instrument calls for an inter-agency agreement to be concluded by the three implementing agencies based on the principles of cooperation elaborated in Annex D. Discussions of such an agreement have surfaced, but no final text has been agreed on.[54]

Miscellaneous proposals

There have been a number of other proposals on how to reform UNEP. The G-77 has suggested that a limited operational role for UNEP should be developed in conjunction with UNDP, which would enable it to catalyse and promote international environmental cooperation and action.[55] This might prove to be a useful option in the medium term. However, developing such an approach, even a limited one, would mean some fundamental changes in the character and operations of UNEP, and would probably be best dealt with after the workings and status of the GMEF and the EMG have been fully entrenched.

A civil society representative suggested in 2001 that an environmental ombudsman or centre for the amicable settlement of disputes could be established within UNEP.[56] Such a role for UNEP could be developed, based in part on the experiences of implementing the guidelines on compliance and enforcement of MEAs. The modalities and scope of such a body within UNEP would need further study but, in principle, such a role could be very credibly occupied by UNEP.

A civil society representative also suggested that UNEP should be included in the UN Development Group.[57] The need for linkages between environmental and development policies within the United Nations is manifest and the suggestion has now been acted on. It is to be hoped that this will contribute an environmental perspective to operational co-ordination on the ground.

Conclusions

In many respects, the current proposals to strengthen UNEP seem promising. Their ultimate success will depend on the extent to which governments and civil society are supportive – politically and financially. However, a lot will also depend on the confidence that UNEP can garner in filling its important niche with credibility and leadership.

Approach to international environmental governance

The current proposals will allow UNEP's approach to international environmental governance to be multifaceted, innovative and integrative, thus providing a forceful voice for the environment both within and beyond the United Nations. The proposals largely play on UNEP's strengths: policy formulation, scientific assessment, a regionalized structure, linkages to a wide range of international institutions within the United Nations, as well as with international financial institutions, a high degree of interaction with civil society, and a commitment to building capacity in developing countries. By combining policy leadership on a limited set of priorities – established through mechanisms that link the national, regional and global levels – with support for ensuring effective implementation of these policies, a strengthened UNEP could play the central role in international environmental governance. Key to all this will be the extent to which UNEP succeeds in defining and enhancing the mechanisms at the appropriate levels that create the linkages and feedback loops necessary to foster innovative solutions, stakeholder ownership and effective implementation.

Interface between politics and science

The proposal to create a subsidiary body to the GMEF that focuses on scientific assessment has the potential to develop a solid interface between politics and science. It will be vital for UNEP to be able to integrate the assessment process under the GMEF with its other work on assessments, such as the GEO process, the Intergovernmental Panel on Climate Change and STAP. Indeed, based on experience with the

GMEF, UNEP might consider expanding its role as a scientific adviser to other global and regional institutions.

Financing

It is universally accepted that a strengthened UNEP will require a more solid financial base than currently exists. The proposal to have UNEP members contribute on a multi-year basis may be an improvement, as would be an intensified relationship with the GEF, but it is far from evident that states are willing to commit the necessary resources to UNEP. Thus, it can be expected that, even if the other proposals on strengthening UNEP are implemented, severe financial challenges will remain. To overcome this, UNEP might consider exploring innovative funding partnerships with the private sector.

Participation levels

Participation of civil society appears to be a high priority in the current proposals on strengthening UNEP. However, these proposals are mainly aimed at the GMEF and the UNEP Governing Council. Certainly, a deeper level of interaction between civil society and those bodies is to be welcomed, but effective participation will also need to be developed at regional and national levels, and capacity there is often lacking. More thought needs to be given to the modalities of civil society at those levels, as well as a greater commitment to build the capacity and mechanisms necessary for effective public participation.

Policy influence at both the national and international levels

The ultimate test of the effectiveness of a strengthened UNEP will be the extent to which it succeeds in influencing national and international policy-making and implementation. UNEP has a particularly important role in facilitating the implementation of international policy at national levels. The current proposals, especially those relating to the GMEF and the EMG, would help to enhance UNEP's influence at international levels. What is less certain is the extent to which its influence would be felt on the ground, at national levels. UNEP national committees do not seem to be well developed in many countries, and UNEP's influence at the regional level has been variable so far. The guidelines on enforcement and compliance with MEAs are a useful example of what UNEP can achieve by aiming at both national and international levels. Ultimately, however, UNEP will need to develop mechanisms to link international and national policy, to provide for effective interaction with civil society from all regions, and to provide a greater investment in capacity-building at national and regional levels.

Notes

This chapter is based on a paper written in 2000, which has been modified to take into account the most significant developments since then. I am grateful to Lee Kimball for insightful comments on an earlier draft, although I retain sole responsibility for any errors.

1. *Governance of the United Nations Environment Programme*, Decision 19/32, adopted 4 April 1997.
2. *Reports of the Civil Society Consultations and Expert Consultations on International Environmental Governance*, UNEP/IGM/2/2, 18 June 2001.
3. For example, a number of UN agencies now carry out environmental work, such as the UNDP, the FAO, the UN Educational, Scientific and Cultural Organization, the World Intellectual Property Organization, the World Health Organization, the World Meteorological Organization and the United Nations University.
4. *International Environmental Governance: Report of the Executive Director*, UNEP/GCSS.VII/2, 27 December 2001.
5. United Nations Conference on Environment and Development (UNCED), *Agenda 21: Programme of Action for Sustainable Development*, New York: United Nations, 1992, para. 38.22.
6. *Nairobi Declaration on the Role and Mandate of the United Nations Environment Programme*, Decision 19/1, adopted 7 February 1997, paras. 3(a)–3(f).
7. *Report of the Secretary-General on Environment and Human Settlements*, A/RES/53/242, 10 August 1999.
8. *International Environmental Governance: Provisional Agenda*, SS.VII/1, in UNEP/GCSS.VII/6, 20 October 2001.
9. *Nairobi Declaration on the Role and Mandate of the United Nations Environment Programme*, para. 4(a).
10. *Report of the Secretary-General on Environment and Human Settlements*, para. 6.
11. *Legal Status of the Global Ministerial Environment Forum*, UNEP/IGM/4/INF/5/Rev.1, 1 December 2001.
12. For example through the *Malmö Ministerial Declaration*, Adopted by the Global Ministerial Environment Forum – Sixth Special Session of the Governing Council of the United Nations Environment Programme, Fifth plenary meeting, Malmö, Sweden, 31 May 2000.
13. *Contribution of the Committee of Permanent Representatives to the United Nations Environment Programme, Open-Ended Intergovernmental Group of Ministers or Their Representatives on International Environmental Governance, Fourth Meeting, Montreal, 30 November–1 December 2001*, UNEP/IGM/4/INF/4, 17 November 2001, p. 3.
14. G-77, Non-Paper, 5 October 2001, adopted provisionally by the G-77 Nairobi Chapter at its General Counsel Meeting on 5 October 2001, para. 10.
15. *Proposals of the President of UNEP GC for Consideration by the Open-Ended Intergovernmental Group of Ministers or Their Representatives on International Environmental Governance, Fourth Meeting, Montreal, 30 November–1 December 2001*, UNEP/IGM/4/2, 12 November 2001.
16. The UN Task Force on Environment and Human Settlements recommended that membership of UNEP GC should be made universal.

17. *Legal Status of the Global Ministerial Environment Forum*, para. 5.
18. What Governance Programme? A Joint Initiative of the World Humanity Action Trust (WHAT), UNED Forum and Global Legislators Organisations for a Balanced Environment (GLOBE) Southern Africa, Submission to the Fourth Meeting of the Open Ended Intergovernmental Group of Ministers or Their Representatives on International Environmental Governance, Montreal, Canada, 30 November–1 December 2001.
19. *Proposals of the President of UNEP GC*, 12 November 2001.
20. G-77, Non-Paper, 5 October 2001, para. 14.
21. *International Environmental Governance*, UNEP/GCSS.VII/1 of the UNEP Governing Council adopted at its Seventh Special Session in Cartagena, Colombia, 15 February 2002, para. 11(a).
22. Joy Hyvarinen and Duncan Brack, *Global Environmental Institutions: Analysis and Options for Change*, London: Royal Institute of International Affairs, 2000, p. 56.
23. See also *Note by the Executive Director, Intergovernmental Panel on Global Environmental Change, Twenty-Second Session of the Governing Council/Global Ministerial Environment Forum*, UNEP/GC.22/INF/15, 9 January 2003.
24. UNEP Committee of Permanent Representatives, Non-Paper, *IEG Building Blocks: Strengthening the Role, Authority and Financial Situation of UNEP, Strengthening UNEP within Its Existing Role and Mandate*, 2 October 2001, para. 3(a).
25. Norway, *An Intergovernmental Panel for Assessing Global Environmental Change, Open-Ended Intergovernmental Group of Ministers or Their Representatives on International Environmental Governance*, UNEP/IGM/4/CRP.1, 30 November 2001, para. 12.
26. *Draft Final Report of the Thirteenth Meeting of the Forum of Ministers of the Environment of Latin America and the Caribbean*, UNEP/LAC-IG/VIII/7, 23 October 2001.
27. "Johannesburg Plan of Implementation", in *Report on the World Summit on Sustainable Development*, A/CONF.199/20, 26 August–4 September 2002, para. 159.
28. Government of Canada, *International Environmental Institutions: Where from Here?*, Discussion Paper, Bergen Informal Ministerial Meeting, 15–17 September 2000.
29. *The Report of the United Nations Task Force on Environment and Human Settlements to the Secretary-General*, 1998, annexed in the *Report of the Secretary-General: United Nations Reform – Measures and Proposals – Environment and Human Settlements*, A/53/463, 6 October 1998, *Recommendation 2*.
30. *International Environmental Governance: Report of the Executive Director*, para. 30.
31. *Improving International Environmental Governance among Multilateral Environmental Agreements: Negotiable Terms for Further Discussion*, UNEP/IGM/2/4, 4 July 2001.
32. Ibid., para. 39.
33. *Note by the Executive Director, Addendum, Draft Guidelines on Compliance with and Enforcement of Multilateral Environmental Agreements, Global Ministerial Environment Forum, Seventh Special Session, Cartagena, 13–15 February 2002*, UNEP/GCSS.VII/4/Add.2, 23 November 2001.
34. *Compliance with and Enforcement of Multilateral Environmental Agreements*, Decision SS.VII/4, 15 February 2002.
35. These included three entities that are not members of the UN system: the Ramsar Convention, the World Bank and the WTO.
36. *Global Environmental Governance and the United Nations Environment Programme: Report of the Executive Director*, UNEP/GC/21/4, 22 December 2000, para. 5.
37. *Contribution of the Committee of Permanent Representatives to the United Nations Environment Programme, Open-Ended Intergovernmental Group of Ministers or Their Representatives on International Environmental Governance*, UNEP/IGM/4/INF/4, 17 November 2001.
38. *Report of the Environmental Management Group on Its Second Meeting, Open-Ended*

Intergovernmental Group of Ministers or Their Representatives on International Environmental Governance, Bonn, Germany, 17 July 2001, UNEP/IGM/2/INF/4, 4 July 2001.

39. UNEP, Issue Management Group, *Harmonization of Information Management and Reporting for Biodiversity-Related Treaties*, Third Meeting of the Environmental Management Group, Geneva, 10 October 2001.

40. *Malmö Ministerial Declaration*.

41. *Nairobi Declaration on the Role and Mandate of the United Nations Environment Programme*, para. 4(d).

42. *Draft Strategy on Enhancing the Engagement of Civil Society in the Work of the United Nations Environment Programme, Seventh Special Session of the Governing Council of the United Nations Environment Programme, Cartagena, 13–15 February 2002*, UNEP/GCSS.VII/Add.1, 3 December 2001. See also *Note by the Executive Director, Enhancing Civil Society Engagement in the Work of the United Nations Environment Programme*, UNEP GC.22/INF/13, 21 November 2002.

43. *Report of the Executive Director, Draft Strategy on Enhancing the Engagement of Civil Society in the Work of the United Nations Environment Programme*, UNEP/GCSS.VII/4/Add.1, 3 December 2001.

44. *International Environmental Governance: Report of the Executive Director*, UNEP/IGM/3/2, 17 August 2001.

45. UNEP Committee of Permanent Representatives, Non-Paper, *IEG Building Blocks*.

46. UNEP/GCSS.VII/1 of the UNEP Governing Council, para. 17.

47. It has even been proposed to broaden the mandate of the GEF so that it becomes the financial mechanism for all global environmental agreements and is more closely linked with UNEP in order to bring coherence between policy and financing.

48. *The Report of the United Nations Task Force on Environment and Human Settlements to the Secretary-General, Recommendation 16*.

49. *Instrument for the Establishment of a Restructured Global Environment Facility*, Washington, D.C.: Global Environment Facility, May 2004, Article 7.

50. Ibid.

51. *Report of the Secretary-General on Environment and Human Settlements*, A/RES/53/242, para. 12.

52. See *Proposals of the President of UNEP GC*, 12 November 2001.

53. *Instrument for the Establishment of a Restructured Global Environment Facility*, Article 14(a) of Annex D.

54. Jake Werksman, "Consolidating Global Environmental Governance: New Lessons from the GEF?", in Norichika Kanie and Peter Haas, eds, *Emerging Forces in Environmental Governance*, Tokyo: United Nations University Press, 2004.

55. G-77, Non-Paper, 5 October 2001.

56. *Reports of the Civil Society Consultations and Expert Consultations on International Environmental Governance*, UNEP/IGM/2/2, 18 June 2001.

57. Ibid.

4

A World Environment Organization

Steve Charnovitz

This chapter explores the idea of bolstering international environmental governance by centralizing the current system under one umbrella institution. The idea received important backing in June 1997, at the United Nations General Assembly Special Session, when Germany's Federal Chancellor Helmut Kohl, Brazil's President Fernando Henrique Cardoso, South Africa's Deputy President Thabo M. Mbeki, and Singapore's Prime Minister Goh Chok Tong joined together in a "Declaration" for a Global Initiative on Sustainable Development. A key point in that Declaration was that "the establishment of a global environmental umbrella organization of the UN with UNEP as a major pillar should be considered".[1] That joint Declaration had been spurred by a proposal at a Rio+5 Forum held earlier that year.[2] Although this Declaration did not meet with enthusiasm at the Special Session, it energized long-time advocates of such a reform and spurred policy makers to acknowledge the need to think more systemically about the defects of global environmental institutions. In the following four years, governments introduced some new institutions and initiated a dialogue about more fundamental changes. With the World Summit on Sustainable Development in Johannesburg on the horizon, one environmental analyst opined that "there is presently a certain institutional effervescence in the air".[3]

Nevertheless, the reformist hopes were left unfulfilled. At the Johannesburg summit in September 2002, the governments gave little attention to environmental governance, and instead focused their efforts on ad-

93

dressing development goals. The conclusion of this chapter will reflect on why the reform movement sputtered in the early 2000s.

The idea of an international agency for the environment is by no means new. The attention to the environment in the early 1970s led some analysts to propose the establishment of new agencies. In a lead article in *Foreign Affairs* in April 1970, George Kennan proposed an "International Environmental Agency" as a first step toward the establishment of an "International Environmental Authority".[4] The most comprehensive proposal was developed by Lawrence David Levien, who proposed a "World Environmental Organization" modelled on the practice of the International Labour Organization (ILO), which was created in 1919.[5] Such inspiring ideas were too ambitious for the governments of that era, however, and they decided on a minimalist approach by creating the United Nations Environment Programme (UNEP) in 1972.[6] Although some observers at the time recognized UNEP as unsatisfactory, it settled the organizational question for a generation.[7] In the early 1990s, however, dissatisfaction with the overall state of environmental governance led to renewed attention to organizational structure and effectiveness.

The most important proposal came from Sir Geoffrey Palmer, the former prime minister of New Zealand, who advocated new methods of making environmental law, and called for action at the United Nations Conference on Environment and Development in 1992 in Rio to establish a specialized UN agency for the environment.[8] Sir Geoffrey proposed the creation of an "International Environment Organization", borrowing loosely from the mechanisms of the ILO. He saw an opportunity for a "beneficial restructuring" of the world's environmental institutions that "would involve cutting away existing overlaps in international agencies". No such action was taken at the Rio Conference, which instead called for the creation of the Commission on Sustainable Development (CSD) and for "an enhanced and strengthened role for UNEP and its Governing Council".[9]

Within a couple of years, new support for institutional change came from a different direction, the international debate on "trade and the environment", which had been rekindled in 1990 and was in full swing by 1993. Both camps in this debate saw the weak state of the environment regime as a serious problem. The environmentalists yearned for an international agency that could stand up to the General Agreement on Tariffs and Trade (GATT), which they saw as a threat to environmental measures. And the trade camp wondered whether a better environment regime might spur the use of appropriate instruments for environmental protection rather than inappropriate instruments such as discriminatory trade measures.

With one foot in both camps, Daniel C. Esty became a new champion of establishing a new international environmental organization. His article "GATTing the Greens" contended that solving the trade and environment conflict would necessitate not only a greening of trade rules, but also a stronger organization of environmental governance.[10] Esty proposed the GATT as a good model for an environmental institution. In 1994, Esty optimistically named the institution the Global Environmental Organization (GEO),[11] and in a series of studies he strengthened the environmental arguments for institutional change. Esty began the Global Environmental Governance Project at Yale in 1998, and has organized a series of study groups to improve understanding of the proposals for change.

Ford Runge was another early advocate of institutional reform. In 1994, he proposed a World Environmental Organization to give stronger "voice" to environmental concerns.[12] Runge suggested that a new organization could serve as a "chapeau" to the growing number of international environmental treaties, but he did not elaborate on how that might be done. In a more recent study, Runge argues that a GEO could alleviate environmental pressure on the World Trade Organization (WTO).[13]

The ranks of academic advocates for a World Environment Organization (WEO) have expanded in recent years. For example, Rudolf Dolzer has proposed a global environmental authority "with the mandate and means to articulate the international interest in an audible, credible and effective manner".[14] Frank Biermann has provided the most systematic analysis of what a WEO would do.[15] John Whalley and Ben Zissimos have defined an economic role for a WEO.[16] Peter Haas has advocated a GEO to centralize support functions such as research, technology databases and training for the various environmental regimes.[17] The German Advisory Council on Global Change has recommended that UNEP be upgraded into an International Environmental Organization as an entity or a Specialized Agency within the UN system.[18] The Council points out that this step might not suffice to remedy the deficits it sees, and suggests consideration of another proposal that would involve integrating various environmental agreements and their Conferences of the Parties into a common Framework Convention Establishing an International Environmental Organization.

Proponents of a WEO received a boost in June 2001 when the UN High-Level Panel on Financing for Development (the Zedillo Commission) proposed that "[t]he sundry organisations that currently share responsibility for environmental issues should be consolidated into a Global Environmental Organization".[19] However, the Commission's report was disappointingly thin on a proposed design for such an organization or its exact rationale.

WEO advocates have been challenged by some environmental experts, the leading ones being Calestous Juma and Konrad von Moltke. Juma has argued forcefully that the advocates of a WEO have produced "no compelling organizing principle, clear design concept, or realistic plan" and have failed to explain how new institutions would operate better than existing ones.[20] Furthermore, he has criticized a WEO as being inherently bureaucratic, and contended that centralization is a "peril" in an era of decentralization. He also warned that "the debate on creating a new agenda diverts attention from more urgent tasks".[21] Von Moltke has expressed scepticism that a WEO would help in solving current problems, but has been less definitive in his criticism.[22] Although emphasizing the need for change, he has underlined the impracticality of a true WEO.

This chapter follows a comparative institutionalist approach in analysing the issues surrounding a WEO. It is organized as follows. I begin by developing a case for a WEO of moderate centralization. Next I discuss the structure and functions of a WEO. Then I consider the extent to which a WEO might contribute to achieving a set of specific objectives for environmental governance. Lastly, a short conclusion is presented.

Refining the WEO debate

This part of the chapter has four sections: the first discusses the terms "WEO" and "centralization"; the second explains why a fully centralized WEO is inconceivable; the third presents some factors to consider in deciding whether a WEO is a good idea; the fourth presents a case for setting up a WEO.

Note on terminology

I shall employ the most commonly used term "World Environment Organization" and its acronym "WEO". Many international agencies start with the modifier "World", such as the World Health Organization (WHO), the World Meteorological Organization (WMO), the World Intellectual Property Organization (WIPO), the World Tourism Organization, and the World Trade Organization (WTO). The oldest of these, the WHO, goes back to 1946. Calling an organization "World" connotes a universality that can be appropriate. It was the Chinese government that had the inspiration of naming the new health organization a "World" agency.

Nevertheless, it should be said that a Global Environment Organization would be a better name because it could be called a "GEO". Geo means earth or land, and is a term that the public can readily understand

and identify with. The public are unlikely to warm to a "wee-oh" any more than they have warmed to a "dubya-tee-oh". Esty, who invented the acronym GEO, argues that the new organization should be limited to global rather than international functions. One can disagree with that limitation and still see the wisdom of using the term GEO.

I shall employ the word "centralized" based on the framework paper written by the United Nations University Institute of Advanced Studies (UNU-IAS),[23] but that is not the best descriptor. Advocates of a WEO are not proposing true centralization. They are not saying that all environmental governance needs to be in one building (like the WTO) or in one organizational entity. They are not saying that the environmental governance that goes on in every country and city in the world needs to be centralized and directed from the top. Indeed, one of the advocates of moving toward "an overarching, coherent international structure", Michael Ben-Eli, says that he favours a "decentralized approach".[24] Perhaps some of the reaction against a WEO comes from analysts who are reading too much into the term centralization.

The WEO proposal would be more accurately called a consolidation. The myriad disconnected organizational boxes of global environmental governance would be consolidated into fewer boxes with more networking among the entities. Environmental governance would not necessarily have one centre, but instead could have several leadership nodes.

Full centralization is inconceivable

If centralization is the aim, why not a single WEO that consolidates all international environmental institutions under one umbrella? Such a complete organization could comprise UNEP, the hundreds of multilateral environmental agreements (MEAs), the WMO, the Global Environment Facility (GEF), the pollution control programmes of the International Maritime Organization (IMO), the International Tropical Timber Organization, the fishery and forestry programmes from the United Nations Food and Agriculture Organization (FAO), the Intergovernmental Panel on Climate Change, the International Oceanographic Commission, the United Nations Inter-Agency Committee on Sustainable Development, the International Council for the Exploration of the Sea, and many others.

Although a comprehensive WEO would have some compelling logic behind it, such a massive reorganization is inconceivable. Yet, even if it could be done, there are strong arguments against it. One problem is that environmental issues are often diverse and might not coexist well.[25] Another problem is that the resulting organization would cut a huge swathe through domestic policy, and no government would be comfortable giving any WEO executive that much responsibility. In pointing out why a broad WEO would be impossible, von Moltke makes an additional telling point that no major government has an environment ministry as broad as the subject matter of a fully centralized WEO.[26] If governments have not deemed it advisable to amalgamate environmental functions at the national level, why should one assume it would be advantageous at the international plane? Of course, it could be that governments have maintained separate national agencies with environmental functions to coincide with disconnected international organizations. But that might imply that national bureaucracies may resist a global reorganization that would disrupt their relationships with international agencies.

The fallacy of full centralization can also be seen by recalling that even the non-environmental agencies will need environmental programmes, staff and offices.[27] The World Bank, the WTO, ILO, WHO, FAO, the United Nations Educational, Scientific and Cultural Organization, the United Nations Conference on Trade and Development (UNCTAD), the International Atomic Energy Agency and the Organisation for Economic Co-operation and Development (OECD) all have environmental components, and properly so. The mainstreaming of environment into all agencies is one of the successes of modern environmental policy, even if these environmental components are inadequate. The existence of such environmental offices does not itself demonstrate redundancy; such offices are a vital interface for organizations. Similarly, the fact that there may be a dozen or more international offices addressing climate change does not prove disorganization. Rather, these offices exemplify a recognition that responding to global warming will require a multifaceted effort.

The centralist would not deny the need for regional environmental programmes such as the regional seas treaties and the North American Commission for Environmental Cooperation, and for environmental components of regional institutions such as the development banks or the Association of South East Asian Nations. The regional level is often the right setting for environmental cooperation because it matches the scope of the problem or the ecosystem at issue. Thus, even with a fully centralized WEO, there might be more intergovernmental environmental institutions outside the WEO than inside it.

That a fully centralized WEO is inconceivable should not come as a surprise, because no other regime is fully centralized. The WTO may be the core of the trade regime, but many trade agencies and bodies of law lie outside it, such as UNCTAD, the International Trade Centre, the trade directorate of the OECD, the UN Convention on Contracts for the International Sale of Goods, the UN Commission on International Trade Law, and various agreements on trade in food, endangered species, hazardous waste, military goods, etc. The WHO may be the core of the health regime, but many health agencies and bodies of law lie outside it, such as the United Nations Population Fund, the Joint UN Programme on HIV/AIDS, the United Nations International Drug Control Programme, the International Consultative Group on Food Irradiation, and numerous ILO conventions. Even the United Nations system, which is comprehensive, excludes the World Bank Group, the International Monetary Fund and the WTO. Although the environment regime may seem comparatively disjointed, consider the development, energy and banking regimes, which enjoy even less cohesion.

Some commentators contend that the environment regime should consolidate in the way that the WTO has consolidated various GATT agreements. This WTO analogy is false however. The GATT was centralized already. The WTO was created from existing GATT agreements (as modified in 1994) and several new agreements. The WTO did not absorb any freestanding agencies in the way that WEO advocates imagine that WEO would absorb MEAs. Although the WTO did incorporate new obligations on intellectual property, it did not transfer these functions from the World Intellectual Property Organization. It is true that WTO membership was conditioned on accepting new versions of GATT plurilateral agreements that had gathered only a small number of parties. But the new versions were negotiated during the Uruguay Round. Such a manoeuvre is quite different from establishing a WEO and requiring that governments ratify, say, the Desertification Convention as a condition of WEO membership.

The WTO is also used misleadingly as a model for integrating the MEAs. For example, the German Advisory Council on Global Change contends that the MEA Conferences of the Parties could be brought under the umbrella of a WEO in the same way that special committees of the WTO Ministerial Conference operate with a "high degree of autonomy".[28] This analogy is inapt, however, because almost all of the WTO committees are committees of the whole, and none of them so far has operated with any autonomy from the WTO membership as a whole.

The only regime that has consolidated in the way that proponents want a WEO to do is intellectual property. In 1967, the United Nations established the WIPO to bring together the intellectual property conventions and unions. Today, WIPO oversees 21 separate treaties. But it is not a convincing model for a WEO because WIPO is too topically narrow. Moreover, it was dissatisfaction with WIPO that led GATT parties to write the new WTO Agreement on Trade-Related Aspects of Intellectual Property Rights (TRIPS). In WIPO, governmental members are *not* required to join the treaties, and there are no WIPO systems for implementation review.

Thus, if WEO centralization is going to be done, it will need to chart its own course rather than follow in the footsteps of another organization. This need for complete reinvention is not a reason to refrain from undertaking a WEO. But it should serve as a caution against trying to do too much at once.

A reorganization calculus

A practical plan for a WEO would seek to centralize some environmental agencies and functions, while recognizing that many important institutions would be omitted. Determining whether such a plan should be pursued requires weighing the costs of reorganization against the gains. The obvious costs of reorganization include administrative costs and opportunity costs as officials focus on reorganization rather than production. The gains are more speculative, but one would hope for administrative savings and anticipated improvements in productivity. No major reorganization is worth doing unless the expected gains are well in excess of the expected costs.

Can we really expect a WEO to lead to better outcomes in environmental governance? Reducing the excessive fragmentation in the environmental regime would seem almost necessarily to be beneficial.[29] Yet fragmentation also has its good side. According to recent management research, innovation proceeds most rapidly under conditions of some intermediate degree of fragmentation. Because a high capacity for innovation may be the most distinguishing feature of the environment regime,[30] and a key source of its successes, one needs to be careful about undertaking a reorganization that would reduce fragmentation, and hence innovation, too much. One reason some fragmentation is good for innovation is that fragmented entities compete with each other. The environment regime has surely benefited from diversity among the entities that do environmental work.[31]

The main target of the WEO proposals is the MEAs and their associated institutions. It is the centralization of the core MEAs that is touted as the main benefit derivable from reorganization. Yet it is the MEAs that have been the most innovative feature of the environment regime. A study in the *American Journal of International Law* provides a comprehensive review of the techniques of rule-making, decision-making and compliance review in MEAs, and characterizes these developments as "unique" within international organization and law.[32] Indeed, the significance of this development leads the authors to devise a new name for the way MEAs work: the authors call them "autonomous institutional arrangements". If the innovativeness of the MEAs stems from their autonomy, that would throw up a caution flag against undertaking a reorganization aimed at reducing that autonomy. At present, we do not have enough evidence to measure the value of autonomy to the MEAs. But it is certainly interesting to note that the fragmented, autonomous MEAs have been very innovative over the past 30 years, whereas the more traditionally structured international organizations, such as WHO and ILO, have not been as innovative. In defence of these two organizations, it should be noted that they have become more innovative in recent years. The WHO has used previously neglected authorities to promulgate a convention on tobacco, and the ILO has enacted a Declaration that defines fundamental worker rights and provides a review mechanism for governments that have not ratified the applicable conventions.[33]

To be sure, autonomy was not necessarily the key reason the MEAs were so dynamic and successful. The main reason perhaps is that the MEAs were driven by advancements in scientific understanding of the underlying environmental problems. Had the environmental problems been less severe, the MEAs would not have been called upon to do as much. Furthermore, the MEAs worked because governmental parties wanted them to and were willing to endow the Conferences of the Parties with important powers. The question remains, however, whether governments would have been as willing to grant as much authority to a *general* environmental organization as they did to the specialized MEAs.

In weighing the costs and benefits of greater centralization of environmental functions, one should start by considering two of the leading arguments for a WEO: first, a WEO would be stronger than UNEP; second, a WEO would serve as a counterweight to the WTO. Neither argument is fully convincing.

The strength of UNEP results from the choices that governments have made. If governments wanted to make UNEP stronger now, they could do so. The act of establishing a WEO, with nothing more, would not strengthen environmental governance. Analysts sometimes make the mistake of thinking that reorganization (or organizational name changes) can drive policy. That almost never happens. Reorganizations can be useful only when they implement authoritative policy changes.

If governments ever decide to create a WEO, it will probably be because they have decided that a more centralized, better-funded environmental governing structure is needed to achieve more effective environmental policy. If so, then a WEO would be stronger than UNEP. But there is also a danger that governments may create a status-enhancing WEO without giving it more authority or funding than UNEP now has. That sort of WEO, endowed with only an enhanced "conscience" role, would not be appreciably stronger than UNEP.

The notion that a well-constituted WEO could act as a check or counterweight to overreaching by the WTO has potential validity.[34] External pressure is needed on the WTO to get trade officials to consider the environmental implications of what they are doing. UNEP recognized the need for such advocacy in 1993 and began to undertake trade-related efforts. That these efforts have had little effect is owing to their poor execution and to the difficulty of the challenge, and not at all to UNEP's status as a "programme" rather than a Specialized Agency.

Although it is true that GATT/WTO officials and national delegates to the WTO have claimed for years that coordinating with the environment regime is hard because it is so disparate, one should be hesitant to accept such claims at face value. The WTO does not cooperate well with other agencies because it is hard-wired to be insular and parochial and to resist other values beyond commercial reciprocity. If organizational unity were sufficient for WTO coordination, then one would expect the WTO to have very tight relations with the WHO and the ILO, whose headquarters (unlike that of UNEP) are located within a kilometre or two of the WTO. But the WTO has fewer interactions with the ILO than it does with UNEP.

Then WTO Director-General Renato Ruggiero surprised observers in 1998 when he said in a speech that the *Shrimp–Turtle* Appellate Body decision "underlines the need to strengthen existing bridges between trade and environmental policies – a task that would be made immeasurably easier if we could also create a house for the environment to help focus and coordinate our efforts".[35] Ruggiero did not explain why the task would be any easier, and no one else has since. The idea that the WTO would have been more ready to defer to MEAs or environmental exigencies had a WEO existed is naive. In the November 2001 Doha Ministerial Declaration, the WTO ministers endorsed continued WTO interactions with a multi-polar environment regime when the ministers stated, "We welcome the WTO's continued cooperation with UNEP and other inter-governmental environmental organizations."[36]

Although trade should be an important issue for UNEP and its institutional successors, trade is not itself among the most serious of the environmental problems. Thus, the challenge of grappling with the WTO would not be a sufficient reason to constitute a WEO. The case for a WEO needs to be made on environmental grounds.

Why a WEO is needed

A WEO is needed for two reasons: first, many ecosystems continue to deteriorate and the human environment is under serious, uncontrolled threats; second, the processes of international environmental governance need rationalization.

Although human stewardship over the earth's environment may not be disastrous, serious environmental problems exist that are not being adequately managed under current institutions.[37] In *Global Environment Outlook 2000*, UNEP concluded that, "if present trends in population growth, economic growth and consumption patterns continue, the natural environment will be increasingly stressed".[38] The most serious problems include a massive loss of biodiversity, overfishing, depleted freshwater supplies, and global warming.

Before critiquing the environment regime, one should first note that environmental governance is far from being fully dysfunctional. UNEP has achieved a number of successes over the years, particularly in acting as a catalyst for new MEAs.[39] The systems for implementation review of environmental treaties are complex, yet the results are often significantly positive.[40] In recent years, important new MEAs were negotiated on biosafety, on persistent organic pollutants, chemicals and pesticides, and on the implementation of the Kyoto Protocol on climate change.

Nevertheless, environmental governance does not function as well as it needs to. The environmental treaties are often too weak to address the problem they were set up to correct.[41] There is a lack of coordination among the MEAs, and opportunities for policy integration are missed. At a meeting in 2001 of the Open-Ended Intergovernmental Group of Ministers, the president of the UNEP Governing Council reported that "[t]he proliferation of institutional arrangements, meetings and agendas is weakening policy coherence and synergy and increasing the negative impact of limited resources".[42]

One long-time observer, Konrad von Moltke, reminds us that at no time has the entire structure of international environmental management ever been reviewed with the goal of developing optimum architecture.[43] The UN Task Force on Environment and Human Settlements reported that environmental activities in the United Nations "are characterized by substantial overlaps, [and] unrecognized linkages and gaps", which are "basic and pervasive".[44] If this is true even within the United Nations, it is probably much worse externally.

The Task Force reported further that environmental ministers are frustrated at having to attend so many different meetings, and that it was difficult for them to get the big picture. This is not surprising because nobody sees the big picture. The current scattered organization of environmental governance is confusing to experts and incomprehensible to the public. If an organization chart of world environmental governance existed, its incoherence would be Exhibit A for reformers.[45]

Joy Hyvarinen and Duncan Brack have keenly observed one symptom of governance failure – what they call the tendency to "recycle" decisions by having each new forum call for implementation of what the previous forum proposed.[46] All regimes do this to some extent, but it is particularly prevalent in the environment regime. Of course, the disorganization of environmental governance is not the only cause of recycling. Governments recycle when they cannot find anything new to agree upon and need some text for a declaration following an intergovernmental meeting.

The current incoherence in environmental organization provides reason enough for reform, but an even stronger reason exists, namely, that the trend is for more proliferation. The question of whether environmental governance should be centralized was discussed extensively in the run-up to the 1972 Stockholm Conference. For example, a special committee of the Commission to Study the Organization of Peace noted that "a new intergovernmental environmental organization" would provide "the best possible coordination" and would "adequately centralize all efforts".[47] Yet the committee rejected that approach because "it would be difficult to persuade organizations to transfer their environmental functions to the new entity". Today, the same conundrum exists, yet the number of environmental functions that would need to be transferred to a WEO has multiplied 10-fold. Back in 1970, when George Kennan recommended the creation of an "International Environmental Agency", he hypothesized that a single entity with great prestige and authority stood the best chance of overcoming the formidable resistance from individual governments and powerful interests. As he analysed it:

One can conceive of a single organization's possessing such prestige and authority. It is harder to conceive of the purpose being served by some fifty to a hundred organizations, each active in a different field, all of them together presenting a pattern too complicated even to be understood or borne in mind by the world public.[48]

Over three decades later, we live in the nightmare scenario that worried Kennan. The crazy quilt pattern of environmental governance is too complicated, and it is getting worse each year.

At the Rio summit in 1992, the governments had an opportunity to restructure environmental governance but, instead of doing so, they bypassed UNEP in a new climate change convention and created the Commission on Sustainable Development. At a meeting of experts held in Cambridge in May 2001, there was a consensus that, on the whole, the CSD adds little value to the debate on sustainable development.[49] Yet no one predicts that the CSD will be abolished anytime soon.

The problem is that the current system of environmental governance cannot correct itself. All of the trends point to continued proliferation, and governments show little appetite for thinning out the ineffective institutions. The tendency toward expansion can be seen in recent reformist actions. Concerned about the fragmentation of environmental institutions, governments created *three* new ones to deal with the problem: the Global Ministerial Environment Forum (GMEF), the Environmental Management Group, and the Open-Ended Intergovernmental Group of Ministers or Their Representatives on International Environmental Governance. It is hard to escape the conclusion that, unless governments take a big step toward creating a holistic WEO, the current governance architecture will get worse and the time-consuming dialogue on governance will remain open-ended rather than conclusive.

Organizing the WEO

This part of the chapter considers approaches to establishing a WEO. I start by noting some unrealistic options for setting up a WEO. Then I present two alternatives for setting up a WEO and dealing with UNEP. Next I examine several structural issues. Then I look at the relationship between a WEO and the MEAs. Following that, I consider some key issues of WEO orientation. The last section lists several functions for a WEO and examines four of them.

Unrealistic approaches

Before considering some conceivable possibilities for reorganization, I start by dismissing some approaches that are politically unrealistic. The first is to create a WEO within the United Nations but separate from UNEP; the second is to create a WEO outside the United Nations.

As von Moltke has pointed out, "UNEP must stand at the heart of any organizational restructuring of international environmental management".[50] This is perhaps unfortunate given UNEP's problems. Yet, even though it is often critical of UNEP, the environmental community is also intensely proud of it. In recent years, UNEP has succeeded in getting its status blessed by governments, and that is not likely to change. For example, the Nairobi Declaration of 1997 stated that UNEP "has been and should continue to be the principal United Nations body in the field of the environment".[51] The Malmö Ministerial Declaration of 2000 stated that the World Summit of 2002 "should review the requirements for a greatly strengthened institutional structure for international environmental governance" and that "UNEP's role in this regard should be strengthened and its financial base broadened and made more predictable".[52] Thus, the approach of creating a WEO separate from UNEP is impossible.

Another impossible approach is to create a WEO outside the United

Nations. Some commentators point to the WTO as a model for externalization, and it is true that many participants in the WTO believe that its non-UN status is a source of its effectiveness. Whatever the truth of that assessment for the WTO, the situations are hardly comparable because the trading system was traditionally outside the United Nations, whereas UNEP is inside the United Nations.

The controversy over the UN Security Council consideration of Iraq in 2002 and 2003 has rekindled debates in some quarters about the usefulness of the United Nations for difficult issues. The universality of the United Nations is contrasted to ad hoc "coalitions of the willing". Yet good ecological stewardship, more so than perhaps any other issue, requires multilateral approaches. Taking environment out of the United Nations would seem to contradict the foundational axioms of the UN system.

WEO organizational alternatives

At this time, there are two realistic organizational structures for a WEO vis-à-vis UNEP. The first is a WEO that adds new flanks to UNEP, with UNEP retaining its organizational identity. The second is a WEO that incorporates UNEP and in which UNEP eventually dissolves in the new organization.

The first option may resemble the 1997 Joint Declaration, discussed at the beginning of the chapter, which called for a global environmental umbrella organization, with UNEP as a "major pillar". Von Moltke has pointed to the option of establishing a WEO with UNEP as a division of it.[53] This WEO could be created as a Specialized Agency pursuant to Article 59 of the UN Charter or it could be a new type of agency more central to the United Nations. The Governing Council of UNEP might become the Governing Council of the WEO, but otherwise UNEP would retain its current programmes and location in Nairobi. The remaining components of the WEO could include some MEAs and other environmental programmes.

The second option would be to establish a WEO to incorporate the UNEP but with the intention of dissolving UNEP into the new organization. This WEO could be created as a Specialized Agency pursuant to Article 59 of the UN Charter[54] or it could be a new type of agency more central to the United Nations. The remaining components of the WEO could include some MEAs and other environmental programmes.

What would be the implications of one approach versus the other approach? At this level of generality, it is hard to say much definitively. Either organization could be well funded or poorly funded (recall that transformation of the GATT into the WTO did not lead to a large increase in funding). Either WEO could attract MEAs or fail to. Either organization could promote and utilize science well. Either organization could carry out monitoring and reporting. Either organization could strengthen MEAs.

One difference may be predictable however. The second option would provide for more reorganization and therefore stands a better chance of attaining greater programme integration. Of course, putting issues within the same organization does not necessarily cause them to be integrated. For example, in eight years of operation, the WTO has done little to integrate consideration of goods and services.[55]

I have indicated that a WEO could be a Specialized Agency or something else. What else? Under Article 22 of the UN Charter, the General Assembly may establish such subsidiary organs as it deems necessary. Thus, it would be possible for the General Assembly to establish a new organization for the environment that is a hybrid. It could have some of the autonomy of a Specialized Agency while still remaining at the centre of the United Nations. This could be justified on the grounds that environmental concerns are too intrinsic and generalized to the United Nations' mission to be assigned to a "specialized" agency.[56]

Structural issues

The benefits of a WEO over the current structure will depend upon how the WEO is designed. This section considers five structural issues. Perhaps the most important structural issue, the relationship of the WEO to the MEAs, will be discussed separately in the following section.

The role of environment ministers

In 1999, UN General Assembly Resolution 53/242 approved the proposal of the UN Task Force on Environment and Human Settlements to institute an annual, ministerial-level global environmental forum in which participants could gather to review important and emerging policy issues in the field of the environment. The first Global Ministerial Environment Forum (GMEF) was held in Malmö in May 2000 as a special session of the UNEP Governing Council. The UN Task Force also recommended that membership in the UNEP Governing Council be made universal, although it appears to have reached this recommendation without any analysis.

Periodic meetings of national environment ministers can be beneficial in promoting solidarity and serving as a forum for discussion, but it is doubtful that such a large assembly could serve as an effective governing body. The establishment of a non-universal Governing Council for UNEP was intentional, although its size of 58 countries is rather large. Organizations without a governing body, such as the WTO, make decisions very slowly.

The ILO structure achieves a good compromise between universality and effectiveness. The ILO Governing Body, with 28 nations, meets three times a year in extended sessions. The ILO also has an annual conference of all party states, which adopts new conventions and effectuates other business. The ILO approach could serve as a model for a WEO because it integrates a workable governing body with a universal membership forum. It should be noted, however, that the ILO plans its work so that the annual conference adopts at least one new convention virtually every year. Thus, labour ministers do not have to worry about holding a conference that fails to accomplish anything. A WEO annual conference that produced nothing other than an empty declaration would soon lose the interest of the world, if not the environment ministers themselves.

Another aspect of the ILO model worth noting is that each government sends *two* governmental members in its delegation, as well as employer and worker delegates. The ability to send two delegates means that governments are represented by a labour ministry official plus an official usually from another agency, typically the ministry of foreign affairs. This issue of representation may be even more important for a WEO because it would have a much broader scope than the ILO. The problem with just sending the environment minister to the WEO is that this person is likely to have less than full competence within the national government for all of the issues that come under the WEO's purview. One way of dealing with this problem might be for the WEO founding document to state that each government should send a delegation reflective of the division of authority within its government for environmental affairs.

Another good model is the Global Environment Facility (GEF). The GEF's Governing Council is reasonably sized (32 members) with more from developing than from developed countries. Even more innovatively, the members on the Council are appointed by a constituency of states whom they represent, with some large states representing only themselves.

The GMEF experiment is too new to evaluate. One can imagine a GMEF as the central decision-making body of a WEO, but it is hard to imagine the GMEF being fruitful if detached from an organization. It is one thing to organize G-7 and G-20 meetings with staffing by governments. It is quite another to attempt to carry out global environmental governance through that sort of a body. A danger exists that governments may settle on a GMEF staffed by UNEP as an inexpensive improvement over the current system.

WEO leadership

International governance does not follow the corporate model in which shareholders delegate authority to a board and chief executive officer. Governments have done this with the World Bank, the International Monetary Fund and the UN Secretary-General to some extent, but are unlikely to do so with the executive of a WEO. Thus, a WEO will be a member-driven, government-driven organization. Nevertheless, in designing the WEO, governments should look for ways to enhance the leadership capacity of the executive of the WEO. Consideration should also be given to establishing a two-person executive on the assumption that management and representational roles are both full time.

Participation by elected officials

International organizations today often have little or no participation by elected officials and this void has contributed to a deficit of legitimacy. This is not an easy problem to remedy because representation in international agencies has traditionally been viewed as an executive function. The establishment of a WEO, however, provides an opportunity to build in a role for national elected officials. The early role of the European Parliament might be one model for this, although some analysts might reject the analogy because, even in its early stages, the European Economic Community sought more policy harmonization than there is a current consensus for a WEO to perform.

One possibility would be to establish a WEO parliamentary forum consisting of one elected official from each WEO member country. Each country could decide how that person is selected. The role of the forum would be to meet periodically to review the operations of the WEO. The forum could hold a question period for the executive of the WEO. The forum might also invite other world officials to participate in its question period – for example, it could invite the president of the World Bank or the director-general of the WTO. If such a forum were established, a role might be found for associations of parliamentarians, such as the Global Legislators for a Balanced Environment (GLOBE).

Non-governmental participation

As noted above, the idea of using an ILO model for non-governmental participation in the WEO goes back to the initial discussions that led to the creation of UNEP. Sir Geoffrey Palmer reintroduced this idea in the early 1990s, when he suggested that each country be represented by two government delegates, one from business and one from environmental organizations.[57] In the recent debates, several analysts have suggested this same idea. For example, Runge proposes that the WEO have representatives from government, business, environmental groups and other non-governmental organizations (NGOs).[58] Esty has recommended a streamlined WEO supported by a network of government officials, academics, business leaders and NGO leaders.[59]

Because non-governmental participation in a WEO is so vital, advocates of this feature need to be realistic. In my view, governments will not replicate the ILO model in which the non-government and government roles are equal.[60] Similarly, governments are not ready to establish an organization in which non-governmental organizations can lodge environmental complaints against scofflaw governments, as was proposed by Philippe Sands, among others.[61]

The environment regime already has considerable NGO and private sector participation, and designers of a WEO can take advantage of this experience. NGO participation has often been constructive in the MEA setting where technical decisions are being made – for example, biosafety.[62] The very deep NGO participation in the CSD has been interesting to watch, but it has not been a constructive experience. The reason for this failure is not attributed to the NGOs, but rather to the fact that the CSD was not set up to make decisions.

Perhaps the best model for light non-governmental participation is what occurs in the OECD. The OECD has business and trade union advisory committees that interact with governmental committees and can make recommendations. Although the idea has been discussed for years, the OECD has been unable to agree on any new advisory committees, such as one for the environment. It should also be noted that, although the functions of the OECD are largely hortatory, it can draft binding treaties. It has enjoyed one recent success in the Convention on Combating Bribery and two failures on investment and shipbuilding subsidies.

One problem with establishing WEO advisory committees is that the CSD has now set the precedent of having the governments hear from a large number of "groups", including women, youth, indigenous peoples, non-governmental organizations, local authorities, workers and trade unions, business and industry, the scientific community, and farmers. Rather than set up homogeneous advisory committees for these interests, the WEO might set up a heterogeneous advisory committee by cluster, based on some of the recent proposals for clustering MEAs. For example, the WEO could have an advisory committee for biodiversity that would include environmental groups, biologists, economists, indigenous peoples and business. A well-respected organization might be asked to set up this committee – for example, the World Conservation Union (IUCN).

However non-governmental participation is organized, it is vital that the WEO build that into its constitution. If the WEO is simply an upgraded version of UNEP that includes only governments and does not establish any strong roots into business and civil society, then the enormous effort and resources needed to set up a WEO would be a poor investment indeed.

WEO membership

Setting up a WEO as a new organization offers an opportunity to establish conditions for membership greater than statehood. The UN system has tended not to do this, and it may be impractical to do so for a WEO. One possibility is to require that WEO members agree to good environmental governance principles such as those in the Aarhus Convention on Access to Information, Public Participation in Decision-making, and Access to Justice in Environmental Matters. This Convention went into force on 31 October 2001 and has been lauded by Secretary-General Kofi Annan as "the most ambitious venture in environmental democracy undertaken under the auspices of the United Nations".[63] Because Aarhus is a regional convention, it would be inappropriate for a WEO to require that governments subscribe to the specific provisions of that Convention.

Even if no substantial conditions are set for membership, the Specialized Agency approach would require governments to ratify a WEO treaty in order to join. This procedural requirement could serve as a basis for some solidarity in the WEO, in that every member would have taken an action to join.

WEO's relationship to the MEAs

The most complex issue involving the proposed WEO is its relationship to the MEAs. This issue is central to the WEO debate. UNEP already serves as a secretariat to some of the MEAs, and so a WEO would have at least that function. But a driving force behind the WEO proposals is that the new organization should have greater responsibilities for coordinating MEAs than UNEP now does.

Two distinct though interrelated issues need to be considered. First, what role should a WEO have with respect to the legal obligations in the MEAs? At the maximum, one could imagine a re-codification of international environmental law in which treaties on the same topic are grouped together, duplicative law is eliminated, conflicting law is reconciled, and eventually the hundreds of MEAs are reduced to a single code. Second, what role should a WEO have with respect to governance within each MEA consisting of Conferences of the Parties, subsidiary bodies, a commission or a secretariat. At the maximum, one could imagine implementing French President Jacques Chirac's suggestion that

UNEP "be given the task of federating the scattered secretariats of the great conventions, gradually establishing a World Authority, based on a general convention that endows the world with a uniform doctrine".[64] One month before Chirac's speech, the Task Force on Environment and Human Settlements had pointed to the possibility of establishing clusters of MEAs in which the MEA secretariats would be fused and an umbrella convention would be negotiated to cover each cluster.

The first issue, codification, is daunting, yet progress may be possible. Although the differences in parties for each environmental treaty would hold back the achievement of a general environmental law, some integration could be pursued following the steps of the ILO. For example, the ILO Declaration on Fundamental Principles and Rights at Work (1998) sets out a list of fundamental principles that all governments subscribe to even if they have not ratified the underlying ILO conventions. The ILO also publishes a compilation of ILO conventions with a subject matter classification. This provides in one single reference series a picture of international labour law.

The second issue has drawn a great deal of attention, and there is now growing support for the idea of setting up clusters of MEAs in order to promote better coordination among related MEAs. Clustering obviously would work better if the MEAs were co-located, but some coordination could probably be achieved by defining the cluster and promoting new linkages among the secretariats and MEA subsidiary entities. Relocation would exact a policy cost – the loss of the alliance between the MEA and its "host" government.

The different membership in the MEAs should not be a barrier to a common organizational structure. In the ILO, the membership in each convention varies, yet the ILO provides a common mechanism for technical assistance, compliance review and dispute settlement. In the WIPO, each treaty has a different set of parties, but the WIPO provides overall housekeeping functions and also promotes new negotiations among WIPO members. In the WTO, there are some plurilateral agreements (e.g. on government procurement) with limited membership that are nevertheless part of the WTO.

If the WEO undertakes clustering, it should try to include all major MEAs, not just those associated with UNEP. A paper on MEAs prepared by UNEP for the Open-Ended Intergovernmental Group limits its analysis to those MEAs associated with UNEP.[65] This seems narrowminded. The paper does include (in Table 4) a broader list of treaties, but this list leaves off important agreements on birds, turtle protection, seals, the Convention on Nature Protection and Wildlife Preservation in the Western Hemisphere, the Aarhus Convention, and others.

Von Moltke has suggested two approaches to the clustering of environmental regimes – one by problem structure and the other by institutions that occur in every environmental regime.[66] Some examples of the first type are a conservation cluster and a global atmosphere cluster. Some examples of the second are science assessment and implementation review. Von Moltke's analysis is helpful in focusing on the two ways that MEAs could be concatenated. A WEO should try to do both of them.

The last issue to consider is how a WEO should embark upon the task of providing a more coherent structure for the MEAs. Juma has pointed to this as a problem, writing that, "[s]ecretariats of conventions cannot be combined without the approval of their respective governing bodies. Advocates of the new agency have not indicated how they plan to deal peacefully with the divergent governing bodies."[67]

Juma's challenge deserves an answer, so let me suggest one. A WEO could simply open the door to the MEAs and invite them to cooperate with the WEO and consider joining the WEO's umbrella. Since all of the parties to an MEA would also be parties to the WEO, one can anticipate that many MEAs would accept this invitation. A precedent for this open door approach existed in the Charter of the International Trade Organization (ITO). Although the 1948 Charter did not go into effect, Article 87.3 established a procedure for an intergovernmental organization concerned with matters within the scope of the Charter to transfer all or part of its functions and resources to the ITO, or to bring itself under the supervision or authority of the ITO. This precedent points to a spectrum of possibilities for how MEAs could relate to a WEO. Each MEA could work out its own initial arrangement, although over time (if the WEO is successful) one might anticipate more convergence toward an optimal relationship.

Orientation issues

Designers of a WEO will need to consider three basic issues of orientation. First, should governments establish a WEO or a World Sustainable Development Organization (WSDO)? Second, should the WEO focus only on global problems? Third, should the WEO have operational functions?

WEO vs. WSDO

Although a WEO could be very broad, one can imagine setting up an even broader World Sustainable Development Organization to encompass development as well as environment programmes. Such an organization might incorporate UNCTAD, the United Nations Development Programme, the United Nations Industrial Development Organization and the International Fund for Agricultural Development, among others. A commitment to sustainable development, however, does not entail forgoing organizations that focus on the environmental function rather than the development function.[68] A successful WSDO would need to include the WTO and the World Bank, and that is obviously unrealistic.

Global or non-global scope

Daniel Esty and Maria Ivanova have suggested that a WEO be limited to "global-scale pollution control and natural resource management issues".[69] They contrast "global" problems (such as the protection of the global commons), which should be controlled by the "GEO", with "world" problems, such as drinking water, air pollution and land management, which would not be covered. Their terminology is a bit confusing, but one can distinguish between *global* problems (which require widespread participation to solve) and *shared* problems (which all countries have but some can solve even if others do not). For example, corrupt government is a problem that many governments share, but it is hardly a global problem.

This aspect of the Esty/Ivanova conception of a WEO/GEO differs from that of other analysts. For example, Runge does not limit the scope of his WEO to global issues, suggesting that it look at irrigation schemes involving the international transfer of water.[70] Biermann suggests that the WEO should look at outdoor and indoor air pollution.[71]

The problem with a WEO for just the global commons is that any decision about what is or is not global commons is somewhat arbitrary. Is biodiversity to be included? Are ocean fisheries? How about nuclear waste or other toxic wastes? Are forests global because of their services in combating climate change, or non-global because they root within national boundaries? Lines can be drawn but they will remain debatable.

The Esty/Ivanova approach would seem to preclude a WEO mandate for regional issues such as the regional seas programmes. Yet it is interesting to note that the Task Force on Environment and Human Settlements suggested that attention by the global environment ministers to regional issues would be a good thing. Indeed, the Task Force suggested that the ministers shift the venue of their meetings from region to region and that regional issues should feature prominently on their agenda.[72] One wonders whether there would be enough of a constituency for a GEO that worked exclusively on global problems.

No easy answer exists to this conundrum about scope. Ideally, a WEO should be given duties that distinguish it from the national environmental agencies that exist in each country. Otherwise, the world agency would look duplicative to the national agencies. But this is an impossible standard to meet. All existing international agencies overlay national agencies. The Esty/Ivanova approach may do the best job of avoiding

the conundrum because national governments could (in principle) delegate global problems to a global agency. Yet it should be noted that no
existing major international agency looks only at global problems. The
mandates of the WTO, the ILO, the WHO, the FAO, etc. are to work
on problems that each country shares.

Policy versus operations

Everyone agrees that a WEO should have policy functions, but there is a
question of whether it should also have operational functions beyond
data collection and dissemination. The operational functions at issue are
capacity-building and assistance to environment-related projects in developing countries.[73] One possibility is to leave capacity-building to existing
UN institutions (such as the United Nations University and UNCTAD)
or to private institutions (such as the LEAD programme). The other possibility is for the WEO to do some capacity-building, if only to promote
competition among capacity builders. For projects, the issue of how the
WEO should relate to the project activities of the UNDP, the World
Bank and the Global Environment Facility depends to a great extent on
the scope of the WEO. Certainly at this time there is insufficient attention
at the international level to the need for greater investment in environmental infrastructure.

The WTO Doha Ministerial Declaration states that trade ministers
"recognize the importance of technical assistance and capacity building
in the field of trade and environment".[74] Whether the WTO will undertake new technical assistance in this area remains unclear, but this WTO
statement provides some possibilities for new WTO–UN collaboration.

WEO functions

A WEO would have several important organizational functions including:
- planning
- data-gathering and assessment
- information dissemination
- scientific research
- standards and policy-setting
- market facilitation
- crisis response
- compliance review
- dispute settlement
- evaluation

All of these are important, but for reasons of space only a few of them
will be commented on.

Standards and policy-setting

Some advocates of a WEO emphasize its legislative role in developing norms and setting standards. In that regard, advocates point to the WTO, the ILO or the new WHO Framework Convention for Tobacco Control. These are useful models, but the environment regime is not lacking in policy-setting experience. Indeed, the environment regime has been perhaps the most innovative of any regime in using soft law and in building upon it. This is not to suggest that the environment regime has used all of the legislative techniques of the ILO or the WTO. Rather, my point is that a WEO can build on many of the techniques already in use in the environment regime.

Market facilitation

The idea that the environment regime could help countries exchange economic and environmental commitments is not a new one. In 1991, David Victor proposed that a General Agreement on Climate Change be modelled on the GATT.[75] In recent work, Whalley and Zissimos have proposed a bargaining-based WEO to facilitate deals struck between parties with interests in particular aspects of the global environment on both the "custody" and "demand" sides.[76] These ideas deserve greater attention.

Dispute settlement

It is sometimes suggested that the environment regime would benefit from having a dispute settlement system like that of the WTO. Since this WTO-envy is fairly common, let me point out a few reasons why the WTO model would not be right for a WEO.

First, the WTO system relies on dispute settlement rather than compliance review. This may be appropriate for a regime in which reciprocity is the central value, but it would not be appropriate for the environment regime, which has substantive, measurable environmental objectives. For the environment regime, the compliance review procedures of the MEAs will be more effective because they are not as confrontational as those in the WTO and because they can be directly linked to technical assistance, which is largely absent from the WTO.

Second, the WTO system is considered strong because there is a possibility of a trade sanction in the event of non-compliance. Such trade sanctions are counter-productive, however, and injure innocent parties.[77]

Third, the WTO model provides for dispute settlement within the WTO. Although this internal adjudication model is not used in MEAs, it is used in the UN Convention on the Law of the Sea, which has its own International Tribunal (of course, this Convention is broader than environment). The MEAs that do provide for dispute settlement typically provide for ad hoc arbitration or adjudication in a forum outside of the MEA.[78] This could be the International Court of Justice, which has an unused environment chamber. Recently, the Permanent Court of Arbitration established a set of rules for the arbitration of disputes relating to natural resources and the environment.[79] These arbitral procedures are available to states, intergovernmental organizations, non-governmental organizations and private entities.

Evaluation

Organizations need regular evaluation, but this function must be carried out externally. Organizations cannot evaluate themselves. For example, if the UN Secretary-General wants an impartial evaluation of UNEP, then he should not set up a task force with the UNEP executive director as chairman, as the Secretary-General did with the Task Force on Environment and Human Settlements. This Task Force concluded "that the United Nations system needs a strong and respected UNEP as its leading environmental organization".[80]

Assessment of the WEO

I shall now examine how the establishment of a WEO might improve the overall functioning of international environmental governance. I do this by looking at the five analytical priorities identified by UNU-IAS in its project on reforming international environmental governance.

Improving the current approach to governance

A WEO would improve environmental governance by making it more coherent. There are two aspects to such coherence – internal and external. Internal coherence could be achieved by better coordination among UNEP, MEA clusters and other agencies. External coherence is about the interface between the environment and other regimes, such as the WTO (trade and environment), the WHO (health and environment), the ILO (workplace environment) and the Security Council (biological and chemical warfare). A WEO would not be guaranteed to perform better than UNEP on external coherence, but it might help if the WEO constitution spelled out that function. On trade and environment, it is clear that both the WTO and the environment regime have gained from the interaction. For example, the term "MEA" and the view of the MEAs as a related system arose out of the trade and environment debate of the 1990s.

Not all governments will want to see such coherence however. For example, in the run-up to the WTO Ministerial Conference at Doha, the G-77 and China issued a statement that, among various points, warned that "[d]eveloping concepts such as global coherence with other intergovernmental organizations like ILO and UNEP should be cautioned against as it may be used to link trade with social and environmental issues for protectionist purposes".[81]

Strengthening the interface between science and politics

The best way to promote a fruitful interface between science and politics is to have good, credible science. This requires separating science from politics at the research end at least. Whether a WEO would strengthen the interface between science and politics depends on the decisions made about structure, orientation and function as detailed above. UNEP has made some important decisions to promote a better interface – for example, in joining with WMO to set up the Intergovernmental Panel on Climate Change in 1988. The ultimate goal for a WEO would be to convince governments that following international norms on environment is in their own national economic interest.

Improving financing

More funding is certainly needed for international environmental governance. However, one cannot say in advance that a WEO would be better funded than the existing organizations are. The best way to secure increased funding is for governments to perceive the WEO as well organized and effective. This is easier said than done. The direct involvement of elected officials and the private sector, as suggested above, might help in securing higher funding.

Increasing participation

The environment regime already has more non-governmental participation than any other regime.[82] Nevertheless, it could be improved. Earlier, I suggested that, unless a WEO establishes a means for direct participation by business, environmentalists and others, there would be little point in going to all the trouble of creating a WEO. Direct participation does not mean that governments have to share decision-making with private groups however. The goal should be for politicians to hear competing ideas so that they can make the best decisions.

Increasing influence over policy

To increase influence over policy, a WEO would need to interpenetrate national government. The environment regime consists not only of international organizations but also of national environmental agencies. For trans-border environmental problems (which are a large share of the totality of environmental problems), all agencies must be pulling in the same direction. If national agencies are ineffective, then those failures will be felt outside the country as well as inside it. A WEO should respond to this by working to improve environmental law and enforcement, particularly in developing countries.

A second priority should be the relationship between economic and environmental policy at the national and international levels.[83] A WEO would need to be much more effective in influencing economic policy than UNEP has been. Some areas of focus should be investment, trade, debt management, taxes and subsidies.

Conclusion

This chapter has sought to promote a better debate on the question of whether governments should set up a WEO. In the first part, I pointed out that although some of the arguments for a WEO are not convincing, compelling arguments do exist. The initial discussion also explained that full centralization of international environmental affairs is impossible, and thus a WEO would entail partial centralization. In the second part, I discussed how a WEO might be organized, and emphasized the need for an inclusive approach to participation. I also examined the key question of how a WEO should attract the MEAs, and I suggested that MEAs would want to associate with a well-functioning WEO. In the third part, I considered the benefits of a WEO compared with the status quo with respect to five analytical priorities.

If properly designed, a WEO has the potential of making an important improvement in the environmental governance of our planet. Nevertheless, in 2002, the governments took no steps in the direction of setting up a WEO. Why not? Let me speculate and offer three reasons. First, UNEP is threatened by such a change and has not promoted any serious consideration of such a reform. Second, the proponents of a WEO, despite their best efforts, have not yet made a convincing case for why such a reorganization would be better than what exists now, and how it could possibly be achieved. Third, the Bush administration in the United States showed an early lack of interest in the idea of strengthening global environmental governance. None of these impediments is insuperable, however, and I hope that this volume will serve as a key reference point for the governance debate as it continues in the years ahead.

Notes

1. *Global Initiative on Sustainable Development, Joint Declaration by German Federal Chancellor Helmut Kohl, Brazilian President Fernando Henrique Cardoso, South African Deputy President Thabo M. Mbeki and Singapore Prime Minister Goh Chok Tong, on the Occasion of the Special Session of the United Nations General Assembly, on 23 June 1997 in New York*, issued by the Department of Foreign Affairs, South Africa, para. 2; available at ⟨http://www.polity.org.za/html/govdocs/pr/1997/pr0623c.html?rebookmark=1⟩.
2. Maurice Strong, interview with Geoffrey Lean, "Remaking Industrial Civilization", *Our Planet*, Vol. 9, No. 1, 1997, p. 9.
3. Urs Thomas, "Improving Integration between the WTO and the UN System", *Bridges*, October 2000, p. 13.
4. George F. Kennan, "To Prevent a World Wasteland: A Proposal", *Foreign Affairs*, Vol. 48, 1970, pp. 259–283.
5. Lawrence David Levien, "Structural Model for a World Environmental Organization: The ILO Experience", *George Washington Law Review*, Vol. 40, 1972, p. 464.
6. Technically, the UN General Assembly established the Governing Council of UNEP rather than UNEP itself. At that time, the governments did not want to establish a new agency.
7. Tony Brenton, *The Greening of Machiavelli. The Evolution of International Environmental Politics*, London: Royal Institute of International Affairs Energy and Environmental Programme/Earthscan Publications, 1994.
8. Geoffrey Palmer, "New Ways to Make International Environmental Law", *American Journal of International Law*, Vol. 86, 1992, p. 259.
9. United Nations Conference on Environment and Development, *Agenda 21: Programme of Action for Sustainable Development*, New York: United Nations, 1992, paras. 38.11, 38.21.
10. Daniel C. Esty, "GATTing the Greens, Not Just Greening the GATT", *Foreign Affairs*, November–December 1993, p. 32.
11. Daniel C. Esty, "The Case for a Global Environmental Organization", in Peter B. Kenen, ed., *Managing the World Economy: Fifty Years after Bretton Woods*, Washington, D.C.: Institute for International Economics, 1994, p. 287.
12. C. Ford Runge, *Freer Trade, Protected Environment*, New York: Council on Foreign Relations Press, 1994, pp. 100–107.
13. C. Ford Runge, "A Global Environment Organization (GEO) and the World Trading System", *Journal of World Trade*, Vol. 35, 2001, p. 399.
14. Rudolf Dolzer, "Time for Change", *Our Planet*, Vol. 9, No. 1, 1997, p. 19.
15. Frank Biermann, "The Case for a World Environment Organization", *Environment*, Vol. 42, November 2000, pp. 23–31; Frank Biermann, "The Emerging Debate on the Need for a World Environment Organization: A Commentary", *Global Environmental Politics*, Vol. 1, 2001.
16. John Whalley and Ben Zissimos, "Trade and Environment Linkage and a Possible World Environment Organization", *Environment and Development Economics*, Vol. 4,

2000, p. 510; John Whalley and Ben Zissimos, "What Could a World Environmental Organization Do?", *Global Environmental Politics*, Vol. 1, 2001, pp. 29–34.

17. Peter M. Haas, "Environment: Pollution", in P. J. Simmons and Chantal de Jonge Oudraat, eds, *Managing Global Issues. Lessons Learned*, Washington, D.C.: Carnegie Endowment for International Peace, 2001, pp. 310, 346.

18. German Advisory Council on Global Change, *New Structures For Global Environmental Policy*, Vol. 2, London: Earthscan, 2000, pp. 176–177.

19. United Nations, *Recommendations of the High-Level Panel on Financing for Development*, June 2001, p. 26.

20. Calestous Juma, "Stunting Green Progress", *Financial Times*, 6 July 2000, p. 15; Calestous Juma, "The Perils of Centralizing Global Environmental Governance", *Environment Matters*, 2000, pp. 13–15.

21. Juma, "Stunting Green Progress", p. 15.

22. Konrad von Moltke, "The Organization of the Impossible", *Global Environmental Politics*, Vol. 1, 2001; Konrad von Moltke, *Whither MEAs? The Role of International Environmental Management in the Trade and Environment Agenda*, Winnipeg: International Institute for Sustainable Development, July 2001, pp. 14–22, 30–32.

23. UNU-IAS, *The Future of Environmental Governance: An Analysis of Recent Reform Proposals*, Project Outline, n.d.

24. Michael Ben-Eli, "Towards a New System", *Our Planet*, Vol. 9, No. 1, 1997, pp. 21, 23.

25. Juma, "The Perils of Centralizing Global Environmental Governance", pp. 13–15.

26. Von Moltke, "The Organization of the Impossible", p. 23; Von Moltke, *Whither MEAs?*.

27. Paul C. Szasz, "Restructuring the International Organizational Framework", in Edith Brown Weiss, ed., *Environmental Change and International Law: New Challenges and Dimensions*, Tokyo: United Nations University Press, 1992, pp. 340, 355, 383.

28. German Advisory Council on Global Change, *New Structures For Global Environmental Policy*, p. 138.

29. Jared Diamond, "The Ideal Form of Organization", *Wall Street Journal*, 12 December 2000, p. A26.

30. Alexandre Kiss, "The Implications of Global Change for the International Legal System", in Brown Weiss, ed., *Environmental Change and International Law*, p. 315; Von Moltke, "The Organization of the Impossible", p. 26.

31. Peter H. Sand, "Environment: Nature Conservation", in Simmons and Oudraat, eds, *Managing Global Issues*, pp. 281, 297.

32. Robin R. Churchill and Geir Ulfstein, "Autonomous Institutional Arrangement in Multilateral Environmental Agreements: A Little-Noticed Phenomenon in International Law", *American Journal of International Law*, Vol. 94, October 2000, p. 623.

33. David P. Fidler, "International Law and Global Public Health", *University of Kansas Law Review*, 1999, pp. 1, 21–22; Raymond Torres, *Toward a Socially Sustainable World Economy*, Geneva: International Labour Organization, 2001, p. 84.

34. Daniel C. Esty, "Toward a Global Environmental Organization", in C. Fred Bergsten, Rainer Masera and Heizo Takenaka, eds, *Toward Shared Responsibility and Global Leadership: A Report to the Leaders of the G-8 Member Countries*, Washington, D.C.: Institute of International Economics, May 2001, pp. 30, 31.

35. Renato Ruggiero, "A Global System for the Next Fifty Years", Address to the Royal Institute of International Affairs, 30 October 1998.

36. *Doha Ministerial Declaration*, WT/MIN(01)/DEC/1, 14 November 2001, paras. 6, 33.

37. Mark Hertsgaard, *Earth Odyssey. Around the World in Search of Our Environmental Future*, New York: Broadway Books, 1998.

38. UNEP, *Overview, Global Environment Outlook (GEO) 2000*, London: Earthscan, 1999, p. 3.
39. Mostafa K. Tolba (with Iwona Rummel-Bulska), *Global Environmental Diplomacy*, Cambridge, MA: MIT Press, 1998.
40. David C. Victor, Kal Raustiala and Eugene B. Skolnikoff, eds, *The Implementation and Effectiveness of International Environmental Commitments*, Cambridge, MA: MIT Press, 1998.
41. Hilary French, *Vanishing Borders: Protecting the Environment in the Age of Globalization*, New York: W. W. Norton, 2000.
42. UNEP, *Proposals of the President of the UNEP Governing Council*, Annex I, UNEP/IGM/3/3, 2001, para. 4j.
43. Von Moltke, *Whither MEAs?*.
44. *Task Force on Environment and Human Settlements*, A/53/463, 6 October 1998, *Recommendations*, paras. 20, 45, *Recommendations 2*, para. 13.
45. UNU-IAS should consider commissioning a poster-size chart of current international environmental organization.
46. Joy Hyvarinen and Duncan Brack, *Global Environmental Institutions: Analysis and Options for Change*, London: Royal Institute of International Affairs, 2000, p. 41.
47. Commission to Study the Organization of Peace, *Report of the Special Drafting and Planning Committee on the United Nations and the Human Environment*, in *The United Nations and the Human Environment*, 22nd Report, New York: CSOP, 1972, pp. 15, 60–61.
48. Kennan, "To Prevent a World Wasteland", p. 409.
49. *Sustainable Developments* (published by the International Institute for Sustainable Development), 7 June 2001, p. 5.
50. Von Moltke, *Whither MEAs?*, p. 32.
51. *Nairobi Declaration on the Role and Mandate of the United Nations Environment Programme*, UNEP/GC.19/1, 7 February 1997, para. 1. The Declaration was endorsed by the UN General Assembly Special Session in June 1997.
52. *Malmö Ministerial Declaration*, Adopted by the Global Ministerial Environment Forum – Sixth Special Session of the Governing Council of the United Nations Environment Programme, Fifth plenary meeting, Malmö, Sweden, 31 May 2000, para. 24.
53. Von Moltke, *Whither MEAs?*.
54. This was the authority used to upgrade the United Nations Industrial Development Organization (UNIDO) into a Specialized Agency in 1985.
55. Pierre Sauvé and Americo Beviglia Zampetti, "Subsidiary Perspectives on the New Trade Agenda", *Journal of International Environmental Law*, Vol. 3, 2000, pp. 83, 104.
56. National Academy of Sciences (USA), *Institutional Arrangements for International Environmental Cooperation*, Washington, D.C.: National Academy of Sciences, 1972, p. 25.
57. Palmer, "New Ways to Make International Environmental Law", p. 280.
58. Runge, "A Global Environment Organization (GEO) and the World Trading System", p. 399.
59. Daniel C. Esty, "An Earthly Effort", *Worldlink*, September–October 2000, pp. 14, 15.
60. The UNAIDS Programme has a Programme Coordinating Board that serves as its governing body. The board has 22 governments, 7 co-sponsors (which are international agencies), and 5 non-governmental organizations; but the agencies and NGOs are non-voting.
61. Philippe J. Sands, "The Environment, Community, and International Law", *Harvard International Law Journal*, Vol. 30, 1989, pp. 393, 417; Peggy Rodgers Kalas, "International Environmental Dispute Resolution and the Need for Access by Non-state Enti-

ties", *Colorado Journal of International Environmental Law and Policy*, Vol. 12, 2001, p. 191.

62. Laurence Boisson de Chazournes and Urs P. Thomas, "The Biosafety Protocol: Regulatory Innovation and Emerging Trends", *Swiss Review of International and European Law*, Vol. 10, No. 4, 2000, pp. 513, 550–557.

63. Aarhus Convention homepage, n.d.; accessed at ⟨http://www.unece.org/env/pp/⟩.

64. Jacques Chirac, "Remarks at the 50th Anniversary Meeting of the Congress of the World Conservation Union", *Environmental Science & Technology*, Vol. 33, No. 1, 1999, p. 24.

65. Open-Ended Intergovernmental Group of Ministers, *International Environmental Governance: Multilateral Environmental Agreements (MEAs)*, UNEP/IGM/2/INF/3, 10 July 2001, para. 19, Tables 1, 4.

66. Von Moltke, *Whither MEAs?*, pp. 1, 16–19.

67. Juma, "The Perils of Centralizing Global Environmental Governance", *Environment Matters*, 2000, p. 15.

68. Daniel C. Esty, "A Term's Limits", *Foreign Policy*, September/October 2001, pp. 74–75.

69. Daniel C. Esty and Maria H. Ivanova, "Making International Environmental Efforts Work: The Case for a Global Environmental Organization", Yale Center for Environmental Law and Policy, May 2001, pp. 10, 13.

70. Runge, "A Global Environment Organization (GEO) and the World Trading System", p. 399.

71. Biermann, "The Emerging Debate on the Need for a World Environment Organization", p. 49.

72. *Task Force on Environment and Human Settlements, Recommendations*, paras. 20, 45, *Recommendations 2*, para. 13.

73. Marc A. Levy, Robert O. Keohane and Peter Haas, "Improving the Effectiveness of International Environmental Institutions", in Robert O. Keohane and Marc A. Levy, eds, *Institutions for the Earth*, Cambridge, MA: MIT Press, 1993, pp. 397, 404–408. Biermann "The Emerging Debate on the Need for a World Environment Organization", p. 46.

74. *Doha Ministerial Declaration*, paras. 6, 33.

75. David G. Victor, "How to Slow Global Warming", *Nature*, Vol. 349, February 1991, p. 451.

76. Whalley and Zissimos, "What Could a World Environmental Organization Do?", pp. 29–34.

77. Steve Charnovitz, "Rethinking WTO Trade Sanctions", *American Journal of International Law*, Vol. 95, 2001, p. 792.

78. WTO Committee on Trade and Environment, *Compliance and Dispute Settlement Provisions in the WTO and in Multilateral Environmental Agreements, Note by the WTO and UNEP Secretariats*, WT/CTE/W/191, 6 June 2001.

79. Permanent Court of Arbitration, *Optional Rules for Arbitration of Disputes Relating to Natural Resources and/or the Environment*, June 2001.

80. *Task Force on Environment and Human Settlements, Recommendations*, para. 19.

81. *Declaration of the Group of 77 and China on the Fourth WTO Ministerial Conference at Doha, Qatar, Communication from Cuba*, WT/L/124, 24 October 2001, para. 26.

82. The ILO provides for a policy-making role for workers and employers, but these are only a narrow part of the spectrum of interest groups interested in the work of the ILO.

83. Von Moltke, *Whither MEAs?*.

5

The World Trade Organization and global environmental governance

Gary P. Sampson

Introduction

In the preparations for the World Summit on Sustainable Development (WSSD) in September 2002 in Johannesburg, one of the priority items to be addressed was how to secure an improved and strengthened institutional structure for international environmental governance.[1] From a trade perspective, an important question, particularly in the aftermath of the WTO Ministerial Meeting in Doha in Qatar in November 2001 where environmental matters were addressed, is whether there is coherence between the global trade regime and the environment regime.[2]

On the grounds of the outcome of the WSSD and the meeting of trade ministers in Doha, it could be argued that, at the political level, there is a recognition of the need for coherent and mutually supportive regimes and there is little to be concerned about. In fact, one of the noticeable features of the Ministerial Declarations that emerged from the two meetings is their mutually supportive character. There are many examples in the ministerial texts. At Johannesburg, ministers committed themselves to continue "to promote open, equitable, rules-based, predictable and non-discriminatory multilateral trading and financial systems that benefit all countries in the pursuit of sustainable development and ... support the successful completion of the work programme contained in the Doha Ministerial Declaration".[3] They recognized "the major role that trade can play in achieving sustainable development and in eradicating

poverty" and "encourage[d] WTO members to pursue the work programme agreed at the Fourth WTO Ministerial Conference".[4] In Doha,
the trade ministers strongly reaffirmed their "commitment to the objective of sustainable development" and expressed their conviction that
"the aims of upholding and safeguarding an open and non-discriminatory
multilateral trading system, and acting for the protection of the environment and the promotion of sustainable development can and must be
mutually supportive".[5]

Important as political declarations may be, it is equally important to
explore at the more operational level what evidence there is of coherent
approaches to global policy formulation in trade and the environment.
More specifically, in the search for an improved and strengthened institutional structure for international environmental governance, is there an
enhanced role that the WTO could usefully play? There is little doubt
that the WTO could become a far more important player in the field of
international environmental governance than is the case at present.[6] The
important question is whether or not this would be desirable, and from
whose point of view.

The objective of this chapter is to analyse various options available to
the WTO for enhancing its role in environmental governance in the light
of the outcome of the World Summit on Sustainable Development and
progress in the Doha Development Round of trade negotiations. This
could come in a number of ways. There could be changes in WTO rules
and processes, or there could be new interpretations of WTO provisions
through the dispute settlement process. There could be Understandings
that spell out specific articles of agreements, as was the case in the Uruguay Round, or a higher priority might be assigned to work on the environment in existing WTO "business as usual" committees (such as the
Committee on Trade and the Environment). In addition, different priorities will almost certainly be assigned to fulfilling the mandate that
emerged from Qatar and the conclusion of the Doha Development
Round in January 2005, including in terms of future work in the area of
environment. In my view, however, in almost all instances it is not in the
interests of the trade or the environment communities for the WTO to
take on greater formal responsibilities in the area of global environmental governance. On the other hand, I will argue that the effectiveness of
the WTO in governance matters relating to the global environment could
be enhanced through action outside the WTO, as well as through a
change in emphasis within the WTO with respect to its existing functions.

It is not the intention of this chapter to be comprehensive in addressing
all the options available to the WTO – space would not permit.[7] The
intention is rather to discuss some of the most important areas where
change in WTO rules and processes could be undertaken to enhance its

role in environmental governance. To avoid launching ideas in a vacuum, the objective is also to describe what changes could be considered feasible within the boundaries of political realities. There are at least three important questions: what changes could be made in a technical sense, would it be desirable to make them, and is it realistic to expect them to be accepted and implemented by governments? I also address some examples of the issues that should be dealt with outside the WTO for it to be more effective in its work relating to the environment.

The outline of the chapter is as follows. There is first a discussion of some of the characteristics of the WTO "system" that are relevant for the following sections of the chapter. This also serves to highlight some of the marked differences between global trade and environmental governance. I then discuss some areas where there is clearly an overlap between issues relating to trade and the environment within the WTO. In each of the areas addressed, change could be implemented in the WTO that would give it a greater role in environmental governance. In both sections the choice of topics is selective but sufficiently broad to give an idea of the nature and implications of the changes addressed. I then review the likelihood of acceptance of some of the types of proposal advanced. The chapter concludes with an assessment of the possible future role of the WTO in global environmental governance.

Some fundamentals

The World Trade Organization is the product of the Uruguay Round of Multilateral Trade Negotiations (1986–1994). It came into being on 1 January 1995, and, at the time of writing, has 142 members, the most recent additions being China and Taiwan.[8] The WTO deals with all trade agreements attached in four annexes to the Agreement Establishing the WTO (signed in Marrakesh on 15 April 1994). These annexes contain the multilateral trade agreements reached in the Uruguay Round, as well as other Understandings and decisions reached during the negotiations. All individual WTO members have accepted these agreements. They constitute a totality in terms of an undertaking and there can be no choosing between them.[9]

The Preamble to the Agreement Establishing the WTO sets out the objectives of the Uruguay Round multilateral trade agreements. Much of the language of the Preamble is taken over from the General Agreement on Tariffs and Trade (GATT), with some minor modifications. The most important for present purposes is that the Agreement adds the objective of sustainable development and that of "seeking both to protect and preserve the environment". The declared means of achieving these objectives are reciprocal and mutually advantageous arrangements directed to the substantial reduction of tariffs and other barriers to trade and the elimination of discriminatory treatment in international trade relations. The objective of sustainable development does not appear in any of the multilateral trade agreements establishing rights and obligations, although there are a number of references to the environment in various agreements.

The structure of the WTO is such that it is headed by the Ministerial Conference, composed of all members of the WTO, which meets at least once every two years. The most recent meetings were in Doha, Qatar, in November 2001 and in Cancun, Mexico, in September 2003. The conference has the power to carry out the functions of the WTO and any of the multilateral trade agreements. Between sessions of the Ministerial Conference, the General Council, also made up of the full membership of the WTO, exercises its functions. It is responsible for the continuing management of the WTO and supervises all aspects of its activities. The General Council also meets as the Dispute Settlement Body and as the Trade Policy Review Body.

An important characteristic of decisions in the WTO is that they are taken on the basis of consensus. An issue is discussed to the point where all members agree, or at least do not oppose, the decision. If voting takes place, it is a mere formality, and usually is concerned with the pre-negotiated terms of accession of a country to the WTO, or a waiver to permit a member to deviate from a certain rule. Formally, each WTO member has one vote and the normal rule is that a decision is made according to the majority of the votes cast. Matters are far more complicated when it comes to amendments to WTO rules; for certain key articles such as those relating to non-discrimination, no change is possible unless all members agree formally.[10]

Like the GATT before it, the WTO is an intergovernmental organization and does not provide for the participation of non-governmental interest groups. The closed nature of GATT negotiations can arguably be traced to the realities of the political economy of protection. The vast literature on this topic makes clear that distributional coalitions form to resist policy change that is not in the specific interest of their members. Because interest groups can be adversely affected through a process of trade liberalization, they naturally use their influence to resist such change. WTO members – and GATT contracting parties before them – are familiar with taking decisions that are not in the interest of all groups in society but are nevertheless thought to be in the interests of the constituencies that the governments represent when elected democratically.[11]

A further relevant feature of the WTO is its dispute settlement process. The current practices are inscribed in the Dispute Settlement Understanding (DSU), which is viewed by many as one of the most significant outcomes of the Uruguay Round and an effective way to promote multilateralism in the resolution of trade conflicts. This lies at the heart of the WTO. In all of the diverse multilateral trade agreements, breaking the rules means being taken to (the same) court. If the offending measures applied by the country found to be in error are not brought into conformity with WTO rules, then compensation and retaliation – with the approval of the General Council – are provided for. In this context, the interrelationship between the trade agreements is critical. Compensation can be sought in the form of improved market access in any of the areas covered by the multilateral trade agreements and not necessarily with respect to the agreement where the breach of obligations was committed. Similarly, retaliation can take place in any of the areas covered by the agreements, not necessarily with respect to the one where there was a breach of obligations.

Non-discrimination

The principle of non-discrimination underpins the rules-based multilateral trading system. It has two components: the most-favoured nation (MFN) clause contained in Article I of GATT, which stipulates that WTO members are bound to grant to the products of other members treatment no less favourable than that accorded to the like products of any other country. Thus, no member is to give special trading advantages to another or to discriminate against a particular product because of the manner in which it was produced, or because of the country of origin of the product. Article III of GATT stipulates that once goods have entered a market, they must be treated no less favourably than domestically produced like goods.[12]

The WTO does not inhibit governments from taking the measures they wish to protect the environment – for example, measures to avoid damage to the environment resulting from the manufacture and consumption of goods produced and used within national boundaries. Final products can be taxed and other charges levied for any purpose thought to be appropriate. Similarly, there are no problems from a WTO perspective with governments levying taxes according to the process used to produce something within their own territory. But the interpretation of non-discrimination in the WTO agreements is that WTO flexibility extends only to regulation of domestic products and processes and not to the processes used to produce imported products. It does not normally extend to the extraterritorial application of measures relating to production processes in exporting countries.

In short, from a trade policy perspective, goods produced in an environmentally unfriendly manner are like any other. From an international relations perspective, this serves to minimize any unwanted encroachment on national sovereignty, with powerful countries riding roughshod over less powerful ones by forcing them to produce goods according to the preferred environmental standards of the importing country. Importantly, it leaves space for other treaties to be negotiated to deal with the establishment and enforcement of environmental norms. The reality would seem to be that global environmental agreements do not have the same legally enforceable discipline and compliance mechanisms as those found in the WTO agreements.

Not surprisingly, a number of environmental groups have called for the WTO to modify its interpretation of like products to permit discrimination on environmental grounds; under this proposal, the WTO would adopt the role of an enforcement agency for what are considered universally held environmental norms. If standards are universally held, there is, in principle, no real problem. If all WTO members have agreed to forgo their rights not to be discriminated against in trade when certain environmental standards are not met, then trade discrimination should be acceptable. WTO members have already agreed to restrictions on trade in endangered species, living modified organisms, stolen goods, narcotics and many other products.

However, as noted above, decision-taking in the WTO is on the basis of consensus, and it may well be that not all countries agree to the preferred environmental standards of other countries and, therefore, the use of trade restrictions. A country may find the scientific evidence unpersuasive, it may not be able to afford to join the agreement concerned, or it may not have access to the necessary technology on favourable terms. It may not agree with a given environmental objective or with the means to achieve the objective, or it may consider there are more pressing national policy problems that deserve higher priority. To give the WTO the role of deciding which "almost" universally held standards could provide a justification for trade discrimination would increase its role in environmental governance enormously.

WTO and the environment: The overlap

Environmental agreements

The important question then becomes what the role is of the WTO in environmental governance if there is not a universal acceptance of environmental norms via a multilateral or regional agreement. Ideally, from a

WTO perspective, such an agreement should establish the conditions under which trade restrictions can be invoked for environmental purposes and the nature of the trade measure. If this is not the case, there are at least two potential problems. The first is when a trade-related measure is taken by a party to a multilateral environmental agreement (MEA) against another party to the MEA. The problem arises when the measure is not specifically provided for in the MEA itself, but is "justified" by the party taking the measure as "necessary" to achieve the objectives of the environmental agreement. The necessity of this measure may be challenged by the party against which the measure is taken. In this case, both parties could be members of the WTO and the measure could violate WTO rights and obligations. This could lead to a dispute over the legitimacy of the measure in terms of either the MEA or the WTO.

It seems reasonable that such a dispute should be pursued under the dispute settlement procedures of the MEA. In this respect, it would be helpful if MEA parties stipulated from the outset that they intended trade disputes arising out of implementation of the obligations of the MEA to be settled under the MEA's provisions. It could be argued that this approach could help ensure the convergence of the objectives of MEAs and the WTO, while safeguarding their respective spheres of competence, thus overcoming problems arising from overlapping jurisdictions. This, however, requires an effective compliance mechanism to be available to MEA parties. Most of the MEAs with trade-related provisions do contain mechanisms for resolving disputes, but these lack the power of the WTO dispute settlement process. In the absence of an effective dispute settlement system in the MEA, the dispute could gravitate to the WTO. It has been suggested on numerous occasions in the Committee on Trade and the Environment (CTE) that there would be value in strengthening MEA dispute settlement mechanisms. This, of course, is outside the terms of reference of the CTE.

Another problem relates to potentially WTO-inconsistent measures that are specifically provided for in an MEA and taken by a party to the MEA against a non-party. A problem may then present itself if the measure is against a WTO member that challenges the legitimacy of the measure in the WTO dispute settlement process. Dealing with this group of problems involves a number of decisions on the part of the WTO dispute settlement process. These include whether the measure can be justified as an exception to WTO rules and what importance to ascribe to the existence of the MEA in determining if the measure in question is really "necessary" (see below on dispute settlement). The likelihood of a positive decision on the necessity of the measure is presumably enhanced if the goals of the environmental agreement are accepted globally in a broad-based MEA to which all, or most, WTO members belong. In fact, most proposals relating to the relationship between WTO and MEA rules are based on the notion that, subject to specific conditions being met, certain trade measures taken pursuant to MEAs should benefit from special treatment under WTO provisions. This approach has been described as creating "an environmental window" in the WTO. However, discussions in the WTO Committee on Trade and the Environment (see later) have made clear that determining what is an acceptable MEA from the perspective of receiving greater WTO acceptability has proved to be far from a simple task, and in any event one that would be better performed outside the WTO.

It is instructive to note that coherence between these two bodies of law is high on the agenda of both trade and environment ministries – at least in terms of political declarations. In Doha, ministers stated that, with "a view to enhancing the mutual supportiveness of trade and environment, we agree to negotiations, without prejudging their outcome, on: the relationship between existing WTO rules and specific trade obligations set out in multilateral environmental agreements".[13] In Johannesburg, ministers agreed to promote the "mutual supportiveness between the multilateral trading system and the multilateral environmental agreements, consistent with sustainable development goals, in support of the work programme agreed through WTO, while recognizing the importance of maintaining the integrity of both sets of instruments".[14]

Settling disputes

Exceptions are provided for in the GATT 1994 Exceptions Article (Article XX), where nonconforming measures can be taken for environmental purposes if they are necessary to protect human, animal or plant life or health, or if they relate to the conservation of exhaustible natural resources and are made effective in conjunction with restrictions on domestic production or consumption. If at least one of these conditions is fulfilled, then the remaining requirement is specified in the head note to the Exceptions Article: that the measures not be applied in an arbitrary or unjustifiable manner in order to discriminate between countries where the same conditions prevail or constitute a disguised restriction on international trade.

With respect to substance, there is little doubt that the WTO dispute settlement process could play a greater role in environment-related matters, particularly in its rulings on exceptions to WTO obligations taken for environmental purposes. In the *Shrimp–Turtle* case, a decision had to be taken on whether the term "renewable resources" applied to renewable biological resources or was limited to depletable mineral resources. The Appellate Body ruled that, in the light of contemporary international law, living species, which are in principle renewable, "are in certain circumstances indeed susceptible of depletion, exhaustion and extinction, frequently because of human activities". In taking this decision, the existence of an MEA was critical. Because "all of the seven recognised species of sea turtles are listed in Appendix 1 of the Convention on International Trade in Endangered Species of Wild Fauna and Flora (CITES)", the Appellate Body concluded that the five species of sea turtles involved in the dispute constitute "exhaustible natural resources" within the meaning of Article XX of the GATT 1994.[15]

The Appellate Body also drew on the Preamble to the Agreement Establishing the WTO referred to above. Principles as expressed in Preambles are general legal commitments rather than specific legal obligations of states.[16] In its ruling, the Appellate Body clearly assigned importance to promoting sustainable development and preserving the environment. Although this objective is certainly recognized and supported by WTO members, the manner in which it is translated into rights and obligations can fundamentally change the character of the exceptions provisions of the WTO.

A principal criticism of the Dispute Settlement Body (DSB) relates to the process and a lack of openness; a common criticism is that hearings are not open to the public and that briefs by the parties are not made publicly available at the time of submission. In this respect, an important question is whether a panel or the Appellate Body is obliged to accept information submitted in the form of *amicus* briefs by non-governmental organizations (NGOs). This became a particular issue in the *Shrimp–Turtle* case, in which three submissions were received from NGOs, all with expertise in turtle conservation.[17] The panel found that it could not accept non-requested submissions from NGOs, because this would be incompatible with the DSU provisions. It explained that the initiative to seek information and to select the source of information rested with the panel alone, and noted that only the parties to the dispute and third parties could submit information directly to panels. The Appellate Body ruled that "the Panel erred in its legal interpretations that accepting non-requested information from non-governmental sources is incompatible with the provisions of the DSU".[18]

The complaining countries objected to the Appellate Body's ruling, arguing that this procedure was not in conformity with the working procedures. They argued that, because WTO members that are not parties or third parties cannot avail themselves of the right to present written submissions, it would be unreasonable to grant the right to submit an unsolicited written submission to a non-member when many members do not enjoy a similar right. Such information might be strongly biased if nationals from members involved in a dispute could provide unsolicited information. The complaining parties reasoned that this would only increase the administrative tasks of the already overburdened secretariat. They also reasoned that the parties to a dispute might feel obliged to respond to all unsolicited submissions, just in case one of the unsolicited submissions caught the attention of a panel member. Due process requires that a party should know what submissions a panel intends to consider, and that all parties should be given an opportunity to respond to all submissions. It was argued that the Appellate Body had diminished the rights of members and intruded upon members' prerogative as negotiators to establish the bounds of participation in the WTO. Members should decide such issues. The Appellate Body, which was only a judiciary body, was in this case writing the rules of participation.[19] With regard to *amicus* briefs, the Appellate Body appeared to have "let itself be overawed by the campaign of NGOs of major trading entities".[20]

Precaution and risk management

WTO agreements seek to avoid standards that create unnecessary obstacles to trade, while recognizing the sovereign right of governments to adopt whatever standards are appropriate to fulfil legitimate objectives and taking into account the risks that non-fulfilment would create. At the same time, they recognize that, for a variety of reasons, a particular standard may not be appropriate across countries. For example, physical conditions may differ between areas and, in the light of scientific evidence, the absorptive capacities for air pollution may differ between countries because of these physical characteristics. However, although such differences across countries can presumably be measured objectively, this is not necessarily the case with respect to how different societies wish to manage the risk.[21] Risk assessment is the scientific determination of the relationship between cause and effect in situations where adverse effects can occur, so it is hard to imagine a role for the WTO in this. Risk management, on the other hand, is the process of identifying, evaluating, selecting and implementing measures to reduce risk.[22] Determining what is "appropriate" in the light of scientific evidence and what constitutes legitimacy in terms of public preferences for the management of risk promises to be one of the most contentious areas for environmentalists and trade officials alike.

At the heart of the issue is the role of "precaution" in risk assessment.[23] The Precautionary Principle responds to the gap between banning a product or procedure until science has proved it is harmless and not banning it until science has proved that there is a real risk. The theoretical underpinnings of this principle are elusive and difficult to define, and there is no consensus on accepting it as a basis for establishing obligations in national and international rules.[24]

As far as WTO agreements are concerned, the Agreement on the Application of Sanitary and Phytosanitary (SPS) Measures and the Agreement on Technical Barriers to Trade (TBT) are both specifically designed to avoid standards that constitute unnecessary barriers to trade.[25] In the SPS Agreement, the management of risk is important in ensuring food safety and animal and plant health. The most important objective of the agreement is to reduce the arbitrariness of governments' decisions by clarifying which factors to take into account when adopting health protection measures. Measures taken to fulfil the objectives of the agreement should be based on the analysis and assessment of objective and accurate scientific data. Thus, an important question in managing risks to human, animal and plant life and health is deciding on the risk levels and the appropriate standards to adopt to manage the risk.[26]

International standard-setting organizations offer ready-made yardsticks. The SPS Agreement explicitly refers to three groups whose activities are considered relevant in meeting its objectives: the Codex Alimentarius Commission, a joint effort of the Food and Agriculture Organization (FAO) and the World Health Organization; the International Office of Epizootics (OIE); and the international and regional organizations operating within the framework of the FAO International Plant Protection Convention (IPPC). Many WTO members are involved in these forums, and their scientists and health experts participated in the development of these voluntary international standards.

The SPS Agreement provides for long-term national measures that exceed the protection levels established in international agreements if these are judged not to provide an acceptable level of protection at the national level. But, if challenged, these measures must be supported by scientific evidence based on an objective assessment of the potential health risks involved. When introducing a standard that is more trade restrictive than the Codex, OIE or IPPC, the SPS Agreement calls for measures based on the analysis and assessment of objective and accurate scientific data. In the absence of an international standard, each country must conduct its own risk assessment and determine its "acceptable level of risk". These assessments commonly include substantial safety margins as a precautionary measure. Once a government has determined its appropriate level of sanitary and phytosanitary protection, however, in order to be consistent with the WTO it should not choose a measure that is more stringent and trade restrictive than necessary. The evaluation of this is thus important in determining the measure, the effects of which should be proportional to the risk.

However, even given the same scientific evidence, different societies have different preferences for the management of risk. This also creates the possibility of abuse of measures for protectionist purposes.

It is in this sense that the recent dispute on meat treated with hormones heralds potential problems for the WTO. The EU ban on meat products containing hormones went into effect in 1989; it applied to animals treated with hormones in order to promote growth, because the European Union maintained that there was a carcinogenic effect associated with human consumption of the hormone-treated beef. When the case was dealt with by a WTO panel, the panellists rejected the EU arguments owing to a lack of scientific evidence of a health and safety risk. They concluded this after consulting scientific experts, and there was general agreement that the hormones posed no risk. The panel did not consider information presented by public interest groups. In the proceedings, international standards played an important role – in particular, the use of the Codex benchmark standard. The European Union argued that the Codex did not represent a consensus-based standard for minimum residue levels of growth-promoting hormones, since it was adopted by a vote of 33–29, with 7 abstentions. From an operational perspective, the SPS Agreement thus required the European Union to implement food safety standards whose minimum levels were agreed to by fewer than half of the Codex experts. The European Union argued that being obligated to adhere to standards that were not accepted on a consensus basis seems far from the consensus-based notion of WTO rules.

The panel also considered whether the Precautionary Principle could provide a justification for the ban in the absence of scientifically based risk assessment. It noted that the Precautionary Principle was incorporated into the SPS Agreement through the use of emergency measures permitting members provisionally to introduce measures that are not supported by "sufficient" scientific evidence until this evidence is obtained. In the hormone case, emergency measures as such were not under discussion, because the ban did not relate to "provisional regulations" – the EU Directive was a definitive regulation.

The panel report was referred to the Appellate Body, which agreed that the specific wording in the SPS Agreement prevailed over the Precautionary Principle. However, neither the panel nor the Appellate Body addressed whether scientific risk assessment and the Precautionary Principle were potentially at odds. The European Union was restricting the importation of hormone-treated beef when scientific risk assessments could not take account of society's fear of the potential risk involved. In fact, the Appellate Body concluded that the Precautionary Principle awaits confirmation as a customary principle of international law.

The lack of clarity as regards the application of the Precautionary Principle in specific situations has a number of potentially important implications for the WTO. The absence of agreement outside the WTO on how the Precautionary Principle is to be interpreted in specific cases means that the WTO will find itself in the situation of being the arbiter in a number of potential environment- or health-related controversies. Indeed, the WTO has already been described as the "World Trans Science Organization, a global meta-regulator". It resolves "scientific issues such as carcinogenicity, adopts policies concerning the acceptable levels of risk or scientific uncertainty, and makes decisions about appropriate levels of health and safety".[27] It is of primary importance for the WTO that ongoing negotiations outside the WTO in areas where precaution is important, such as how to deal with the trade in and labelling of products derived from genetically modified organisms, are successfully completed.

The Committee on Trade and the Environment

The Committee on Trade and the Environment (CTE) was established in January 1995, and it reports to the WTO General Council. It is mandated to address a variety of areas of work and to recommend whether any modifications to the rules of the multilateral trading system are required to permit a positive interaction between trade and environment measures. There are no observers from non-governmental organizations, despite a number of requests. The CTE has a standing agenda, and it meets formally at least two times a year and informally whenever considered necessary. It addresses, *inter alia*, the relationship between the provisions of the multilateral trading system and trade measures for environmental purposes – in particular, the relationship between WTO rules and compliance procedures and those of the multilateral environmental agreements.[28]

The CTE has been soundly criticized[29] and accused of failing, among other things, in its task of recommending modifications of the provisions of the multilateral trading system "to enhance a positive interaction between trade and environmental measures and for the promotion of sustainable development".[30] As a result, various environmental groups have proposed "mainstreaming" environment issues by factoring environmental concerns into the WTO across the board. In this scenario, each relevant WTO committee would deal with environment under its area of authority. Although this may hold some appeal, it is difficult to see how it would operate in practice. In a formal sense, it is not clear how the process could be established and, in a very practical sense, resources devoted by governments to questions relating to the environment are already spread thinly in WTO meetings. This is evidenced, for example, by the small number of developing country delegations that are active in the CTE. Mainstreaming may just lead to a dilution of already inadequate resources and a further minimization of attention paid to trade and environment issues.

Nevertheless, there is certainly a need to monitor the manner in which environmental concerns are dealt with in the various post-Qatar negotiating groups. In this respect, there is a potentially important role for the CTE. It could, for example, provide the forum in which those countries that have chosen to conduct reviews of the trade and environment linkages of the negotiations present their results. It could also provide the focal point for the identification and discussion of links between the various elements of the negotiating agenda and the environment. This role could be further broadened if a similar mandate were given to the Committee on Trade and Development (CTD). The CTE and the CTD could each provide a forum for identifying and debating the developmental and environmental aspects of the negotiations, including the synergies between trade liberalization, economic development and environmental protection. The work of the two bodies would be complementary and would help to ensure that the negotiations reflect the Preamble of the WTO Agreement about acting in accordance with the objectives of sustainable development and responding to the needs of the developing countries and, especially, of the least developed countries.

There is also an important role for the CTE in terms of future relations with MEAs. At the time of its inception, there was active discussion in the CTE on the relationship between the WTO and MEAs. This has served a useful purpose. It could be argued that one of the reasons there has never been a dispute relating to an MEA brought to the WTO is the increased understanding created through information sessions in the CTE, where the secretariats of environmental agreements have been invited to present relevant information with respect to the rules of their agreements.[31] These sessions have clearly facilitated a mutual understanding of the linkages between the multilateral environment and trade agendas and built awareness of the use of trade-related measures in MEAs.

This debate has recently been enlivened with a number of far-reaching formal proposals to the CTE by governments. This is perhaps a reaction to the commercial, political and social importance of some recent MEAs, which could well impact on trade, and the claim that the lack of clarity between WTO and MEA rules has led to confusion in the negotiation of MEAs. It has been argued that the negotiations surrounding the Biosafety Protocol, for example, proved to be difficult, "precisely because of the lack of clarity with regard to the relationship of the Protocol to the WTO".[32] The renewed interest could also be due to high-profile trade and environment disputes that have come to the WTO in recent times, and recognition of the fact that they probably never would have arisen had an effective MEA been in place. An additional consideration is that the debate in the WTO has been enriched with a large amount of useful work being undertaken by reputable non-governmental organizations, intergovernmental institutions and academics.

In Qatar in November 2001, trade ministers launched a new round of multilateral trade negotiations and brought precision to how they want to deal with the WTO and MEAs. With a view to enhancing the mutual supportiveness of trade and environment, they agreed to negotiations on the relationship between existing WTO rules and specific trade obligations set out in multilateral environmental agreements; procedures for regular information exchange between MEA secretariats and the relevant WTO committees; and the reduction or, as appropriate, elimination of tariff and non-tariff barriers to environmental goods and services.

In discussions pertaining to improved market access through negotiated trade liberalization, there have been calls for a multilateral framework to assess the effects of expanded trade on the environment.[33] After making such a proposal in 1994, the Commission on Sustainable Development was mandated by governments to provide the institutional coordination necessary to undertake an assessment of the environmental and social development aspects of trade policies. At the High Level WTO Symposium on Trade and Environment held in March 1999, the United States announced that it would join the European Union and Canada in carrying out an assessment of the implications of the post-2000 WTO negotiations on the environment.

Although there has been some discussion in the WTO of the possibility of all members agreeing to carry out such environmental impact assessment studies, the idea has not gained broad-based support. For most countries, whether or not to conduct such studies is a national choice having little to do with the work of the WTO as such. In addition, the task of evaluating the environmental benefits derived from removing trade restrictions and distortions is complicated not only by the complexity of the changes in the resource usage and consumption patterns that follow trade liberalization, but also by the limited capacity to measure the environmental impact.

Work has proceeded in the CTE, however, with a narrower focus on identifying sectors where environmental benefits follow trade liberalization.[34] Notwithstanding the complexities of the task, a number of conclusions can be drawn that enable priorities to be assigned to various sectors.[35] In the Doha Declaration, ministers instructed the CTE, in pursuing work on all items on its agenda within its current terms of reference, to give particular attention to the effect of environmental measures on market access, especially in relation to developing countries, in particular the least developed among them, and those situations in which the elimination or reduction of trade restrictions and distortions would benefit trade, the environment and development.[36]

The work on these issues should include the identification of any need to clarify relevant WTO rules. The CTE is to report to the Fifth Session of the Ministerial Conference and make recommendations, where appropriate, with respect to future action, including the desirability of negotiations. The outcome of the work carried out in accordance with the Ministerial Declaration is to be compatible with the open and non-discriminatory nature of the multilateral trading system, not to add to or diminish the rights and obligations of members under existing WTO agreements, in particular the Agreement on the Application of Sanitary and Phytosanitary Measures, nor to alter the balance of these rights and obligations, and will take into account the needs of developing and least developed countries.

In more colloquial language, this is a response to the fact that WTO members have been exploring the possibilities of trade liberalization in industrial countries where "win–win" scenarios exist. Industrial countries win when they remove trade restrictions that are environmentally harmful in their own countries; and developing countries win when exports grow following the removal of environmentally harmful trade restrictions in the importing developed countries.

There is, in fact, a third win. Numerous empirical studies have demonstrated that the link between trade liberalization and economic growth is unequivocal. Empirical evidence supports the contention that countries that have opted for an outward-oriented development strategy have been the fastest growing in the developing world. This does not mean, however, that the link between growth and liberalization cannot be challenged. Economic growth may lead to more wealth but does not in itself ensure an egalitarian society. Nor does it mean that growth will automatically lead to an improvement in the environment. Nevertheless, higher gross domestic product per capita and fewer resources used to produce each unit of output mean a higher national income and more resources available for the implementation of sound environmental policies.

One important question is whether win–win situations do in fact exist. The answer is that they do – in principle. From a trade perspective, different environmental resource endowments (such as the physical capacity to absorb pollution) are themselves a basis for differences in true comparative advantage. Furthermore, different societies and individuals within them also have different levels of tolerance with respect to environmental degradation. As long as national sovereignty prevails with respect to environmental priorities, the extent to which externalities are internalized will be determined by awareness of the environmental problem, the government's capacity to adopt the necessary policy measure to deal with it, the nation's physical capacity to absorb the environmental damage, and societal preferences relating to environmental conditions and the quality of life. This in turn will influence the impact on relative prices nationally and internationally. Trade restrictions can distort the good functioning of markets, and thus the exploitation of comparative advantage, just as they can frustrate the implementation of sound environmental management policies.

Discussion in the CTE has revealed that win–win situations exist in practice as well as in principle. In the case of fisheries, a sector of considerable importance to developing countries,[37] the link between depleted fish stocks and bad government policy seems to be well accepted. Fisheries subsidies are widespread, distorting trade and undermining the sustainable use of the resource base. One reason for giving priority to this sector is that useful substantive work has already been done in the WTO, by non-governmental organizations and elsewhere and there is now concrete evidence that the political will to address the problem appears to be strengthening.[38]

At the Ministerial Conference in Doha, ministers agreed to negotiations aimed at clarifying and improving disciplines under the Agreement on Subsidies and Countervailing Measures while taking into account the needs of developing and least developed country participants. In the context of these negotiations, the intention is to clarify and improve WTO disciplines on fisheries subsidies, taking into account the importance of this sector to developing countries.

There are also win–win possibilities in the agriculture sector. Agricultural subsidies have led to intensified land use, increased applications of agrochemicals, the adoption of intensive animal production practices and overgrazing, the degradation of natural resources, loss of natural wildlife habitats and biodiversity, reduced agricultural diversity, and the expansion of agricultural production into marginal and ecologically sensitive areas. Agricultural assistance through output-related policies in many industrial countries has imposed high environmental costs on other nations that have a comparative advantage in agricultural production and trade.

Of course, not all subsidies are harmful. The Agreement on Agriculture adopted during the Uruguay Round seeks to reform trade in agricultural products and provides the basis for market-oriented policies. In its Preamble, the Agreement reiterates the commitment of members to reform agriculture in a manner that protects the environment. Under the Agreement, domestic support measures with minimal impact on trade (known as "green box" policies) are excluded from reduction commitments. These include expenditures under environmental programmes, provided that they meet certain conditions. The exemption enables members to capture positive environmental externalities.

In addition, WTO agreements do not prohibit subsidies per se. The WTO Agreement on Subsidies, which applies to non-agricultural products, is designed to regulate the use of subsidies. Under the Agreement, certain subsidies are referred to as "non-actionable"; these are generally permitted by the Agreement. Amongst the non-actionable subsidies mentioned are those to promote the adaptation of existing facilities to new environmental requirements imposed by law and/or regulations that result in greater constraints and financial burden on firms. Such subsidies, however, must meet certain conditions. Making them non-actionable enables members to capture positive environmental externalities when they arise.

A further sector where liberalization could be beneficial for all is trade in environmental goods and services (for example, pollution control equipment or solid waste management). The value of world production in this sector is considerable and has been estimated to be in the order of US$450 billion a year.[39] In this sector, as in others, it is in the interest of all WTO members that environmentally sound goods and services are made available on the international market at the cheapest prevailing world prices. After studying liberalization in this sector, the OECD Report to the Council of Ministers in May 1999 concluded that goods and services would become cheaper, meaning that "limited environmental protection budgets can be stretched further" and "expanded market opportunities can encourage technological progress, as well as providing economies of scale and increased efficiency".[40]

Buying goods and services at world market prices is of course an option available to all countries, because governments can unilaterally remove barriers to imports in these goods and services and so serve their own interests. In practice, however, governments seek "concessions" in negotiations even when acting in their own interests, and the possibility of obtaining such concessions is greatest in multilateral rounds of negotiations where the removal of barriers to imports in one sector can be traded off against liberalization in another. In recent years, however, traditional cross-sectoral trade-offs have not always been necessary to encourage governments to enter into sectoral trade-liberalizing negotiations. Reaping the advantages that ensue from trade liberalization and more efficient resource use on both the consumption and production sides has been the driving force in a variety of sectors; examples include information technology, pharmaceutical products, basic telecommunications and financial services. It seems reasonable that WTO sectoral negotiations should extend to environmental goods and services.

Importantly, in all these areas of improved market access that are linked to better environmental governance, no change in WTO rules is required, simply a change in negotiating and other priorities.

Assessment

A number of the potential changes for the WTO in terms of its role in global environmental governance – such as a reinterpretation of non-discrimination – would require consensus in the WTO. Experience has shown that changes to GATT rules were rare, even with far fewer countries involved. After the establishment of GATT in 1948, there were only two amendments, one in 1955 and the other in 1964,[41] and there is no indication that things will be different in the future. This is not surprising. As noted, consensus would require agreement from almost 150 countries at very different levels of development and with very different priorities. Further, given the contractual nature of WTO agreements, members will agree to a rule change only if the outcome is clear and without risk. The dispute settlement process, with its threat of retaliation and compensation, is the Damocles' sword hanging over those that have to live with the interpretation of the new rules. A further consideration is that change in WTO rules will be resisted by those who believe that first GATT and now the WTO have been particularly successful at doing what they were mandated to do. Changing rules in an organization just several years old will be a priority for few members. One observer, for example, has expressed the view of many not only in the trade community by remarking that the "multilateral trading system at the beginning of the twenty-first century is the most remarkable achievement in institutionalized global economic cooperation that there has ever been".[42]

Notwithstanding the probable resistance to changing WTO rules, GATT and now the WTO have proved to be flexible instruments where "changes" have been possible through techniques that have ranged from simple non-enforcement of certain rules (such as Article XXIV of GATT 1994) to a variety of relatively informal actions or interpretations through the dispute settlement process. The question then is whether these non-rule change options can be used to alter the traditional interpretation of terms such as "like products" and provide for discrimination among imports on the basis of production methods. Such changes would profoundly alter the role of non-discrimination that lies at the heart of the WTO legal system and would be strongly resisted.[43] In my view, they are inadvisable. Some members have already argued that the Appellate Body has extended its authority beyond that granted to it by members and is playing a role in policy formulation through litigation. The DSU limited the jurisdiction of the Appellate Body to issues of law covered in panel reports and to legal interpretations developed by panels, and it prohibited the Appellate Body from adding to, or diminishing, the rights and obligations provided in the covered agreements. A number of countries have argued that the Appellate Body has adopted an "evolutionary" interpretative approach and it has overstepped the bounds of its authority by undermining the balance of rights and obligations of members.[44]

In my view, the solution to dealing with the use of non-conforming WTO measures to address environmental concerns lies in ensuring the existence of effective multilateral environmental agreements covering trans-boundary environmental problems.[45] If agreed standards and trade measures are adopted by WTO members in an environmental agreement, and the WTO members agree to forgo their WTO rights not to be discriminated against, then there seems little reason for the WTO members not to recognize this fact formally if it is considered useful for the purposes of environmental governance. If, however, the standards or the measures taken are disputed – for example through the dispute settlement process – the WTO becomes both the body that establishes the standards and the body that enforces them.

What is sure, however, is that the members of the WTO have no desire to become arbitrators on matters well outside the realm of conventional trade policy considerations. It is not reasonable to expect to find solutions requiring multilateral agreement in the case of disputes involving food safety or protection of endangered species that cannot be settled bilaterally. Nor should the problem be relegated to a dispute settlement process in which trade officials take decisions on a de facto basis that will almost by definition (because there is no agreement at the national level) be unpopular with large parts of the public. The way to deal with problems such as risk management in a WTO context must be discussed in terms of policy choices relating to the use of the Precautionary Principle, not litigation. There must be a coherent approach to dealing with problems where scientific evidence alone does not make the policy choices clear. Such issues cannot be dealt with through the rough and tumble of daily negotiations.

Where there *is* scope for a greater role in environmental governance for the WTO, however, is in improving market access within the context of win–win scenarios. There are many good reasons for promoting a win–win approach. It would give force to the commitment of WTO members to use the world's resources optimally and in accordance with the objective of sustainable development. It would provide evidence of their desire to protect and preserve the environment and to enhance the means for doing so precisely when they are being criticized for not doing enough. Viewed constructively, by adopting a win–win approach, public support can be garnered for undertaking reform in sectors where some interest groups might be adversely affected by policy reform but where reform is in the interests of the community at large. The initiative is already viewed positively by some environmental non-governmental organizations that have been hostile to the WTO in other areas. In addition, improving market access holds attraction for developing countries where few other advantages are seen in the trade and environment debate.

There is also scope for imaginative proposals for changes in processes that would remove some of the pressure for rule and process change in the WTO. In the words of the president of Worldwide Fund for Nature International with respect to the WTO Dispute Settlement Mechanism: "The speed, power, and efficiency of the system are both frightening and fascinating to environmental groups. It is the very power and authority of the system that has led to calls for reforms."[46] He notes that, because of its adversarial nature, formal WTO dispute settlement may not be the best means of resolving disputes of this kind. He suggests that WTO members should explore the establishment of multi-stakeholder consultative processes in which relevant facts could be put on the table by all interested parties from governments, non-governmental organizations, industry, academia and local communities. In fact, the Dispute Settlement Understanding formally creates the option for parties to the potential dispute to request the good offices of the Director-General to engage in consultations to settle the dispute. Such a consultative process could assist in providing the countries involved with an opportunity to consider a range of policy instruments suitable for resolving any trade-related environmental issue that may have arisen.

Conclusion

In a perfect world, meeting the challenges facing the global economy requires a coherent approach and institutional structure at the global level. This means the existence of institutions that determine the substantive policies and public processes, with a clear delineation of the responsibilities of the various actors involved. The goals of the institutions should be to facilitate the attainment of agreed policy objectives through cooperation, while providing for the avoidance and resolution of any disputes that may arise in the pursuance of these objectives. Good governance requires a set of such institutions that are coherent, mutually consistent and supportive, and that operate in an effective, accountable and legitimate manner. At the international level, these are the characteristics of an effective global governance structure. One of the conclusions of this chapter is that we are far from having such a structure today.

In fact, a strong argument can be made that a trade policy organization such as the WTO should not be responsible for the non-trade issues that are gravitating towards it. The United Nations and its Specialized Agencies are charged with advancing the causes of development, the environment, human rights and labour. A case can be made that they should be strengthened, and given the resources they need to carry out their tasks successfully, in order for the WTO go ahead and deal with a narrower agenda than it is now acquiring. Not surprisingly, this view has been expressed on a number of occasions by Kofi Annan, the Secretary-General of the United Nations.

In attempting to bring more coherence to global formulation, there are those who see the vacuum at the international level being at least partially filled by the WTO taking on even more responsibilities. The argument at its most fundamental level is that there currently exists a strong multilateral rules-based trade regime – attained through the WTO – and that this is essential to developing an effective system of governance of the global market. It is reasoned that the trading system cannot act in isolation when there exists a wide variety of issues, such as the environment, that belong on the international agenda and that are directly affected by trade itself or the rules that govern it. Without a common appreciation of the role of the WTO, the end result is that many think it is acting irresponsibly or somehow not fulfilling its functions.

The fact of the matter is that there is no world government or supranational body to determine the appropriate division of labour among existing multilateral institutions. The key question is how this can be done. Many proposals have been put forward on the part of former and current Director-Generals of the WTO: Peter Sutherland proposed a global summit conference;[47] Renato Ruggiero called for a World Environment Organization; and Supachai Panitchpakdi proposed an Eminent Persons Group outside the negotiating process to find a way forward.[48] It is timely that this be done through the creation of an Eminent Persons Group such as this, because there clearly needs to be a coordinated response on the part of the institutions involved and a coherent approach to policy formulation at the global level.

Notes

1. See the *Malmö Ministerial Declaration*, Adopted by the Global Ministerial Environment Forum – Sixth Special Session of the Governing Council of the United Nations Environment Programme, Fifth Plenary Meeting, Malmö, Sweden, 31 May 2000.

2. One response to this question came in a high-profile manner when the then Director-General of the WTO called for a "framework" or an "architecture" within which environment agreements could be dealt with coherently, effectively and efficiently. Renato Ruggiero considered it the responsibility of environmentalists to "put their house in order", and a World Environment Organization could be considered as a means to bring this order. See the remarks by Renato Ruggerio to the *WTO High Level Symposium on Trade and Development*, Geneva, 17–18 March 1999.

3. "Johannesburg Plan of Implementation", in *Report on the World Summit on Sustainable Development*, A/CONF.199/20, 26 August–4 September 2002, para. 47(a).

4. Ibid., para. 90.

5. *Doha Ministerial Declaration*, WT/MIN(01)/DEC/1, adopted 14 November 2001, para. 6.

6. When global environmental governance was discussed by EU environment ministers in July 2000, the "main issue" was whether to copy the WTO model in the environmental field. European Commission, *An EU Contribution to Better Governance Beyond Our Borders*, White Paper on Governance, Report of Working Group 5, May 2001.

7. Thus, some important areas, such as trade-related aspects of intellectual property rights, are not addressed.

8. In what follows, the governments that constitute the membership of the WTO will be referred to as the WTO members. Although the 15 countries of the European Union are individual members, they are represented at WTO meetings (with the exception of the Budget Committee) by the European Commission, which speaks on behalf of the 15 member states.

9. The exceptions are the three relatively unimportant plurilateral agreements in Annex IV.

10. For an explanation of how decisions are taken in the WTO, see John H. Jackson, *The World Trade Organization: Constitution and Jurisprudence*, Chatham House Papers, London: Royal Institute of International Affairs, 1998, section 3.4; see also John H. Jackson, "Global Economics and International Economic Law", *Journal of International Economic Law*, March 1998.

11. If, for example, saving an efficient domestic motor vehicle manufacturing industry requires removing tariff protection for a highly protected and inefficient local steel industry, it is most unlikely that the government concerned would invite steel and car manufacturers to the multilateral negotiating table.

12. Under the General Agreement on Trade in Services (GATS), members are also required to offer MFN treatment to services and service suppliers of other members. However, it permits listed exemptions to the MFN obligation covering specific measures for which WTO members are unable to offer such treatment initially. National treatment is an obligation in GATS only where members explicitly undertake to accord it for particular services. Therefore, national treatment is the result of negotiations among members.

13. *Doha Ministerial Declaration*, para. 31.

14. "Johannesburg Plan of Implementation", para. 92.

15. See WTO, *United States – Import Prohibition of Certain Shrimp and Shrimp Products*, Appellate Body Report, WT/DS58/AB/R, 12 October 1998, adopted 6 November 1998, para. 128.

16. Philippe Sands, "International Law in the Field of Sustainable Development: Emerging Legal Principles", in Winifred Lang, ed., *Sustainable Development*, Netherlands: Kluwer Law International, 1995.

17. During the panel proceedings, the panel received briefs from the Centre for Marine Conservation, the Centre for International Environmental Law (CIEL), and the Worldwide Fund for Nature, with copies to the complainants. During the Appellate Body pro-

ceedings, the United States attached to its submission *amicus* briefs from three groups of NGOs (*United States – Import Prohibition of Certain Shrimp and Shrimp Products*, Appellate Body Report, para. 79). In addition, CIEL sent a revised version of its brief directly to the Appellate Body.

18. See *United States – Import Prohibition of Certain Shrimp and Shrimp Products*, Appellate Body Report, para. 110.

19. See the views of members as reported in WTO, *Minutes of Meeting of the Dispute Settlement Body*, WT/DSB/M/50, 14 December 1998, p. 11.

20. Ibid., p. 10.

21. See Steve Charnovitz, "The World Trade Organization, Meat Hormones and Food Safety", *International Trade Reporter*, 15 October 1998.

22. National Research Council, *Risk Assessment in the Federal Government*, Washington, D.C.: NRC, 1983.

23. The Precautionary Principle has already secured its place in a number of international agreements. See, for example, the Report of United Nations Conference on Environment and Development, Annex 1, *Rio Declaration on Environment and Development*, Rio de Janeiro, 3–14 June 1992, Principle 15. The Convention on Biodiversity, for instance, states that, "where there is a threat of significant reduction or loss of biological diversity, lack of full scientific certainty should not be used as a reason for postponing measures to avoid or minimise such a threat" (Preamble, 1992).

24. For an elaboration, see European Commission, Directorate General XXIV, *Guidelines on the Application of the Precautionary Principle*, HB/hb D(98), Brussels, 17 October 1998.

25. The Trade-Related Intellectual Property Rights Agreement also establishes minimum standards for the protection of intellectual property. These standards are not addressed here.

26. The SPS Agreement allows countries to take measures in cases of emergency where sufficient scientific evidence does not yet exist to support definitive measures. Following the scare in 1996 relating to bovine spongiform encephalopathy ("mad cow disease"), and in the absence of sufficient scientific evidence, several emergency bans were introduced. In accordance with the SPS Agreement, however, these could be only provisional. In the long term, governments must conduct scientific risk assessment and adapt their measures accordingly, although there is no determination as to how long "provisional" may be.

27. See Vern R. Walker, "Keeping the WTO from Becoming the World Trans Science Organization: Scientific Uncertainty, Science Policy, and Fact-finding in the Growth Hormones Dispute", *Cornell International Law Journal*, Vol. 31, 1998, pp. 251–320. Questions of trans-science in this context are considered to be "those which can be asked of science and yet which cannot be answered by science".

28. A number of MEAs have trade-related provisions that raise questions with respect to their WTO conformity. A detailed description of the WTO-relevant measures in 11 environmental conventions containing trade measures can be found in WTO, *Report of the Meeting Held on 5–6 July 2000*, WT/CTE/M/24, 19 September 2000.

29. See, for example, Steve Charnovitz, "A Critical Guide to the WTO's Report on Trade and the Environment", *Arizona Journal of International and Comparative Law*, Vol. 14, No. 2, 1997.

30. *Ministerial Decision on Trade and the Environment*, MTN.TNC/W/141, 29 March 1994.

31. The most recent of these information sessions was held on 27–28 June 2001. The following secretariats responded to questions from CTE members: the Convention on the International Trade in Endangered Species of Wild Fauna and Flora; the Basel Convention on the Control of Trans-boundary Movements of Hazardous Wastes and Their

Disposal; UNEP Chemicals on the Rotterdam Convention on the Prior Informed Consent Procedure for Certain Hazardous Chemicals and Pesticides in International Trade and the draft Convention on Persistent Organic Pollutants; the Intergovernmental Forum on Forests; the UN Framework Convention on Climate Change. For a report on the meeting see WTO, *Report of the Meeting Held on 24–25 October 2000*, WT/CTE/M/25, 12 December 2000.

32. See WTO, *Clarification of the Relationship between the WTO and Multilateral Environmental Agreements*, Submission by Switzerland, WT/CTE/W/168, 19 October 2000.

33. See, for example, WWF International, "Initiating an Environmental Assessment of Trade Liberalisation in the WTO", WWF Discussion Paper, March 1999.

34. Comprehensive work has been done in this area by the OECD secretariat. The secretariat has studied the environmental effects of trade liberalization in three sectors: environmental goods and services, the freight sector, and the fossil fuel sector. See, for example, OECD, *Environmental Effects of Liberalising Trade in Fossil Fuels*, COM/TD/ENV/(98)129, 25 November 1998.

35. For an analysis on a sector-by-sector basis of the environmental implications of removing trade barriers, see OECD, *Environmental Benefits of Removing Trade Restrictions and Distortions*, WT/CTE/W/67, 8 November 1997.

36. *Doha Ministerial Declaration.*

37. Developing countries account for over one-half of world trade in fish and fish products; in 1996, exports exceeded imports by US$17 billion. See FAO, *State of World Fisheries and Aquaculture*, Rome, 1999.

38. See David Schorr, "Fishery Subsidies and the WTO", in Gary P. Sampson and W. Bradnee Chambers, eds, *Trade, Environment and the Millennium*, Tokyo: United Nations University Press, 1999.

39. See OECD, *Future Liberalisation of Trade in Environmental Goods and Services: Ensuring Economic Protection as well as Economic Benefits*, COM/TD/ENV(98)37, 4 March 1999.

40. Results reported in OECD, *Report on Trade and Environment: Council at Ministerial Level, 26–27 May 1999*, C/MIN(99), 12 May 1999.

41. There were, however, Understandings negotiated in the Uruguay Round relating to some of the principal GATT articles.

42. See Martin Wolf, "What the World Needs from the Multilateral Trading System", in Gary P. Sampson, ed., *The Role of the WTO in Global Governance*, Tokyo: United Nations University Press, 2001, p. 183.

43. This concern manifests itself in a resistance to any attempts to provide for the extension of domestic production standards in industrial countries into developing ones in order for their exports to be acceptable for import. The strength of feeling on this matter on the part of many developing countries cannot be overstated, and was recently evident in the discussion of an Appellate Body ruling that appeared to leave the question open. See the remarks by a number of developing countries in WTO, *Minutes of Meeting of the Dispute Settlement Body*, WT/DSB/M/50, 14 December 1998, discussing the *Shrimp–Turtle* dispute, where it was argued that dictating fishing practices in other countries was an encroachment on national sovereignty.

44. See comments by Malaysia, India, Pakistan, and others in WTO, *Minutes of Meeting of the Dispute Settlement Body*, WT/DSB/M/50, 14 December 1998.

45. See Gary P. Sampson, "Multilateral Environment Agreements and Why the WTO Needs Them", *The World Economy*, Vol. 24, No. 9, 2001, pp. 1097–1108.

46. See Claude Martin, "The Relationship between the Trade and Environment Regimes: What Needs to Change?", in Gary P. Sampson, ed., *The Role of the WTO in Global Governance*, Tokyo: United Nations University Press, 2001, p. 143.

47. Peter Sutherland, John Sewell and David Weiner, "Challenges Facing the WTO and Policies to Address Global Governance", in Gary P. Sampson, ed., *The Role of the WTO in Global Governance*, Tokyo: United Nations University Press, 2001, pp. 81–112.
48. Supachai Panitchpakdi, "Balancing Competing Interests: The Future Role of the WTO", in Sampson, ed., *The Role of the WTO in Global Governance*, pp. 29–36.

6

Judicial mechanisms: Is there a need for a World Environment Court?

Joost Pauwelyn

Most environmental law is domestic law. At the demand of either the government or private entities, domestic courts enforce compliance with national environmental laws. Although this model can generally be applied to transgressions of domestic environmental law, environmental degradation does not always respect national borders. Increasingly, environmental problems are regional and even global in scope. Thus, the scale of legal responses must correspond to the scale of the problem. In sum, since environmental *pollution* does not respect state borders, so environmental *protection* must extend beyond national boundaries.

Hence, environmental law includes an important international component. This component may take the form of conventions that regulate the choice of forum or applicable law before domestic courts, guarantee certain procedural rights for plaintiffs or provide for the mutual recognition of judgments (the discipline of private international law).[1] More importantly, the international component of environmental law may also provide global solutions for global environmental problems such as those set out in conventions on the ozone layer or climate change (the discipline of public international law). Although domestic courts play a crucial role in implementing environmental law, the question arises whether there is a need for an international or world environment court to adjudicate legal issues that increasingly appear on the international level.

In the first section of the chapter, I examine the appropriateness of enforcing international environmental law (IEL) by judicial means. The following section addresses the judicial mechanisms currently in place to enforce IEL. The need for a World Environment Court (WEC) is assessed in the third section, and the fourth sets out the salient features that a WEC could/should have. Finally, I offer some conclusions in terms of the five key points of analysis for examining proposals for international environmental governance.

Is the judicial enforcement of international environmental law a good idea?

Many authors have questioned the appropriateness of enforcing international environmental law (IEL) by means of third-party adjudication where inter-state claims are brought based on the principle of state responsibility.[2] Scholars of this view argue three main points. First, they contend that judicial settlement of disputes is inherently bilateral and confrontational, whereas problems of environmental protection often involve many states and situations in which it is unclear who exactly is the wrongdoer and who is the victim. Second, judicial enforcement operates *ex post facto* and is negative in nature, focused on reparation. Protection of the environment, in contrast, requires a system of prevention and positive incentives in order to achieve compliance. Finally, third-party adjudication may not be appropriate because environmental disputes often raise complex scientific questions as well as profound questions of social choice. Courts are not well equipped to solve such disputes.

As an alternative to judicial enforcement, other authors have favoured multilateral compliance schemes based essentially on monitoring and reporting. One may question, however, whether these two enforcement mechanisms are necessarily mutually exclusive. Strong arguments do indeed exist in support of the current system of institutional monitoring, a system that has been relatively successful in terms of achieving compliance and avoiding disputes. At the same time, there seems to be little reason a system of judicial enforcement could not complement (rather than replace) the monitoring system we have today. This could be done either by injecting a stage of third-party adjudication into current compliance procedures[3] based on the rule of law, or by providing for a distinct process of judicial settlement if the compliance procedure does not resolve the matter.[4]

Though these are viable options for enhancing the enforcement of IEL, there may be less need for judicial settlement than, for example, in the World Trade Organization (WTO). But why rob IEL of the judicial leg that any system of law is built upon? Why deprive IEL of the standard benefits linked to the rule of law: that is, not only bringing an end to violations (even by powerful players), but also enhancing the predictability and further development of IEL itself? To deprive IEL of this judicial branch risks creating a two-class society of international norms – those that can be judicially enforced (e.g. WTO rules) and those that cannot (in particular, IEL). For instance, would it be acceptable for a state restricting trade to be sued before the WTO, whereas its infringements of environmental norms are not subject to any compulsory jurisdiction?

If judicial settlement is to be incorporated into IEL, the traditional state-to-state process must be adapted. These types of reform should not be summarily dismissed before attempts have been made to put them in place. Such changes can indeed be implemented (as was done with varied success in domestic law). Even if there are shortcomings, it is arguably more damaging, in the case of serious and persisting disagreements, not to have a resolution at all than to have one through judicial settlement. From that perspective, it is worth recalling Richard Bilder's reflection: "[W]hat is special about environmental problems and disputes? How do they differ from other kinds of international problems? One possibility, which you may wish to keep in mind, is that they are not really very different."[5] The relevant point, as conveyed by Bilder, is that international environmental disputes, like all other international disputes, require resolution through adjudication.

Unlike other international disputes, however, IEL has successfully avoided judicial enforcement. This can be largely attributed to the fact that states have not been forthcoming in granting the necessary jurisdiction to courts or tribunals that would allow other states or non-state actors to challenge their environmental policies or conduct. States are, of course, free to make that political choice. Indeed, that political choice has been the prevailing reason for the current state of affairs. Certainly, the technical and legal arguments summarized above are not a convincing alibi for governments to continue rejecting some form of third-party adjudication based on the rule of law in the field of IEL.

To a large extent, the arguments raised above against judicial settlement also apply to large parts of WTO law and, in particular, to the United Nations Convention on the Law of the Sea (UNCLOS). Yet both of these bodies of law have judicial settlement procedures. UNCLOS, for example, provides for compulsory jurisdiction over marine environment matters.[6] Few disputes under these conventions are of a purely bilateral nature. Both conventions of law require collaborative and proactive efforts to best achieve their objectives, and quite a number of their provisions also raise intricate scientific questions.[7] Hence, to a certain extent, environmental disputes are already subject to compulsory jurisdiction, but only where they overlap with trade laws or the law of the sea. Should this be counterbalanced by making other international environmental instruments, such as the Montreal Protocol or the Climate

Change Convention, *directly* subject to some form of judicial adjudication?

Before addressing the prospects of creating an entirely new judicial body, I shall first examine some of the existing avenues for judicial settlement of IEL disputes.

Current enforcement of international environmental law

Why create a new court if existing courts could enforce IEL (assuming, of course, that states were willing to grant these courts the necessary jurisdiction)? The leading contender to be given jurisdiction over international environmental disputes is, obviously, the International Court of Justice (ICJ). Other contenders that have been mentioned are the Permanent Court of Arbitration in The Hague and the International Criminal Court to be set up pursuant to the 1998 Rome Convention. In addition, one could expand the jurisdiction of other, more specialized worldwide tribunals such as the International Tribunal for the Law of the Sea (ITLOS, which already has a Chamber on the Marine Environment[8]), the WTO Dispute Settlement Body[9] or even the World Bank inspection panels, the International Centre for the Settlement of Investment Disputes or the United Nations Human Rights Committee (operating under the 1966 International Covenant on Civil and Political Rights).[10] The fact that IEL cuts across – and may often be rephrased in terms of – the law of the sea, international trade and investment law, international human rights, or even international criminal law has received considerable attention in the literature.[11]

The International Court of Justice (ICJ)

The ICJ is the only international court with universal jurisdiction, in terms of both the states that can bring cases to it and the subject matter that it may be asked to examine. The major limitation on that universal jurisdiction is that it can be exercised only if both disputing states have agreed to it *ex ante* or agree ad hoc to send their dispute to the ICJ. So far, relatively few states have subjected themselves to the compulsory jurisdiction of the ICJ.[12] Nonetheless, if states were really determined to provide judicial redress for IEL, they could always empower the ICJ to that effect. This has happened in previous instances, as when the ICJ ruled that France had to desist from nuclear testing in the area of New Zealand, the Cook Islands, Niue and the Tokelau Islands, because the potential for radioactive fallout violated New Zealand's right under international law.[13]

The drawback currently built into the Statute of the ICJ is that contentious cases can be brought only by and against states. Non-state actors can be neither complainant nor defendant. The only non-state actors that have access to the ICJ are certain UN bodies, which may ask the ICJ to give an advisory opinion on certain questions of international law. At the same time, it is important to note that grievances of, or environmental damage caused by, private entities can be brought to the ICJ pursuant to the doctrine of espousal or diplomatic protection, whereby a state takes up the case of an individual before the ICJ. In addition, the *Trail Smelter* principle allows non-state actors to be the subject or initiator of grievances, pursuant to which "no State has the right to use or permit the use of its territory in such a manner as to cause injury ... in or to the territory of another or the properties or persons therein".[14] As a result, even damage caused by a private company in state A or against an individual in state B could be recovered before the ICJ, as long as state B is willing to take up the case of its citizen.

States could, of course, change the ICJ Statute and adapt it to the particular needs of environmental disputes. In particular, they could allow certain non-state actors to get involved in the process, either as *amici curiae* or, more controversially, as full-fledged parties. States could also allow entities other than selected UN bodies – such as individual states, non-UN Specialized Agencies such as the United Nations Environment Programme (UNEP) or the WTO, or even other international tribunals and certain non-governmental organizations (NGOs) – to request advisory opinions or preliminary rulings from the ICJ.[15]

The discussion above highlights some possible revisions to the purview of the ICJ, although it is important to note that the current statute already provides for some of these needs. First, the ICJ appointed a Chamber for Environmental Matters in 1993, composed of 7 of the 15 ICJ judges.[16] So far no state has resorted to the Chamber, mainly because it requires the agreement of both parties.[17] Second, when faced with factually complex cases, involving, for example, scientific questions related to the environment, the ICJ can appoint assessors[18] (sitting on the Court to lend expertise or "specialized knowledge" in technical cases) as well as scientific experts, although only judges have a vote.[19] Thus far, the ICJ has yet to take advantage of either of these provisions. Finally, as noted earlier, the ICJ does permit intergovernmental organizations (such as UNEP or the WTO) as well as NGOs or other interested parties to submit information or so-called *amicus curiae* briefs, either at the request of the Court or on their own initiative.[20]

Nonetheless, in the wake of recent ICJ judgments that have touched upon IEL, some authors have questioned the capacity and willingness of the ICJ to take up the role of judicial branch of IEL, in particular when it comes to "the much needed development of the law by way of judicial insight".[21]

The Permanent Court of Arbitration (PCA)

The PCA was set up by the 1899 Convention for the Pacific Settlement of International Disputes, now revised by a 1907 convention of the same name. As of September 2003, the PCA counted 101 member states. The PCA offers a broad range of services for resolving disputes between states, disputes between states and private parties, as well as disputes that involve intergovernmental organizations. These services include arbitration, conciliation, fact-finding commissions of inquiry, good offices and mediation. All PCA dispute resolution rules are based closely on the 1976 United Nations Commission on International Trade Law (UN-CITRAL) Arbitration Rules and the 1980 UNCITRAL Conciliation Rules.

On 19 June 2001, the member states of the PCA adopted by consensus a set of Optional Rules for Arbitration of Disputes Relating to Natural Resources and/or the Environment.[22] These Optional Rules are largely based upon UNCITRAL Arbitration Rules, taking account of the special needs for resolving environmental disputes. They can be relied on by, as well as used against, states, intergovernmental organizations, non-governmental organizations, multinational corporations and private parties. Even disputes between two private parties can be brought. The crucial condition remains, however, that both disputing parties have explicitly agreed that their dispute shall be referred to arbitration under the Optional Rules, be it *ex ante* in a prior convention or contract or in an *ex post facto* compromise.

The Optional Rules emphasize flexibility and party autonomy. They provide for arbitration in a shorter period than under previous PCA Optional Rules or the UNCITRAL Rules. They allow for *optional* use of:
(a) a panel of arbitrators with experience and expertise in environmental or conservation of natural resources law (Article 8, para. 3); and
(b) a panel of environmental scientists who can provide expert scientific assistance to the parties and the arbitral tribunal (Article 27, para. 5).[23]

Mindful of the possibility of multi-party involvement in disputes having a conservation or environmental component, the Rules provide specifically for multi-party choice of arbitrators and sharing of costs and, where appropriate, security for interim measures. At the request of either party, interim measures of protection may, indeed, be taken if the tribunal deems it "necessary to preserve the rights of any party or to prevent serious harm to the environment falling within the subject matter of the dispute" (Article 26).

Although better adapted to enforcing IEL than, for example, the ICJ (in terms of both potential parties and fact-finding), it remains to be seen how many states and non-state actors will be willing to subject themselves to this specialized jurisdiction of the PCA. In the end, all the PCA has done so far is to provide a medium for the settlement of environmental disputes. States and non-state actors must still decide actually to use the PCA to settle their environmental disputes. Notwithstanding its name, the PCA is neither a standing court nor, arguably, a judicial organ. As an arbitration body completely de-linked from the major international environmental organizations and conventions, it remains doubtful that it will ever live up to the role of judicial branch of IEL. It might have a bright future, though, as a means to provide ad hoc settlement of certain long-standing, cross-border environmental disputes, not only between two states unwilling to resort to the ICJ, but also between a state and a private party or between two private parties unwilling to get their case decided by the national courts of either party.

It is also interesting to note that, in November 1994, a group of environmental organizations formed the International Court of Environmental Arbitration and Conciliation (ICEAC), which is similar to the PCA, with permanent seats in Mexico and Spain.[24] The ICEAC's function is to "facilitate, by Conciliation and Arbitration the settlement of environmental disputes between States, natural or legal persons and submitted to it by agreement of the parties to the dispute".[25] It can also "give Consultative Opinions on questions of Environmental Law or on legal aspects of the use or protection of elements of the environment in any case which is of international concern, at the request of any natural or legal person, whether national or international, public or private, including States and Local Authorities".[26] So far, however, only one case has been brought to the ICEAC, namely a consultative opinion requested by a Mexican lawyer in respect of the movement of waste from the United States to Mexico.[27] Thus, although the ICEAC has the potential to complement the mission and function of the PCA, it is unlikely that its full utilization will come to pass.

The International Criminal Court (ICC)

The ICC is unique in that it will allow the prosecution of individuals under international law. As noted, the ICJ can deal only with inter-state disputes. Other mechanisms also allow private parties, including individuals, to challenge the conduct of states under international law – such as the European Court of Human Rights and investment arbitration under Chapter 11 of the North American Free Trade Agreement (NAFTA). Nevertheless, hearing claims against individuals before an international tribunal is the privilege of the ICC. This feature makes the ICC an attractive venue for IEL. It would certainly be easier to sue individual polluters directly before an international court rather than having to sue their country of origin, with all the political and diplomatic constraints this entails. Yet, the limits of international criminal law must be recalled.

The jurisdiction of the ICC is limited to "the most serious crimes of concern to the international community as a whole".[28] These fall in one of four categories: (a) the crime of genocide; (b) crimes against humanity; (c) war crimes; and (d) the crime of aggression. Only under the definition of war crimes is any reference made to the environment.[29] However, some have argued that the jurisdiction of the ICC ought to be expanded to cover "environmental crimes" as well.[30] Making individual polluters directly responsible – not just for civil damages but also for criminal punishment – could give a serious boost to the effectiveness of IEL. Indeed, if states are genuinely concerned about environmental protection as a public good, why not make serious environmental degradation a crime, subject to imprisonment? If countries such as the United States put the chief executive officers of multinational companies in jail for violations of anti-trust rules (which are purely aimed at securing the economic advantages of a competitive market), why not put them in jail for violations of environmental law (which is aimed at arguably more important societal goals, on which the survival of the planet could depend)?

Nonetheless, to grant the ICC jurisdiction over environmental crimes might pose certain risks.[31] Environmental offences would be likely to become just an add-on to more shocking crimes such as genocide and, as a result, might be overshadowed. Nor does the ICC seem to have particular expertise in the area of IEL. Furthermore, combining environmental crimes with other crimes under the ICC umbrella might make consensus-building in the environmental arena more difficult. A possible alternative could be to negotiate an independent "ecocide" or "geocide" convention.

To examine the responsibility of states in serious environmental degradation, it is instructive to point to the recent evolution in the International Law Commission (ILC) away from "international crimes", including so-called "environmental crimes". Indeed, whereas the Draft Articles on State Responsibility adopted by the ILC in 1996 referred to "international crimes", including certain serious breaches of IEL,[32] the Articles finally adopted by the ILC in August 2001 omit the notion of "international crimes". Instead, particularly grave consequences are attached to any "serious breach by a State of an obligation arising under a peremptory norm of general international law" (Article 40). In contrast to the 1996 Draft Articles, the 2001 *ILC Commentary* does *not* refer to any breaches of IEL as examples of breach falling under Article 40. The Commentary does point out, though, that "[t]he examples given here are ... without prejudice to existing or developing rules of international law which fulfil the criteria for peremptory norms". Hence, it could still be argued that certain norms of IEL are peremptory norms (that is, norms of *jus cogens*), even if they have not been listed explicitly by the ILC, so that their breach does entail the more serious consequences attached to Article 40.[33]

Domestic courts

The potential importance of domestic courts in enforcing IEL cannot be overestimated. One prominent commentator has argued, for example, that claims by private actors against states or multinational corporations for non-observance of IEL "can be more adequately addressed through national courts, at least in the first instance".[34] The major advantage to enforcing IEL through domestic courts is that domestic courts are fully operational and well funded, and are accessible to private parties. Although it may be difficult for reasons of state immunity to sue foreign governments, most domestic courts do offer some redress against both foreign and domestic governments.

In this light, environmental conventions should more frequently force states to implement domestic law to legislate not only substantive environmental norms but also certain minimum guarantees for the effective enforcement of those norms by domestic courts.[35] Examples of such reliance on domestic law and domestic courts for the enforcement of international law can be found in Part XII of UNCLOS (on the enforcement in domestic law of UNCLOS norms on the protection and preservation of the marine environment) and the WTO Agreement on Trade-Related Intellectual Property Rights (obliging WTO members to provide for the effective enforcement by national courts of certain minimum international intellectual property standards).

Moreover, the fact that pollution abroad – say in India – may not be easily actionable in US courts should not be all that surprising. The optimal solution resides in raising environmental standards in India through international conventions acceptable to India, rather than forcing US standards upon India through the operation of US courts, without India's approval. Certain norms of IEL may be universal; others must, however, be tailored to the particular needs and stage of economic development of each country.

A World Environment Court?

There would be little use in setting up a World Environment Court (WEC) if it were simply to *facilitate* the settlement of environmental disputes broadly defined, subject to the specific agreement of the parties involved.[36] As noted before, there are currently at least two mechanisms tailor-made for the resolution of environmental disputes, including disputes that involve non-state actors (the PCA and the ICEAC). In addition, with the agreement of the parties, inter-state claims can always be brought to the ICJ, which is reasonably well equipped to deal with environmental cases. Finally, for claims brought by or against private parties, a strong case can be made for bolstering the role and effectiveness of domestic courts rather than creating a WEC.[37]

What is still lacking, though, is a compulsory dispute resolution mechanism to which states, and possibly non-state actors, can automatically resort in order to enforce the myriad regulatory environmental treaties (such as the Convention on International Trade in Endangered Species of Wild Fauna and Flora, the Montreal Protocol on the Protection of the Ozone Layer and the United Nations Framework Convention on Climate Change). With respect to multilateral environmental agreements (MEAs), the question is not so much "do we need a WEC?" but rather "how can we get states to agree to binding and law-based dispute settlement procedures?" And here experience tends to show that states grant compulsory jurisdiction more easily to specialized courts, tribunals or compliance mechanisms empowered to enforce certain treaty-specific claims.[38] The best examples at the quasi-universal level are the dispute settlement mechanisms in UNCLOS and the WTO. The implementation mechanism that is currently being developed under the Kyoto Protocol to the United Nations Framework Convention on Climate Change (UNFCCC) may confirm this tendency.[39] As a number of ICJ judges have pleaded (conspicuously only in the case of UNCLOS, and less so with the WTO),[40] it would have been better for the system of international law as a whole if the compulsory UNCLOS/WTO jurisdiction had been granted to the ICJ. But states were unwilling to do this.[41] The same political reality applies to MEAs. Granting jurisdiction to the ICJ's Environmental Chamber for disputes concerning the application and interpretation of MEAs could be the optimal solution for enforcing IEL (with some changes to ICJ procedures, in particular in respect of expediency and access for non-state parties, albeit as *amici curiae* only). Yet this expansion of ICJ jurisdiction is politically unlikely.

In that context, the creation of a WEC might be a second-best solution. A WEC, though perhaps unnecessary given the arguments presented here, is preferable to not having *any* law-based adjudication under IEL or to having a distinct judicial procedure and adjudicating body for each individual MEA.

In particular, in combination with a World Environment Organization (WEO), or any other structure that would coordinate the myriad MEAs now in existence,[42] the creation of a WEC might be politically acceptable to states. A new and strong WEC is, indeed, more likely to see the light of day as part of an overall bargain leading to the creation of a WEO. It could then be a trade-off in a wider package of commitments acceptable to all. Moreover, state parties would be able to confine the jurisdiction of the WEC to claims under certain MEAs (thus limiting the risks of overlap with other dispute settlement mechanisms), as well as subject the WEC to some measure of control by the political bodies of the WEO (similar to the control exercised by the WTO's Dispute Settlement Body over panels and the Appellate Body). Furthermore, a WEC, as part of a broader WEO, could constitute a much-needed judicial engine to co-ordinate and further develop the MEAs put under the WEO's umbrella, thus completing the WEO as an international regime with a legislative, executive and judicial branch serving one and the same community of interests.[43]

At the same time, one must guard against portraying IEL, or the collection of norms that would be monitored by a WEO, as a "self-contained regime", de-linked from the wider corpus of international law. Whatever the advantages of a special WEC in terms of expertise, expediency, political acceptability and a building-block for a new WEO regime, it is crucial that any specialized WEC operate

1. as a court under international law broadly speaking, not just the "four corners" of IEL, as well as
2. in close coordination with other international organizations, courts and tribunals and the wider non-governmental community.

If these two guidelines are followed, the proliferation of international tribunals, including the creation of a WEC, is unlikely to pose serious systemic problems (although sooner or later a certain hierarchy among those tribunals will need to be developed).[44] Any new WEC should learn from the mistakes committed by the GATT/WTO system that was, and to some extent still is, wrongly considered to be a special regime de-linked from other rules of international law (including IEL).[45] As one author put it, if this potential pitfall is not avoided, "setting up a 'green' [WEC] to counter-balance the 'non-green' existing tribunals, compounds, not resolves, the problem".[46]

The way in which these pitfalls can be avoided is best explained by looking at some of the specific features of a WEC.

What would a World Environment Court look like?

Assuming that there is a need and the political will for the creation of a WEC, what should it look like and how would it operate?[47] One of the advantages of setting up a new WEC (instead of reforming an existing institution) is, indeed, that it could be tailor-made *ab initio*.[48] In this section I set out some of the major points for consideration.

Subject matter jurisdiction

First, the jurisdiction *ratione materiae* of a WEC should be defined by reference to certain claims under specified conventions (the way, for example, WTO panels can examine only claims under the WTO treaty). It should not be based on general criteria such as "all disputes arising under IEL" or "disputes on the protection of the environment". It is notoriously difficult to define what an environmental dispute is,[49] and very often parties will disagree as to the subject matter qualification of their dispute.[50] Thus, limiting the jurisdiction of the WEC would also reduce the risk of conflicts of jurisdiction between specialized tribunals, such as the WEC, on the one hand, and ITLOS or the WTO, on the other.[51] (One distinction of import is that limited jurisdiction would not prevent different aspects of the same dispute being brought to different tribunals, requiring those tribunals to cooperate closely.[52])

Second, the exhaustive list of treaty-based claims that can be brought to the WEC could be centred around a new convention setting up a WEO that could, in turn, set out certain general principles of IEL and cover a number of pre-existing MEAs, in the same way that the WTO treaty covers a multitude of trade agreements in different sectors.

Third, the WEC could also operate as a distinct step within a wider compliance procedure, or as a last resort if diplomacy-based compliance procedures under a given treaty have not resolved the dispute.[53] This would give the WEC an important power of coordination between different MEAs.

Finally, in addition to contentious cases under certain conventions, the WEC could also be given the power to issue advisory opinions, or even preliminary rulings,[54] at the request of other international institutions or tribunals, states or even non-state actors, including NGOs, or national courts.

Composition

The expertise and independence of the WEC must be decisive. Geographical distribution could also enhance the legitimacy of the WEC. In terms of legitimacy, the success of IEL and the WEC depends on acceptance by national regulators and courts; thus, the WEC will yield greater authority if its members are known and respected in their country of origin, such as former national judges or legislators. Special expertise in IEL may be less important. Indeed, appointing only IEL experts would pose a serious risk of "capture" by the environmental protection constituency.[55] Recall that most members of the WTO Appellate Body are not international trade experts (rather they are experts in international law generally, former legislators, diplomats or national judges). Their general and diverse background has, in my view, been a factor in the increasing openness of the WTO towards non-trade concerns. Thus, for a new WEC, the ideal could be a mix of international law and/or IEL experts and distinguished national practitioners.

Standing to bring a case

The issue of who will be able to bring complaints before the WEC is an important one. Obviously, state parties to the conventions enforced by the WEC should be able to bring complaints. Given the "collective interest" or even "global commons" at stake under many rules of IEL, all state parties should have standing to bring a case, irrespective of individual harm.[56] Cases with multiple complainants are likely to arise and should be catered for in terms of court proceedings and remedies.

Non-state actors – be they individuals, companies or NGOs – could also be allowed to submit claims. This is likely to increase the effectiveness of IEL, but at the same time would take the enforcement of IEL out of the hands of governments, opening the door for frivolous or politically sensitive cases brought against the will of the claimant's government (a government that, we must assume, represents the collective interest of its citizens). Serious thought is required before granting non-state actors such cause of action and, if so, under what conditions.[57] It is one thing to allow all stakeholders, including non-state actors, to express their opinion on a particular dispute, for example as *amici curiae*. It is quite another to give them the actual right to initiate a procedure (in the same way that involving all stakeholders in the formation of the rules of IEL is vastly different from giving them an actual vote on the adoption of new rules). To involve all stakeholders in the formation of IEL and the decisions of a WEC would be a necessary requirement to ensure what has been called the "procedural" and "popular" legitimacy of IEL.[58] To give non-state actors a direct vote in the adoption of IEL or an independent cause of action before a WEC might, however, undermine the equally important "democratic" or "normative" legitimacy of IEL.

One option is to delineate clearly the possible conditions that may be required before a non-state actor can bring a case. These could include: prior exhaustion of domestic remedies, individual harm or, for NGOs, a minimum number of members or other proof of being representative of a sufficient section of society. Another alternative (or complement) to giving standing to private parties at the international level is to oblige state parties to give "direct effect" to certain norms of IEL so that these norms can be directly invoked by non-state actors before domestic courts.

Since violations of IEL may often harm the global environment in general, rather than any particular state, it might thus be useful to set up an independent commission or public prosecutor, linked, for example, to a WEO or to UNEP, which would be able to trigger procedures against a particular state or number of states. This would also avoid the inherent animosity and political side-effects, especially for weaker states, related to bringing a state-to-state complaint. The non-compliance procedure under the Montreal Protocol, for example, gives certain powers to its secretariat to activate the Implementation Committee.

If an independent prosecutor were given the power to trigger a proceeding, a political filter could be added, allowing, for example, that a majority of state parties can prevent the commission/prosecutor from initiating a case.[59] If non-state actors were given standing, to prevent them from bringing frivolous claims a screening commission could be installed through which all claims have to pass before they can be sent to the WEC. (The European Commission on Human Rights or the Pre-Trial Chamber to be set up under the Statute of the ICC used a similar screening exercise in the past.)

Who can be sued before the WEC?

State parties to the IEL conventions in question would be the main targets of complaints. Given the often uncertain cause of environmental damage, cases with multiple defendants are likely to arise.[60] This situation would provide another role for an independent commission or public prosecutor that could conduct a preliminary investigation of the environmental degradation in order to identify possible defendants. If certain violations of IEL were elevated to the status of "international crimes", the WEC could also hear complaints against individuals, for example at the request of a public prosecutor, a state or even another non-state actor.

For non-criminal violations of IEL, it would be difficult to hold individuals or corporations responsible before an international tribunal.[61] One either passes through the state (by suing the state of the private actor concerned) or requires the consent of the private actor to settle the dispute through international arbitration. When following the latter route, the Optional Rules on environmental disputes adopted in 2001 by the Permanent Court of Arbitration would seem particularly appropriate.[62]

Nonetheless, the jurisdiction of a WEC could also be broadly defined (like that of the PCA) so as to include claims against non-state actors *subject to their specific agreement*. To the extent that IEL is incorporated in domestic law, individuals (including companies) may, however, be sued before domestic courts.

Finally, in its capacity as a coordinating mechanism, the WEC could have the power of judicial review of certain decisions taken by the WEO or UNEP institutions. As predicted by a number of authors, for IEL to be effective it will need to be formed and monitored increasingly by majority decisions.[63] If not, the so-called "tragedy of the commons" looms. Judicial review of other international institutional practices or decisions would allow state parties in the minority to challenge the legality of certain acts of international environmental organizations. This process could only increase the legitimacy of those institutions[64] and bolster the prospect of a more expedient (i.e. majority-based) formation of IEL. More broadly, a WEC could also be given jurisdiction to check whether acts of other, non-environmental international organizations such as the WTO, the World Bank or the International Monetary Fund respect IEL.[65]

Applicable law

Although the jurisdiction of the WEC is best limited to claims under certain IEL conventions, this does not mean that the WEC should consider only IEL, that is, limit itself to the "four corners" of IEL. Rules of *general* international law, as well as those that reflect the common intentions of all parties to the IEL convention, remain crucial for the purposes of interpreting the IEL convention.[66]

In addition, beyond the rules on treaty interpretation and the limits that it implies (e.g. in terms of being unable to *overrule* the clear meaning of the treaty text), rules other than IEL should also be referred to as part of the applicable law, as long as they are binding on the disputing parties. Even if these other rules could not form the basis of a claim before the WEC, they should, in certain circumstances (depending on which rule ought to prevail pursuant to the conflict rules of international law, such as *lex posterior* and *lex specialis*), be able to provide a valid defence against claims of violation of IEL. To read IEL in isolation of other rules of international law would wrongly portray IEL as some "self-contained regime" and reduce its legitimacy. It would, furthermore, endanger the unity of international law. This holistic view of international law is essential for the success of any specialized international tribunal, be it the WEC, ITLOS or WTO panels.[67]

Provisional measures

Given the potentially irreversible effects of environmental degradation, the WEC should have extensive powers to order provisional measures. Models can be found in UNCLOS Article 290 and Article 26 of the PCA Optional Rules for environmental disputes.

Procedure

WEC procedures must be expedient and flexible, allowing for the prompt solution of disputes with the possibility for the Court, with or without the consent of the parties, to adopt dispute-specific procedures adapted to the needs of each particular case.

The first objective of WEC procedure ought to be to obtain a mutually acceptable solution to the dispute. Needless confrontation should be avoided. The WEC should hence also be bestowed with mediation powers. Nonetheless, bilateral solutions must be consistent with IEL and not violate the rights of third states.

Certain preferential treatment ought to be given to developing countries both in coming before the Court and in its composition. For example, developing nations should be allotted longer time limits for the submission of briefs. Moreover, in the event that a limited number of judges decide each case, there should be requirements that at least one judge is from a developing country. The same procedure should be applied to the selection of experts.

Independent fact-finding

Given the factual complexity of many environmental disputes and the changing nature of science, it is crucial that the WEC disposes of independent, high-quality and up-to-date scientific advice.[68] It could appoint a group of individual experts on a case-specific basis or be assisted more permanently by a standing scientific body operating, for example, under the umbrella of a WEO or a reformed UNEP.

Since expertise is a well-recognized source of legitimacy, it is imperative that a WEC base its decisions on solid and objective expert opinions. Scientific experts should be appointed after consultations with the parties. Party participation in the selection process weakens subsequent accusations of partiality on the part of certain experts. Other international organizations (in particular UNEP and the WHO) could play a role in suggesting possible names.[69] Nonetheless, it is clear that expert input without transparency and participation can undermine the legitimacy of the process. Thus, the WEC should aim for a careful balance between these two demands.

Finally, the WEC should be given wide investigative powers allowing it, for example, to compel the parties to produce all necessary documents or to ask advice or opinions from any individual or body it deems appropriate (along the lines of DSU Article 13 applicable to WTO panels).

Participation

All state parties to the IEL convention in question, as well as all other states with an interest in the case, should be allowed to act as third parties. Most environmental disputes are of a multilateral nature; to resolve them by taking account of the interests of only two parties, the complainant and the defendant, would not be appropriate.

WEC proceedings should also be as transparent and open as possible. Even if non-state actors are not allowed to bring a case, they should be allowed to express an opinion or add facts related to claims validly before the Court, e.g. in the form of *amicus curiae* briefs (even if the Court has not explicitly requested their input).[70] Transparency and public access and scrutiny would be important legitimizing factors for the WEC – factors that are currently lacking in, for example, the WTO.

Relations with other courts and international organizations

Generally speaking, a WEC should engage in judicial cross-fertilization and inter-institutional dialogue. It could do so by referring to the judgments of other international courts (in particular the ICJ) and by asking the opinion of other international organizations on factual matters.[71]

More formally, the WEC could be allowed to refer questions of general international law to the ICJ. This would ensure the unity of international law, with the ICJ at the apex. It would, however, extend the time within which the WEC can reach its own decision. To give this power to the ICJ would also require a revision of the ICJ Statute, unless the WEC were construed as a UN agency that can ask advisory opinions of the ICJ.

In addition, the WEC could also be empowered to ask advisory opinions from other specialized tribunals, such as the WTO Appellate Body or the ITLOS. In turn, the WEC itself could be given the power to issue advisory opinions at the request of other international institutions, states or even non-state actors.

If IEL had sufficient "direct effect" in domestic law, it could be useful to allow domestic courts to request preliminary rulings from the WEC on matters of IEL. This would ensure the uniformity of IEL, as well as create an important bridge between the WEC and national courts.

Binding effect of judgments

It is crucial that WEC decisions are legally binding on the disputing parties. This could be achieved as a result of the decision itself, as is the case with ICJ and ITLOS decisions. Binding effect could also be granted upon adoption of WEC decisions by some political organ of a WEO, in the same way that the WTO Dispute Settlement Body must adopt WTO dispute settlement reports. Such adoption could be made virtually automatic, as in the WTO, or subject to a majority vote, as with the Energy Charter Treaty.[72] Adoption of decisions by a body on which all WEO members are represented might increase the legitimacy of WEC decisions. Yet it could also threaten the judicial independence of the WEC. In any event, in order for the WEC to be effective, the possibility for one or more states to block or veto the adoption of WEC decisions (as was the case under GATT 1947) should be avoided.

Remedies

Remedies mandated by the WEC must include cessation of the illegal act as well as reparation for damage caused. Assurances of non-repetition might also prove useful. If the notion of "environmental crimes" were recognized, imprisonment and fines should be considered.

Reparations would represent considerable challenges, because the calculation of damages may be difficult. The input of scientific and other experts might again be crucial. The risk of huge damages awards might be a major reason for states not to accept compulsory jurisdiction. Coupled with the fact that the first objective ought to be compliance, one might want to limit the scope for reparation, e.g. by imposing temporal limits and a strict causality test.

In order to promote future compliance, another type of remedy should be considered. Positive incentives could be designed so as to help ensure compliance with IEL. For example, with the damages or fines collected, a fund could be set up to facilitate implementation, especially by developing countries.

Non-compliance

A political body of a WEO should monitor compliance with WEC judgments. Issuance of a WEC decision should not be the end of the matter, as is the case for most ICJ judgments. Rather, any response to non-compliance ought to be monitored multilaterally and not imposed on a unilateral basis by the winning party. In this monitoring process, the

WEC should continue to play an important role, e.g. in the assessment of appropriate counter-measures.

Guidance could be found in the WTO compliance mechanism, where expedited procedures exist in the event of disagreement on the implementation of reports. Counter-measures, particularly those of a collective nature (such as suspension of voting rights or the right to bring cases to the WEC as a complainant), should be possible in the case of non-compliance with WEC decisions. Even the use of trade sanctions could be considered.[73]

Financing

To promote use of a WEC, as well as to expedite its work and ensure the high quality of its decisions, it must be sufficiently funded. If not, it cannot hope to make much of a mark. A large budget could attract the best judges, the best research staff and an attractive home and library, and, crucially, allow for extensive education, promotion and public relations campaigns (including rapid dissemination of decisions and "non-legal" summaries, seminars, dinners and promotion visits to different member states). The WEC budget should provide also for technical assistance to developing countries, in particular funding for high-quality legal advice. This should stimulate the involvement of both rich and poor countries in the WEC.[74] In terms of locating the requisite funds, financing could come from the regular budget of the United Nations or a WEO. The WEC could also be partially funded by the litigating parties, in particular defendants that lose their case, based on the "polluter-pays" principle.

Conclusions: Examining proposals for international environmental governance reform

The creation of an efficient and responsive judicial branch to enforce and monitor compliance with international environmental law would undoubtedly improve the overall functioning of the international environmental governance system. Lack of enforcement and compliance[75] and lack of effectiveness (in terms of real environmental improvements[76]) are among the most prominent criticisms raised against the current system. Both concerns could be alleviated by a sufficiently strong judicial branch, be it one part of a broader treaty-based compliance regime or a full-fledged court or tribunal to enforce international environmental law. Domestic courts also have an important role to play. The main obstacle remains mustering the political will to this effect.

In this context, a World Environment Court could be useful, in particular to adjudicate disputes under multilateral environmental agreements, especially if it were created in the context of a World Environment Organization or other structure bringing together the myriad of multilateral environmental agreements in place today. It might well constitute the only short-term way to inject the rule of law into international environmental law, even if it is a second-best solution compared with having all international law enforced by one and the same court, say the International Court of Justice. Moreover, in the context of a World Environment Organization, it could provide an important engine for the further development and refinement of international environmental law, including coordination between its composite elements and its relationship to other norms of international law. Transparency and the involvement of all stakeholders, including non-state actors, intense collaboration with the scientific community as well as other international organizations and courts (including domestic courts), and sensitivity to regional and national environmental needs and possibilities would be crucial to the legitimacy and future success of any World Environment Court.

Improving the approach to international environmental governance

If established, a World Environment Court should aim at universality in terms of both the actors involved (state and non-state) and the environmental topics to be covered. It should entertain claims under clearly defined treaties, not with reference to the "environmental nature" of a dispute. At the same time, the Court should be sufficiently receptive to regional and national peculiarities as well as to non-environmental norms of international law. The unity of international law, in a context of diversity between states, should be crucial on its agenda.

Strengthening the interface between politics and science

If established, a World Environment Court could offer a much-needed bridge between decision makers and the scientific community. Science is paramount in environmental regulation but, in the end, politicians take the decisions as well as the responsibility. The Court, especially when aptly advised by scientific experts, could review not only domestic environmental policies and conduct but also decisions taken at the international level. It could, in particular, check the procedural requirements to be fulfilled in the making of policies affecting the environment. The Court should be transparent towards the scientific community as well as civil society, in terms of both fact-finding and responsiveness to different values. It should, at the same time, guard against taking the role of law maker and give a degree of deference to the national regulators involved.

Improving financing

International court systems, especially where the litigating parties cover their own costs, are relatively inexpensive. Still, an adequate budget would be required for the Court to establish its legitimacy (something that would require high-quality people, facilities and public relations). To level the playing field, developing countries should be able to benefit from free or cheap legal and scientific advice. A fund set up with money from fines or damages awards could finance such a scheme. To alleviate the burden of international adjudication, one should rely also on national courts for the enforcement of international environmental law.

Increasing participation levels

No doubt, a World Environment Court would benefit, in terms of both effectiveness and legitimacy, from opening its doors to non-state actors and civil society as a whole. Actually giving non-state actors the right to sue states requires careful consideration. An alternative might be to set up an independent commission or public prosecutor, which could initiate procedures independently of state requests. To sue non-state actors before a World Environment Court would be another possibility, especially if certain violations of international environmental law were seen as "crimes". Apart from that, public international law is not well equipped to hold individual operators responsible under environmental conventions. One should rather enhance the role of domestic courts in the enforcement of international environmental law by requiring states to adopt certain minimum standards in domestic law.

The participation of developing countries is equally important. It could be promoted by technical and legal assistance, as well as preferential treatment (e.g. during the proceedings of the Court).

Increasing influence over policy at both the national and international levels

Like any court system, a World Environment Court would put pressure on states as well as individual operators to comply with international environmental law. The rule of law, applied through an independent judiciary (not a political body), would improve the effectiveness and concrete implementation of international environmental law, by both rich and poor states. It should, moreover, introduce predictability and stability into the system, not through political force or economic might, but through legal principle backed by sound scientific advice. The Court should not only provide for negative remedies (such as reparation for damage) but also continue to monitor implementation even after the issuance of a judgment, using, where appropriate, positive incentives or mediated solutions to facilitate implementation.

Notes

1. See the 1974 Nordic Convention on the Protection of the Environment, *International Legal Materials*, Vol. 13, 1974, p. 511, and the OECD Recommendation on Principles Concerning Transfrontier Pollution, *International Legal Materials*, Vol. 14, 1975, p. 242.
2. See Alan E. Boyle, "Saving the World? Implementation and Enforcement of International Environmental Law through International Institutions", *Journal of Environmental Law*, Vol. 3, 1991, p. 229; and Jeffrey Dunoff, "Institutional Misfits: The GATT, the ICJ & Trade–Environment Disputes", *Michigan Journal of International Law*, Vol. 15, 1994, p. 1043.
3. The compliance mechanism under construction for the implementation of the Kyoto Protocol to the United Nations Framework Convention on Climate Change (UNFCCC) may offer a good example. Current draft decisions would set up a compliance committee functioning through two distinct branches, a facilitative branch and an enforcement branch, the latter being responsible for determining whether a state party is not in compliance with Kyoto Protocol commitments. See *Report of the Conference of the Parties on the Second Part of Its Sixth Session*, FCCC/CP/2001/5/Add.2, 25 September 2001, pp. 62–74, available at ⟨http://www.unfccc.int/resource/docs/cop6secpart/05a02.pdf⟩.
4. See, for example, Article 14 on Settlement of Disputes of the UNFCCC, referring disputes concerning the interpretation or application of the Convention to, *inter alia*, the International Court of Justice, subject, however, to explicit acceptance of such referral by both parties.
5. Richard Bilder, "The Settlement of Disputes in the Field of International Law of the Environment", *Recueil des Cours*, Vol. 144, 1975, pp. 139, 154.
6. Note that, in addition to judicial enforcement, the WTO, much like certain regimes under IEL, also provides for institutional monitoring through specific WTO committees and the WTO Trade Policy Review Mechanism (Annex 3 to the WTO Agreement). Hence, the WTO too has a combination of a compliance cum enforcement mechanism.
7. In respect of the WTO, see in particular Article XX of the General Agreement on Tariffs and Trade (GATT), as applied, for example, in *European Communities – Measures Affecting the Prohibition of Asbestos and Asbestos Products*, complaint by Canada, WT/DS135, adopted on 5 April 2001, and the WTO agreements on the Application of Sanitary and Phytosanitary Measures and on Technical Barriers to Trade (as applied, for example, in *European Communities – Measures Affecting Livestock and Meat (Hormones)*, complaint by Canada, WT/DS48, and the United States, WT/DS26, adopted on 13 February 1998). In respect of UNCLOS, see, for example, Article 119 of UNCLOS as it was raised in the *Southern Bluefin Tuna cases* (Australia and New Zealand *v.* Japan, Request for Provisional Measures), Order of the International Tribunal for the Law of the Sea, 27 August 1999, available at ⟨http://www.un.org/Depts/los/itlos_new/Case3_4_SBluefin_Tuna/Order-tuna34.htm⟩.
8. Established in 1997 pursuant to Article 15, para. 1, of the Statute of ITLOS (Annex VI to UNCLOS), composed of 7 of the 21 ITLOS judges and presided over by Rüdiger Wolfrum (Germany). See ITLOS Press Release 5, available at ⟨http://www.un.org/Depts/los/itlos_new/press_releases/ITLOS_5.htm⟩.
9. Note, for example, that Article 25 of the WTO Understanding on Rules and Procedures

Governing the Settlement of Disputes (DSU), available at ⟨http://www.wto.org/english/ tratop_e/dispu_e/dsu_e.htm⟩, enables WTO members to settle "certain disputes that concern issues that are clearly defined by both parties" through "expeditious arbitration". Under this provision one could imagine, for example, WTO members asking arbitrators to settle certain complex environmental disputes that have a trade component but that are not necessarily limited to claims under WTO law and include elements of IEL. The advantage of this could be that (1) expert arbitrators chosen by the parties can be appointed; and (2) the arbitral award could be enforced the way normal WTO dispute settlement reports are, that is, including through multilaterally authorized economic sanctions (DSU, Article 25, para. 4).

10. Not to mention regional courts and tribunals to which IEL has already been referred, such as the European Court of Justice, the European Court of Human Rights and the Inter-American Commission and Court of Human Rights.

11. See Alan Boyle and Michael Anderson, eds, *Human Rights Approaches to Environmental Protection*, Oxford: Clarendon Press, 1996; and Prudence Taylor, "From Environmental to Ecological Human Rights: A New Dynamic in International Law?", *Georgetown International Environmental Law Review*, Vol. 10, 1998, p. 309.

12. As of 31 July 2000, 189 states were parties to the ICJ Statute, and 62 of them had recognized its jurisdiction as compulsory in accordance with Article 36, para. 2, of the Statute. Further, some 260 bilateral or multilateral treaties provide for the Court to have jurisdiction in the resolution of disputes arising out of their application or interpretation. See *Report of the ICJ, 1 August 1999–31 July 2000*, para. 5, available at ⟨http:// www.icj-cij.org/icjwww/igeneralinformation/igeninf_Annual_ Reports/iICJ_Annual_ Report_1999-2000.htm⟩. Note, however, that even if a state has granted compulsory jurisdiction to the ICJ it may have excluded certain environmental disputes from that jurisdiction – the way Canada did, for example, by excluding certain "disputes arising out of or concerning conservation and management measures taken by Canada". On that basis, the ICJ rejected jurisdiction over a dispute brought by Spain against Canada (*Fisheries Jurisdiction Case*, Spain v. Canada, Jurisdiction of the Court, Judgment of 4 December 1998, ⟨http://www.icj-cij.org/icjwww/idocket/iec/iecframe.htm⟩).

13. *Nuclear Tests Case*, New Zealand v. France, International Court of Justice, 20 December 1974.

14. *Trail Smelter Arbitration* (United States v. Canada) 3 *RIAA* 1905, 1965 (1941). The arbitrators qualified the principle as follows: "when the cause is of serious consequence and the injury is established by clear and convincing evidence". See also the *Draft Articles on International Liability for Injurious Consequences Arising out of Acts Not Prohibited by International Law (Prevention of Transboundary Harm from Hazardous Activities)*, adopted by the ILC in 2001, available at ⟨http://www.un.org/law/ilc/reports/ 2001/english/chp5.pdf⟩.

15. See, for example, the statements by President Chirac of France in a February 2000 speech at the ICJ, where he called for the ICJ to be invested with a "regulatory role, advising the international organizations" ("When international law on the environment, trade, and labour standards conflict, we need a place where they can be reconciled. Why not request advisory opinions from your Court in such cases?"). He also suggested that "treaties containing dispute-settlement mechanisms ought to establish an explicit linkage with the Court ... When these treaties set up a new jurisdiction, would it not be desirable for that jurisdiction to be able to refer questions to the Court for preliminary ruling, for guidance on points of law of general interest?" (*Report of the ICJ, 1 August 1999–31 July 2000*, para. 320).

16. Pursuant to Article 26, para. 1, of the ICJ Statute. The composition of the Chamber was most recently renewed for a period of three years in February 2003 and currently con-

sists of the President, Shi Jiuyong, the Vice-President, Raymond Ranjeva, and Judges Pieter H. Kooijmans, Francisco Rezek, Bruno Simma and Peter Tomka. See ⟨http://www.icj-cij.org/icjwww/ipresscom/ipress2003/ipresscom2003-11_admin_20030206.htm⟩.

17. In most disputes, one of the parties is unwilling to call the dispute an "environmental dispute" because, by doing so, it risks acknowledging that, factually speaking, environmental protection is, indeed, at stake. Additional elements explaining why the Chamber for Environmental Matters has so far not yet decided a single case are that its procedures are exactly the same as those of the complete Court and the seven judges appointed to the Chamber do not appear to be any better versed in IEL than are the other ICJ judges.

18. Article 30, para. 2, of the ICJ Statute and Article 9 of the Rules of the Court.

19. Article 50 of the ICJ Statute and Article 67 of the Rules of the Court.

20. For contentious proceedings, see Article 34 of the ICJ Statute and Article 69 of the Rules of the Court (referring only to "international organizations of States"). For advisory proceedings, see Article 66, para. 2, of the ICJ Statute referring to "international organizations" more broadly. See Dinah Shelton, "The Participation of Non-governmental Organizations in International Judicial Proceedings", *American Journal of International Law*, Vol. 88, 1994, p. 611; and Rosalyn Higgins, "Remedies and the International Court: An Introduction", in Malcolm Evans and Stratos Konstadinides, eds, *Remedies in International Law: The Institutional Dilemma*, Oxford: Hart Publishing, 1998, p. 2 (stating that, in the 1996 *Nuclear Weapons* cases, the Court took a decision not to accept the large number of NGO briefs that it had received as part of the docket. Still, all of these briefs were placed in the Court's library, fully accessible to the judges).

21. Philippe Sands, "International Environmental Litigation and Its Future", *University of Richmond Law Review*, Vol. 32, 1999, pp. 1619, 1633, questioning whether in the *Case Concerning Gabcikovo-Nagymaros Project* (*ICJ Reports*, 1997, para. 3) "the ICJ has missed an opportunity to indicate a real willingness to show its environmental credentials".

22. The Optional Rules for Arbitration of Disputes Relating to Natural Resources and/or the Environment are posted at ⟨http://www.pca-cpa.org/EDR/ENRrules.htm⟩. The option of revamping the PCA for the settlement of environmental disputes was raised prominently in a 1999 Conference on International Environmental Dispute Resolutions. For a summary of that conference, see *George Washington Journal of International Law and Economics*, Vol. 32, 2000, p. 325.

23. Note also the PCA Optional Rules for Fact-finding Commissions of Inquiry, adopted in 1997, available at ⟨http://www.pca-cpa.org/BD/inquiryenglish.htm⟩.

24. See the ICEAC website at ⟨http://www.greenchannel.com/iceac⟩.

25. ICEAC Statute, Article 2, para. 1(a), available at ⟨http://www.greenchannel.com/iceac/Ingles/Stat.html⟩.

26. Ibid., Article 2, para. 1(b).

27. See ⟨http://www.greenchannel.com/iceac/Ingles/caso_sonora_ingles.html⟩.

28. Article 5 of the ICC Statute, available at ⟨http://www.iccnow.org/romearchive/romestatute/rome-e.doc⟩.

29. Article 8, para. 2(b)(iv) of the ICC Statute defines the following as being a war crime: "Intentionally launching an attack in the knowledge that such attack will cause ... long-term and severe damage to the natural environment which would be clearly excessive in relation to the concrete and direct overall military advantage anticipated". For a similar definition of war crimes, see Article 20, para. (g) of the *Draft Code of Crimes Against the Peace and Security of Mankind*, adopted by the International Law Commission in 1996. See, generally, Jean-Marie Henckaerts, "Armed Conflict and the Environment", *Yearbook of International Environmental Law*, Vol. 10, 1999, p. 188.

30. See, for example, Robert McLaughlin, "Improving Compliance: Making Non-State International Actors Responsible for Environmental Crimes", *Colorado Journal of International Environmental Law and Policy*, Vol. 11, 2000, p. 377.

31. See Mark Drumbl, "Waging War against the World: The Need to Move from War Crimes to Environmental Crimes", *Fordham International Law Journal*, Vol. 22, 1998, p. 145.

32. Article 19, para. 3(d) of the 1996 Draft Articles included the following under the definition of "international crimes": "a serious breach of an international obligation of essential importance for the safeguarding and preservation of the human environment, such as those prohibiting massive pollution of the atmosphere or of the seas", available at ⟨http://www.un.org/law/ilc/reports/1996/chap03.htm#doc38⟩.

33. In support, see the following statement in the 2001 *ILC Commentary*: "The obligations referred to in article 40 arise from those substantive rules of conduct that prohibit what has come to be seen as intolerable because of the threat it presents to the survival of States and their peoples and the most basic human values", available at ⟨http://www.un.org/law/ilc/reports/2001/english/chp4.pdf, at p. 283, para. 3⟩. This could be said to include certain rules of IEL.

34. Ellen Hey, *Reflections on an International Environmental Court*, New York: Kluwer Law International, 2000, p. 15.

35. See, in this respect, Principle 10 of the 1992 Rio Declaration: "Effective access to judicial and administrative proceedings, including redress and remedy shall be available". For examples, see note 1 above.

36. On the need for a WEC, commentators in favour include: Kenneth McCallion and Rajan Sharma, "Environmental Justice without Borders: The Need for an International Court of the Environment to Protect Fundamental Environmental Rights", *George Washington Journal of International Law and Economics*, Vol. 32, 2000, p. 351; Alfred Rest, "The Indispensability of an International Environmental Court", *Review of European Community and International Environmental Law*, Vol. 7, 1998, p. 63; Amedeo Postiglione, "A More Efficient International Law on the Environment and Setting up of an International Court for the Environment within the United Nations", *Environmental Law*, Vol. 20, 1990, p. 321, as well as the International Court of the Environment Foundation, available at ⟨http://www.com.it/icef⟩. Those against include: Sean Murphy, "Does the World Need a New International Environmental Court?", *George Washington Journal of International Law and Economics*, Vol. 32, 2000, p. 333; Hey, *Reflections on an International Environmental Court* (against, essentially, because of "the danger of fragmentation by causing too much competition among international law-based forums for the settlement of disputes", p. 25); Sands, "International Environmental Litigation and Its Future" (concluding at p. 1640: "The possibility of an international environmental court should be kept on our radar screens, but the time is clearly not ripe to establish such a body"); and Sir Robert Jennings, "Need for an Environmental Court?", *Environmental Policy and Law*, Vol. 20, 1992, p. 312.

37. See further text at note 61 below.

38. Note, however, that the PCA Environmental Rules, referred to in note 22 above, explicitly state in their introduction that "the Rules may be used in relation to disputes between two or more States parties to a multilateral agreement relating to access to and utilization of natural resources concerning the interpretation or application of that agreement". See, in this respect, the call by PCA official Dane Ratliff to adopt the PCA's Environmental Rules as the implementation annex called for in the UNFCCC, Article 14(2)(b) (*Earth Negotiations Bulletin*, 23 July 2001, p. 2, available at ⟨http://www.iisd.ca/climate/cop6bis/enbots⟩).

39. See note 3 above.

40. See Shigeru Oda, "The ICJ Viewed from the Bench (1976–1993)", *Recueil des Cours*, Vol. 244, No. 13, 1993, p. 144 ("the creation of a court of judicature in parallel with the ICJ ... will prove to have been a great mistake") and, less categorically, Gilbert Guillaume, "The Future of International Judicial Institutions", *International and Comparative Law Quarterly*, Vol. 44, 1995, p. 848; and Sir Robert Jennings, "The Role of the International Court of Justice in the Development of International Environmental Protection Law", in *The Collected Writings of Sir Robert Jennings*, Vol. I, New York: Kluwer Law Publishing, 1998, p. 67. See also Philip Jessup, "Do New Problems Need New Courts?", *Proceedings of the ASIL*, Vol. 65, 1971, p. 261.

41. Note that at the regional level too there is a tendency towards specialized judicial decision makers. The Treaty of Nice (which entered into force on 1 February 2003, see ⟨http://europa.eu.int/eur-lex/en/treaties/dat/nice_treaty_en.pdf⟩) provides that "[t]he Council ... may create judicial panels to hear and determine at first instance certain classes of action or proceeding brought in specific areas" (inserting Article 225(a) in the Treaty on European Union or Amsterdam Treaty). Decisions by these "judicial panels" may be subject to a right of appeal before the Court of First Instance, whose decisions may, in turn, exceptionally be subject to review by the European Court of Justice, "where there is a serious risk of the unity or consistency of Community law being affected" (Article 225, para. 2).

42. For some of the legal literature on the creation of a WEO, see Karen Tyler Farr, "A New Global Environmental Organization", *Georgia Journal of International and Comparative Law*, Vol. 28, 2000, p. 493; Daniel Esty, "The Case for a Global Environmental Organization", in Peter Kenen, ed., *Managing the World Economy*, Washington, D.C.: Institute for International Economics, 1994, p. 287; and Catherine Tinker, "Environmental Planet Management by the United Nations: An Idea Whose Time Has Not Yet Come?", *New York University Journal of International Law and Politics*, Vol. 22, 1991, p. 793.

43. The "repeat-player" effect is important too. States might be more willing to cooperate in a specialized tribunal where they know that one day they could be the claimant, and another the other defendant.

44. Commentators in support include: Ben Kingsbury, "Foreword: Is the Proliferation of International Courts and Tribunals a Systemic Problem?", *New York University Journal of International Law and Politics*, Vol. 31, 1999, p. 679 (as well as the series of papers on the same topic in the same issue); and Jonathan Charney, "Is International Law Threatened by Multiple International Tribunals?", *Receuil des Cours*, Vol. 271, 1998, p. 101. More cautious commentators include the President of the ICJ, "Speech of the President of the ICJ, Judge Gilbert Guillaume, to the Sixth Committee of the UN General Assembly, 27 October 2000", *The Proliferation of International Judicial Bodies: The Outlook for the International Legal Order*, available at ⟨http://www.icj-cij.org/icjwww/ipresscom/SPEECHES/iSpeechPresident_Guillaume_SixthCommittee_20001027.htm⟩; and Hey, *Reflections on an International Environmental Court* (as explained in note 36 above).

45. See Joost Pauwelyn, "The Role of Public International Law in the WTO: How Far Can We Go?", *American Journal of International Law*, Vol. 95, 2001, p. 535, and "Enforcement and Countermeasures in the WTO: Rules are Rules – Toward a More Collective Approach", *American Journal of International Law*, Vol. 94, 2000, pp. 335–347.

46. Murphy, "Does the World Need a New International Environmental Court?", p. 344. See also Dunoff, "Institutional Misfits", p. 1108 ("the proposed environmental world court might present a mirror image of the institutional myopia that undermines attempts by the GATT and NAFTA to resolve fairly disputes involving conflicting obligations under international trade and environmental law").

47. This section relies in part on Laurence Helfer and Anne-Marie Slaughter, "Towards a

Theory of Effective Supranational Adjudication", *Yale Law Journal*, Vol. 107, 1997, p. 273.

48. For a systematic overview of international courts and tribunals, as well as their procedures, see the Project on International Courts and Tribunals (PICT), available at ⟨http://www.pict-pcti.org⟩.

49. See note 12 above (*Fisheries Jurisdiction Case*, Spain *v.* Canada).

50. See note 17 above.

51. Thus limiting the jurisdiction of a WEC would largely appease the main argument Ellen Hey has raised against a WEC, namely the vagueness of the definition of an "international environmental dispute" (*Reflections on an International Environmental Court*, pp. 4–14).

52. On conflicts of jurisdiction, see Pauwelyn, "The Role of Public International Law in the WTO", pp. 556–559.

53. See notes 3 and 4 above.

54. Hey, *Reflections on an International Environmental Court*, pp. 15–16, supports this.

55. See note 46 above. Limiting the appointment of IEL academics or former IEL diplomats to the WEC could further avoid the rather serious criticism raised by Judge Oda against the ITLOS that "the idea of the ITLOS seems to have been reinforced by the personal desires of some delegates to UNCLOS III and the Preparatory Commission, and other jurists who appear to have been personally interested in obtaining posts in international judicial organs" (Oda, "The ICJ Viewed from the Bench (1976–1993)", p. 145).

56. See, in this respect, Articles 42 ff. of the 2001 ILC Draft Articles on State Responsibility (note 33 above) setting out rules on the invocation of responsibility by "injured states" as well as "other" states if, for example, "[t]he obligation breached is owed to a group of States including that State, and is established for the protection of a collective interest of the group" (Article 48, para. 1(a)). See also Article 46 on "Plurality of injured States".

57. Chapter 11 of NAFTA, under which private investors can bring claims against NAFTA members, provides a good example of the dynamics of giving standing to non-state actors. Chapter 11 has, indeed, led to a number of cases of which it is safe to say that they would never have been brought by the government involved. One of the subsequent arbitration awards even led to the adoption by NAFTA members of an interpretation overruling the arbitration award (see ⟨http://www.naftaclaims.com⟩).

58. See Daniel Bodansky, "The Legitimacy of International Governance: A Coming Challenge for International Environmental Law?", *American Journal of International Law*, Vol. 93, 1999, pp. 596, 601 and 611.

59. See, in this respect, Article 16 of the ICC Statute, allowing the Security Council to defer investigation or prosecution.

60. Note, in this respect, Article 47 of the 2001 ILC Draft Articles on State Responsibility on "Plurality of responsible States".

61. As noted by Bodansky, "The Legitimacy of International Governance", p. 610: "The question is whether the executive branch ... [through its consent to, for example, IEL] can legitimately bind private actors. This is a question that the traditional theory of state consent does not address. It focuses on the authority of international law vis-à-vis states, not the authority of states over individuals (which the theory of state consent treats as a matter of domestic law)".

62. See note 22 above.

63. See Geoffrey Palmer, "New Ways to Make International Environmental Law", *American Journal of International Law*, Vol. 86, 1992, p. 259, and Bodansky, "The Legitimacy of International Governance", p. 607 ("successful international action will depend on

the ability to require common action even in the absence of consensus among states – it will depend, that is, on some form of supranational authority").

64. Bodansky, "The Legitimacy of International Governance", p. 605, refers to "legal legitimacy" in this respect ("to the extent that authority is exercised at the international level by institutions rather than by international rules directly, then, in addition to general consent, we also need a concept of 'legal legitimacy' – 'the condition of being in accordance with law or principle' ").

65. Hey, *Reflections on an International Environmental Court*, pp. 16–17, supports this.

66. See Article 31.3(c) of the Vienna Convention on the Law of Treaties, requiring that a treaty interpreter take account, not only of the text, context and object and purpose of the particular treaty provision, but also of "any relevant rules of international law applicable in the relations between the parties".

67. See Pauwelyn, "The Role of Public International Law in the WTO".

68. For a model, see the PCA Optional Rules for Fact-finding Commissions of Inquiry, adopted in 1997, available at ⟨http://www.pca-cpa.org/BD/inquiryenglish.htm⟩.

69. As is done in WTO dispute settlement; see Pauwelyn, "Expert Advice in WTO Dispute Settlement", paper presented at Columbia Law School, New York, October 2001 (on file with the author).

70. For a procedure to avoid opening the floodgates, which involves prior authorization to file a brief, subject to certain procedural and substantive requirements, see the Additional Procedure on *amicus curiae* briefs adopted by the Appellate Body in the *EC – Asbestos* case, WT/DS135/9, 8 November 2000.

71. WTO panels have, for example, asked the opinion of the World Intellectual Property Organization on a number of occasions; see Pauwelyn, "Expert Advice in WTO Dispute Settlement".

72. See Article 36, para. 4 of the Energy Charter Treaty, available at ⟨http://ecs.icl.be/english/fulltext/treaty36.html⟩.

73. This may raise questions of WTO consistency. In my view, however, as long as both parties have agreed to the rule that trade sanctions can be imposed in the event of non-compliance with WEC judgments, that rule should be able to constitute a valid defence (e.g. as *lex specialis*) against a claim of WTO violation raised against the trade sanction (even before a WTO panel where only WTO claims can be brought). See Pauwelyn, "The Role of Public International Law in the WTO".

74. See, in this respect, the Advisory Center on WTO Law (see ⟨http://www.itd.org/links/acwlintro.htm⟩), set up by a number of WTO members to give cheap or even free legal WTO advice to participating developing members and all least developed countries. At the opening of the Center on 5 October 2001, Mike Moore, Director-General of the WTO, called the event a "(small) historic moment in its own right", marking "the first time a true legal aid centre has been established within the international legal system, with a view to combating the unequal possibilities of access to international justice as between States" (see ⟨http://www.wto.org/english/news_e/spmm_e/spmm71_e.htm⟩).

75. See Boyle, "Saving the World?", p. 229 ("The development of rules of international law concerning protection of the environment is of little significance unless accompanied by effective means for ensuring enforcement and compliance").

76. See Lawrence Susskind and Connie Ozawa, "Negotiating More Effective International Environmental Agreements", in Andrew Hurrell and Benedict Kingsbury, eds, *The International Politics of the Environment: Actors, Interests and Institutions*, New York: Oxford University Press, 1992, pp. 142, 143 ("A great deal of effort has been invested in 'getting written agreements'. Far too little attention has been paid to guaranteeing that real environmental improvements are made").

7

Reforming the United Nations Trusteeship Council

Catherine Redgwell

Introduction

The purpose of this chapter is to consider reform of the UN Trusteeship Council as one mechanism for the enforcement of international environmental law. Let it be said at the outset that this chapter does not consider a direct *enforcement* function for the Council but rather examines whether an *implementation* function would improve the effectiveness of international environmental law. Moreover, in considering further below the proposal aired by the UN Secretary-General in his 1997 report on UN reform,[1] namely that "collective trusteeship" be exercised over global environmental and commons issues, a broad interpretation of "global environmental issues" is employed. There is no reason in principle why the Council should not exercise oversight of the state of the environment located *within* as well as beyond states, although acknowledging that considerable political will would be necessary for states to accord an oversight function to an external body concerned with matters located within the sovereignty of states.[2] Nor is it suggested that *all* environmental matters within states should be subject to "collective trusteeship"; rather, only those that are the "common concern of humankind".[3] The inclusion of the common concern of humankind is very much in keeping with one of the characteristic features of the environmental era since the United Nations Conference on Environment and Development in Rio in 1992 – namely, the establishment of a global framework of environmental responsibilities, as distinct from regional or trans-boundary issues (e.g. air pollution, international watercourses) and common spaces (e.g. Part XII of the 1982 Law of the Sea Convention). Lest this be viewed as far too modest a proposal, it should be observed that a variety of international environmental agreements regulating matters within and beyond states, ranging from the regulation of wildlife to hazardous waste disposal, reflect common or international concern, and even an intergenerational dimension.[4] The scope of an Environmental Trusteeship Council's oversight is thus potentially quite broad; the scope *ratione materiae* of the Council's oversight powers is an important feature returned to below.

In any event, the sovereign rights of states are not infringed by collective trusteeship. Trust arrangements do not challenge sovereignty directly, for one of the advantages of trusteeship arrangements is the absence of sovereignty in the exercise of trusteeship functions – there is no transfer of sovereignty to the trust authority. This is a reflection of the separation of legal and beneficial interest fundamental to the trust law concept.[5] Central to discussion of a revamped Trusteeship Council is thus the notion of the trust, the modalities for the exercise of trusteeship, and the subject matter over which trusteeship will be exercised. It is in this latter regard that a link is made not only between "collective trusteeship" and global environmental and commons issues, but also between trusteeship and resources, whose conservation is acknowledged by the international community to be the common concern of humankind. As Boyle observes, the use of the term "common concern" in the Convention on Biological Diversity, for example, does not effect the transfer to international ownership of biological resources located within states. On the contrary, the Convention expressly reaffirms states' permanent sovereignty over natural resources. What it does effect, however, is the "much more limited sense of legitimizing international interest in the conservation and use of biological resources otherwise within the territorial sovereignty of other States".[6]

To be sure, it is the common heritage of humankind principle, applied to resources in areas beyond national jurisdiction[7] (common spaces in fact), that is aptly acknowledged as one of the most developed applications of a trusteeship or fiduciary relationship in an environmental context.[8] What is argued here is the further extension of trusteeship notions – or, at the very least, the extension of oversight by a trusteeship institution, the Trusteeship Council – to a wider category of resources that are the common concern of humankind. This is one possible institutional expression for the responsible management of the environment in accordance with the aims of sustainable development.[9] Although it is indisputable that the need for more effective global management institutions has not yet been met, the reasons for reinvigorating the Trusteeship Council must be based upon more than the mere existence of a defunct UN institution in search of a function.[10] Nor should a reinvigorated Trusteeship Council cut across the effective implementation of existing international environmental agreements through the mechanisms established thereunder. Nonetheless, there are in fact practical as well as theoretical arguments in favour of maintaining an international trust institution, reoriented towards environmental matters. These arguments are canvassed below.

In order to consider reform of the existing Trusteeship Council properly, it is important first to examine what the Trusteeship Council is and the way in which the international trusteeship system functioned under the Charter. This is not to suggest that the existing institutions must be deployed unmodified, but rather to examine whether there are elements of that system that should be preserved even in the light of new imperatives. It is also express acknowledgement of the role that League mandates and UN trusteeships have played as models for international supervisory institutions in diverse contexts, including for the environment.[11] This discussion is followed by analysis of existing proposals for change in environmental governance, of which proposals for an "Environmental Trusteeship Council" form a part – a discussion that necessarily encompasses the question of *why* the Trusteeship Council should perform an environmental implementation function. The chapter then considers concrete proposals as to *how* such functions may be performed (namely, the institutional structure and function of a revamped Council), identifying first the design questions to be addressed in structuring an Environmental Trusteeship Council and concluding with some suggestions for redrafting Chapters XII and XIII of the UN Charter.

The international trusteeship system in a nutshell

The international trusteeship system was established by Chapter XII of the UN Charter (Articles 75–85), and Chapter XIII addressed the formation of the Trusteeship Council (Articles 86–91).[12] Each will be addressed in turn.

The trusteeship system

The obligations of the trustee are set out in Article 76 ("basic objectives of the trusteeship system") and include the promotion of "the political, economic, social and educational advancement of the inhabitants of the trust territories, and their progressive development towards self-government or independence".[13] Establishing a trusteeship system building upon but distinct from the League of Nations' mandate system proved one of more controversial questions considered at the San Francisco Conference on International Organization in 1945 and in the early meetings of the General Assembly and Security Council.[14] A major issue was the criteria for trust status. The UN Charter does not employ the same categorization for trust territories as did the League; rather, Article 77 provides for three categories of trusteeship territory according to provenance, namely: (1) territories previously held under mandate;[15] (2) territories that may be detached from enemy states as a consequence of the Second World War;[16] and (3) territories placed voluntarily under UN jurisdiction by the state(s) responsible for their administration.[17] The last remaining territory under UN trusteeship – the strategic trust territory of Palau – voted in favour of a Compact of Free Association with the United States (its administering authority) in 1993.

In respect of environmental matters, it is the third category of UN trusteeship that offers perhaps the most scope, although no new territory has in fact been placed voluntarily under the trusteeship system nor is the United Nations itself empowered unilaterally to do so. It was under this category that unofficial suggestions were made for the Arctic and Antarctic areas to be placed under the trusteeship system.[18] The UN Charter also explicitly contemplates joint administration by one or more states or by the Organization itself.[19] In practice, however, there are no instances of either.[20]

Although these Charter provisions provide a general framework, it was the trusteeship agreement that functioned like a trust deed of covenant, setting out the terms of administration and forming the legal basis for its exercise.[21] In accordance with Article 79, trust terms were to be agreed upon "by the States directly concerned".[22] The trusteeship agreement formed the legal basis for the administration of the trusteeship territory and for the relationship between the administering authority and the United Nations; it was not a deed to which the "beneficiaries",[23] or interested third parties, were privy. The principal provisions of the several trusteeship agreements were quite similar and, understandably for the time and in the light of the trust purposes set out in Article 76 of the UN Charter,[24] addressed a range of matters relating to the administration of the territory, but did not specifically address environmental concerns. Nonetheless, provisions regarding the safeguarding of "native land and resources in the interest of the native population" might be read in this light.[25] For example, Chowdhuri argues that nuclear tests conducted in the strategic trust territory of the Trust Islands under the administration of the United States were inconsistent with the basic objectives of the trusteeship system set out in Article 76 of the UN Charter and with Article 6 of the Trusteeship Agreement.[26] The latter explicitly guaranteed the protection of the inhabitants' health, land and natural resources.[27]

Approval of the agreement, and of any alteration or amendment, was required either from the General Assembly[28] or, in the case of strategic trust territories, from the Security Council.[29] This emphasizes the degree of international control and supervision exercised over trusteeship arrangements, with the United Nations in a sense a "guarantor" of the trusteeship agreement.[30]

The Trusteeship Council

The Trusteeship Council is governed by Chapter XIII (Articles 86–91) of the UN Charter. Membership is set out in Article 86 and comprises the five permanent members of the Security Council, those members administering trust territories and such additional members as is necessary to ensure an even balance in membership between administering and non-administering members. The functions of the Trusteeship Council include examination of reports from the administering authority of trusteeship territories regarding the political, economic, social and educational advancement of the peoples of the trusteeship territory, and the examination of petitions from, and periodic missions to, the trust territories in consultation with the administering authority.[31] Since the independence of Palau, with effect from 1 October 1994, the trusteeship system had in effect achieved its purpose, namely, the self-government or independence (as separate states or by joining neighbouring countries) of all trust territories. Accordingly, on 1 November 1994 the Trusteeship Council – now comprising only the five permanent members of the Security Council[32] – suspended operations and amended its rules of procedure[33] to remove the obligation to meet annually.

In terms of its actual functioning, the cornerstone of the trusteeship system is clearly international accountability.[34] In this regard, it was able to build on the experience of the League's mandate system. This system relied principally upon two kinds of securities of performance of trust obligations under Article 22 of the Covenant: annual reports, reviewed by the Mandates Commission and subject to the satisfaction of the League Council, and judicial supervision by the Permanent Court of International Justice. The reporting function was an essential element of the League's mandate system, required by Article 22 of the Covenant and reflected in the mandate instruments. For example, Article 6 of the Mandate for South-West Africa provided:

The Mandatory shall make to the Council of the League of Nations an annual report to the satisfaction of the Council, containing full information with regard to the Territory, and indicating the measures taken to carry out the obligations assumed under Articles 2, 3, 4 and 5 [which embody the substantive obligations of the Union of South Africa with respect to the Territory].

Reports were considered by the Permanent Mandates Commission of the League, which performed an advisory function in respect of them. Ultimate supervision lay with the Council of the League, a body that the Commission could advise "on all matters relating to the observance of the mandate".[35] This division of roles was no doubt a reflection, at least in part, of the fact that the advisory Commission was composed of individuals not state representatives.

Under the UN trusteeship system, accountability is ensured via the Trusteeship Council, the General Assembly and, ultimately, the International Court of Justice (ICJ). Membership of the Council is open to government representatives drawn from the three categories indicated in Article 86; additionally, observers were permitted at Council meetings from the beginning, specifically representatives of the Economic and Social Council (ECOSOC) and of the UN Specialized Agencies.[36] Its primary functions were to consider the annual reports submitted by the administering authorities in response to a questionnaire formulated by the Council; to consider petitions in consultation with the administering authority; and to make periodic site visits to trust territories. Petitioners could, exceptionally, request an oral hearing before the Trusteeship Council or during a site visit. Further requests for information from the petitioner might be forthcoming following the submission of a petition, drawing the petitioner further into the process, but with no power in the Council or in the General Assembly to make binding decisions.[37]

It is not difficult to see the parallels between these mechanisms and those that have developed for oversight of the effective implementation of international environmental treaties, particularly information-gathering and reporting and, to a lesser extent, site visits (see, for example, mission site visits under the 1971 Ramsar Convention on Wetlands of International Importance, and site visits by the World Heritage Committee of the 1972 UNESCO Convention for the Protection of the World Cultural and Natural Heritage). This suggests that certain features of the trusteeship system might be preserved while expanding its functions to include, *inter alia*: regular reporting by treaty secretariats to the Trusteeship Council; opening membership of the Council to suitably qualified individuals (following the League example and that of e.g. the Human Rights Committee under the 1966 International Covenant on Civil and Political Rights[38]); granting observer status therein for non-governmental organizations (comparable to existing procedures under many international treaties regarding attendance at the Conference of the Parties, and to the practice of ECOSOC[39]); and providing for a petitions system from individuals and/or groups within states alerting the Council to problems of implementation of international environmental agreements within states (analogous to the petitions system under the trusteeship system and to the World Bank Inspection Panel procedure[40]). What is not proposed here is that the Trusteeship Council adopt an active role as the administering authority for either existing common spaces, common heritage or the common concern of humankind, each of which is subject to an international management regime (the Antarctic Treaty and the 1982 Law of the Sea Convention, for example) and/or located within states (biodiversity). Rather, "collective trusteeship" is exercised to ensure that states and international treaty institutions responsible for protecting and conserving the global environment within and beyond states fulfil their obligations for the benefit of present and future generations. That is, the Council would exercise an oversight function similar to that exercised in respect of the discharge of trusteeship functions by administering authorities under the classic trusteeship system.

To what extent have concrete proposals for reform of the Trusteeship Council already been made? It is to this question we now turn, bearing in mind the need first to locate proposals for Trusteeship Council reform within the broader context of global governance reform proposals, before turning to specific proposals regarding the Council itself.

General proposals for reform

Proposals for the reform of the Trusteeship Council to enable it to perform an environmental oversight role may be located within a wider concern to embrace the underrepresented (procedurally and substantively) within international governance structures, namely, the environment and the interests of both present and future generations (international civil society in an intragenerational and intergenerational sense). From a procedural viewpoint, there are two aspects to this question: representation of such interests – the environment, future generations – in diverse forums, and enforcement action in respect of breach of trust. In her seminal work on intergenerational equity, Weiss has suggested a number of possibilities addressed to both, including surrogates such as ombudspeople[41] or trustees with standing to represent the interests of future generations in, *inter alia*, judicial proceedings.[42] The non-binding "Goa Guidelines on Intergenerational Equity"[43] also propose the designation of ombudspeople or commissioners for the protection of the interests of future generations, and Stone suggests the broader notion of guardians acting as legal representatives for the natural environment.[44] Guardians might be drawn from international bodies with the requisite expertise – the United Nations Environment Programme (UNEP)[45] for example – or from non-governmental organizations (NGOs) such as Greenpeace or the Worldwide Fund for Nature.[46]

NGOs may also play a "surrogate" role,[47] with the perpetuation of such organizations providing their programmes with a degree of "intergenerational authenticity".[48] Indeed, although sceptical especially of a role for representatives of future generations in negotiations, Susskind considers that

[Weiss] is more convincing when she speaks of nongovernmental interests of specially appointed ombudsmen being tapped to perform as advocates for future generations. In the same way that U.S. courts often appoint a guardian *ad litem* to represent the interests of children in divorce actions (or that localities or nongovernmental interests can represent future generations in Superfund cleanup decision making), Brown [Weiss] believes that individuals or [non-governmental institutions] could be selected to speak for future generations.[49]

There is clearly a strand in the literature that emphasizes the involvement of non-state actors as crucial to ensuring not only the infusion of *alternative* perspectives but also the articulation of *universal* perspectives; indeed, the 1995 report of the Commission on Global Governance suggests that global NGOs are the best expression of international civil society.[50] This taps into increasing trends recognizing public participation not only in environmental decision-making but also in implementation and enforcement. A strong linkage between public participation and sustainable development is evidenced in, *inter alia*, Section 3 of *Agenda 21*.[51]

The appointment of planetary trustees, commissioners or "ombudsmen" has been suggested by the Experts Group on Environmental Law of the Brundtland Commission, which recommended the appointment of an international ombudsperson – specifically, a United Nations High Commissioner for Environmental Protection and Sustainable Development. S/he would be charged with a range of tasks: receiving and assessing communications from private organizations and individuals regarding compliance with stated international agreements; referring appropriate cases to the then proposed UN Commission for Environmental Protection and Sustainable Development or another body such as UNEP;[52] the performance of special responsibilities for the protection and use of areas beyond national jurisdiction and the representation and protection of the interests of future generations; and the preparation and publication of reports highlighting critical environmental areas with recommendations for action.[53] A similar suggestion comes from Schrijver, based on the notion of an International Environmental Commission or ombudsperson operating through UNEP.

The office of the Executive Director of UNEP could gradually evolve into that of an *International Environmental Commission* (Ombudsman).... This office could come to include (a) receiving petitions of individuals and groups such as Greenpeace and other environmental non-governmental organisations, and (b) the right to raise questions to governments and boards of transnational companies. UNEP could develop the competence to compose and send multilateral inspection teams, comparable with those of the International Atomic Energy Agency, for the purposes of fact-finding and reporting, amongst others, on illegal dumping of industrial waste at sea or on land. The annual report of UNEP's Executive Director or the International Environmental Commissioner could become an authoritative report on "The State of the World's Environment".[54]

Rao proposes the United Nations as a "guardian for posterity" and the establishment of a "Special Office of the Guardian of Future Generations" under the direction of the UN General Assembly.[55]

Although relying in part on the concept of the trust and the role of the trustee in protecting trust property for the benefit of present and future generations and beneficiaries, these proposals do not necessarily require the involvement of the UN Trusteeship Council. Indeed, a closer analogy would be to domestic law concepts of guardians *ad litem* or ombudspeople. Although Weiss considers mechanisms for enforcing charitable trusts to be "especially instructive" for the planetary trust,[56] there are clearly considerable difficulties in translating such mechanisms onto the international level. Mere representation of the interests of potential beneficiaries of the trust – future generations in particular – has produced some scepticism regarding the practicality of planetary ombudsperson or commissioner proposals, particularly in the context of the role of the ombudsperson in projecting future interests in international negotiations.[57] It is also questioned whether the political will exists to implement and to abide by such arrangements. Birnie considers the appointment of a planetary ombudsperson to be impractical for the same reasons Susskind criticizes the concept, namely the weakness of such a representative in influencing the scope of international obligations.[58] Finally, and most pertinently from a legal point of view, there does not presently exist any international precedent clearly acknowledging the rights of future generations either procedurally[59] or substantively.[60]

At the United Nations Conference on Environment and Development (UNCED) in 1992, a number of these institutional proposals were aired, though in the end only the comparatively modest Commission on Sustainable Development was established following a suggestion in Chapter 38 of *Agenda 21*.[61] "More far-reaching, earlier proposals such as establishing an Environmental Security Council or reconstituting the Assembly's Fourth Committee as an Environmental Committee were ... put aside."[62] The Maltese, so instrumental in the evolution of the common heritage of humankind doctrine, suggested that a procedural guarantee of the role of guardian of future generations should be included in the Rio Declaration, worded as: "Each generation has, in particular, the responsibility to ensure that in any national or international forum, where it is likely that a decision be taken affecting the interests of future generations, access be given to an authorized person appointed as 'Guardian' of future generations to appear and make submissions on their behalf."[63] However, this suggestion was not adopted.

In the end, Chapter 38 of *Agenda 21* simply states that UNCED took note of, but did not act upon, "other institutional initiatives" such as the appointment of a guardian for future generations or adapting the role of the Security Council or the Trusteeship Council.[64] Nor was the role of UNEP significantly enhanced.[65] Resulting directly from UNCED was the creation of a Commission on Sustainable Development, but without the powers to negotiate or intervene, which are integral to the institutional proposals indicated above. Monitoring, particularly of the implementation of *Agenda 21*, is one of its functions; additionally, there is scope for the Commission "to consider, where appropriate, information regarding the progress made in the implementation of environmental conventions, which could be made available by the relevant Conferences of Parties".[66] It does not – and, as presently structured, cannot – review the implementation and effectiveness of international environmental treaties. The task, reiterated at Rio+5 (Earth Summit + 5: Special Session of the General Assembly to Review and Appraise the Implementation of Agenda 21) in 1997 and at the 2002 Johannesburg World Summit on Sustainable Development, of the coordination of UN environmental treaties and their implementation has been left to UNEP.[67] Although these developments are consonant "with the post-UNCED emphasis on effective implementation of environmental treaties and ensuring greater coherence and collaboration between them",[68] they fall far short of the creation of a new environmental body with significant powers of oversight. In practice, pragmatic mechanisms such as the conclusion of memoranda of understanding between treaty secretariats (e.g. the Convention on International Trade in Endangered Species of Wild Fauna and Flora and Interpol) and the observer status (e.g. in the World Trade Organization's Committee on Trade and the Environment) have continued to address certain problems of treaty congestion and overlap, supplementing UNEP's weak coordinating role.

What then of specific proposals for reform of the United Nations Trusteeship Council? Could it perform the institutional role of trustee discussed above in the context of various proposals for guardians or ombudspeople? Is it a necessary component in ensuring "greater coherence and collaboration" between environmental treaties and their institutions?

Proposals for reform of the UN Trusteeship Council

Renewed attention to a potential role for the Trusteeship Council in environmental matters may be attributed to at least two factors since UNCED: reform of the United Nations; and the post-UNCED process itself. First, with the independence of Palau in 1994, the last trust territory was removed from the Council's oversight. This provided a fresh opportunity to consider the role of the Trusteeship Council within the general context of wider proposals for UN reform, not merely within the context of environmental matters. Secondly, the failure to achieve ambitious institutional reform in 1992 had not silenced proposals for a stronger institution within the UN system charged with environmental responsibilities, in particular with oversight of the range of treaties under UN auspices and with ensuring the achievement of sustainable development. The newly created Commission on Sustainable Development, which has met annually since 1993, does not meet this need; nor has UNEP successfully done so.

As such, a number of proposals have been made since UNCED that would accord a specifically environmental mandate to the Trusteeship Council. In 1994, the then President of the General Assembly called for the mandate of the Trusteeship Council to be broadened in order for it to "hold in trust for humanity its common heritage and its common concerns: the environment; the protection of extraterritorial zones and resources of the sea and the seabed; the climate and the rights of future generations".[69] In 1995, the Maltese proposed that the Trusteeship Council should be entrusted with common heritage of humankind and environmental issues.[70] The 1995 report of the Commission on Global Governance also suggests that a single body "should exercise overall responsibility acting on behalf of all nations, including the administration of environment treaties related to the commons",[71] with the United Nations Trusteeship Council named to perform this role. Other proposals for the institutional reform of the United Nations make reference to "a new concept of trusteeship" in an explicitly environmental context.[72] Perhaps most significant of all, in his July 1997 report *Renewing the United Nations, A Programme for Reform*, the UN Secretary-General proposed that the Council "be reconstituted as the forum through which Member States exercise their *collective trusteeship for the integrity of the global environment and common areas* such as the oceans, atmosphere and outer space. At the same time, it would *serve to link the United Na-*

tions and civil society in addressing these areas of global concern, which require the active contribution of public, private and voluntary sectors."[73] This links collective trusteeship with emerging concepts of global governance. Further elaboration is contained in the Secretary-General's note on a new concept of trusteeship, which supports the concept of a "high-level deliberative forum that could take a comprehensive, strategic and long-term view of global trends and provide policy guidance in those areas to the world community. A new high-level council with a *well-defined mandate that does not create overlaps or conflicts* with existing intergovernmental bodies could serve that purpose."[74]

However, the Secretary-General observes that his note is limited in scope in the light of a newly created task force, chaired by the executive director of UNEP. This Task Force on Environment and Human Settlements, which was established in April 1998 and reported on 15 June 1998,[75] was charged with examining two areas constituting the "missing link" in the Secretary-General's 1997 report on UN reform, human settlement policies and the environment. With respect to the latter, the Task Force report focused on UNEP's work and its relationship to the other UN agencies and programmes, as well as to multilateral convention secretariats.[76] The report noted the proliferation of environmental institutions created in the wake of UNCED, from the Commission on Sustainable Development to the reconstituted Global Environment Facility, as well as the "greening" of existing institutions ranging from the United Nations Educational, Scientific and Cultural Organization (UNESCO) to the Food and Agriculture Organization (FAO).[77] It identified problems of "substantial overlaps, unrecognized linkages and gaps" arising from this proliferation[78] and, as one of 24 recommendations, suggested the establishment of a new body, the "Environmental Management Group (EMG)", to perform an oversight function.[79] Amongst other things, the Task Force envisaged that UNEP would be one of the entities subject to EMG coordination, with the proposal to transfer to the EMG the task of coordination among treaty secretariats, which is currently assigned to UNEP. As for the Trusteeship Council, the Task Force avoided any final recommendations about its possible future use, calling instead for further consultations.[80]

What remains on the table (or up in the air at present) is a relatively modest proposal for a high-level deliberative forum that would not trespass on the mandate of existing Specialized Agencies. Nor would a revamped Council exercise control over any trust *res* as such; that is, no issue arises of the nature and extent of any trust "territories" under its supervision such as global commons areas. Yet, even with such relatively modest proposals for the Council's environmental role, issues concerning the composition of the Council will undoubtedly arise, as will the vital question of the functions and powers of a revamped "Environmental Council". To progress with any such proposals would require amendment of the UN Charter if any alteration in the composition and/or functions of the Trusteeship Council is to be made.[81] Indeed, the need to amend the Charter is one reason this idea, previously proposed in advance of UNCED, was then dropped.[82] Not considered here is amendment of the treaties establishing the Specialized Agencies, although I acknowledge that this might be needed if the trusteeship idea were intended also to reduce "juridical fragmentation" within the UN system. Rather, the proposals in the next section envisage the Trusteeship Council performing an umbrella function, leaving the remit of existing bodies substantially unchanged.

Specific design features of a revamped Trusteeship Council

Quite apart from satisfying the procedural obligations of Article 108 regarding amendment of the UN Charter, a constellation of issues needs to be considered in redesigning the Trusteeship Council. These include: the intended life-span of a revamped Council; the extent of the Charter amendments proposed; the legal relationship between the Charter, as amended, and existing (and future) international environmental agreements; membership of the Council; and, finally, its functions. Membership should be linked with the functions of the Council and serve to realize the twin aims of the Secretary-General's 1997 proposal: effective international environmental governance and performing an oversight function in respect of the global environment.

Duration

Unlike the original trusteeship system, the objectives of which could ultimately be satisfied, the Council would need to function in perpetuity, much like the United Nations itself. Given the normative character of environmental obligations and the continuing capacity of states (and other entities) irrevocably to alter or harm the human environment, there is no prospect of the Council achieving a fixed goal of perfect environmental conditions (a further departure from the traditional notion of the Trusteeship Council). Moreover, if an intergenerational dimension is to be expressly integrated in the functions of the Council, unlimited duration is essential.

Solution: UN Charter amendment, rather than an ad hoc arrangement (e.g. the Environmental Management Group) to improve coordination between treaty institutions.

The scope of Charter amendments

Is it sufficient merely to amend the provisions of Chapters XII and XIII, or is further amendment, e.g. of Article 1 setting out the purposes of the United Nations, required? One precedent is the EC Treaty, which, like the UN Charter, contains no reference to the environment in its original version. In addition to dynamic interpretation by the European Court of Justice, the EC member states moved progressively to amend the Treaties to include, *inter alia*, an Environmental Title with three substantive articles and expansion of the explicitly recognized objectives of the European Communities to include "sustainable development of economic activities" and "a high level of protection and improvement of the quality of the environment".[83] It is doubtful, however, whether the political will exists to revisit the Pandora's box of Article 1, with attention more properly to be devoted to the elucidation of the Trusteeship Council's mandate in an amended Article 87. From a treaty law point of view, it is not necessary to amend Article 1 in order to support amendments to Chapters XII and XIII, not least because of the dynamic and purposive approach to UN Charter interpretation that has been adopted.[84] The establishment of UNEP (1972) and of the Commission on Sustainable Development (1992), both reporting through ECOSOC, are evidence of the recognition of environmental protection as "an essential element in the promotion of social progress and in solving economic and social problems as referred to in Articles 1 and 55".[85]

Solution: Rely on amendment of Chapters XII and XIII alone, without the need to amend Article 1 (purposes).

The relationship between treaty instruments

UN Charter obligations prevail over obligations under any other international agreement (Article 103). This would apply to any amendment of the trusteeship provisions to establish an environmental mandate, unless express wording to the contrary were used. In his 1997 report, the UN Secretary-General specifically called for a well-defined mandate for the revamped Council "that does not create overlaps or conflicts with existing intergovernmental bodies".[86] There are two potentials for conflict: between substantive obligations (addressed in Article 103), and between treaty institutions and mechanisms (not overtly addressed). Reforming the mandate of the Trusteeship Council would be more likely to produce the potential for conflicts of the latter type. Of particular concern is to ensure that the Council *complements* existing supervisory, implementation and enforcement mechanisms.

Solution: Define the Trusteeship Council's mandate so as to preclude overlap with existing treaty norms *and* institutions (see further below under "functions").

Membership

As was indicated in the first section of this chapter, the League Mandates Commission comprised individuals, whereas the Trusteeship Council comprised state representatives, with observer status granted to ECO-SOC and other Specialized Agencies. Should the Council comprise state representatives, elected by the General Assembly for a three-year term on a rolling basis, or a modified League or other approach?

Solution: If the Trusteeship Council is to reflect current concerns regarding global governance as well as perform a representative function in respect of the interests of future generations, its membership should be representative of international civil society. One precedent that might be followed is the composition of the Human Rights Committee of the International Covenant on Civil and Political Rights – individual experts – with observer status for NGOs as well as for ECOSOC, UNEP, FAO, the International Maritime Organization, and other relevant Specialized Agencies and programmes.[87]

Functions

Apart from membership, the functions of the Trusteeship Council are the most crucial issue of Charter amendment. Indeed, unless a revamped Council impacts beneficially upon treaty implementation, it risks merely imposing an additional bureaucratic burden upon treaty institutions and states (proliferation to address the problem of ... proliferation). There are two innovative possible functions.

The first function is oversight of the panorama of treaty instruments and obligations, with the prospect of not only coordinating reporting obligations ("procedural streamlining") but also identifying substantive gaps and overlaps in the present legal regime for the protection of the global environment. An analogy might be drawn with the surveillance of national trade policies conducted under the WTO's Trade Policy Review Mechanism (TPRM). A product of the Uruguay Round of trade negotiations, this mechanism was placed on a firm treaty footing in Article III of the Marrakesh Agreement of 1994. Annex 3 thereof sets out the TPRM, the purpose of which is to ensure the smooth operation of the international trading system through the increased transparency of members' trade policies.[88] All WTO members are subject to such review, the frequency of which is linked to their share of world trade. The European Union, the United States, Japan and Canada are reviewed biennially, and other members are reviewed every four or six years, with further extensions for less developed countries. The report following the review is drafted by the WTO Secretariat, in consultation with the member, and is publicly available on the WTO's website.

Although not every feature of this mechanism is necessarily appropriate for adaptation – for example, the use of two discussants, selected in advance, to stimulate debate of national policies may be considered unnecessary in an Environmental Trusteeship Council of limited membership – the basic concepts of holistic reporting and transparent scrutiny are attractive features worthy of emulation. A reporting and review function is thus included as one of the essential functions of the Trusteeship Council, although the language of the proposed Article 88 is sufficiently flexible to ensure a rolling report pattern that takes account of, *inter alia*, the timing of relevant Conferences of the Parties under environmental treaties and the relative reporting burdens and capacities of states.

The second innovation is not only to provide a forum for active consideration of reports from states and from treaty institutions,[89] but, in addition, to introduce a petition mechanism for, or on behalf of, both present and future generations (proposed Article 87(b)).[90]

It is not proposed to amend Articles 89–91, which encompass voting procedures (one member, one vote, with majority voting), the adoption of rules of procedures, and requesting the assistance of ECOSOC and of UN Specialized Agencies. As under the existing trusteeship system, the Council would operate under the authority of the General Assembly.

Proposed Charter amendments

Chapter XII. International environmental trusteeship system

The bulk of Chapter XII is applicable only to the classical trusteeship system, with trusteeship territories as its focus.[91] For present purposes, some form of Articles 75 and 76 might be retained, setting out the "International environmental trusteeship system" and its basic objectives. Without purporting to be exhaustive, Articles 75 and 76 might include the following:

Article 75: The United Nations shall establish under its authority an international trusteeship system for the protection of the global environment.

Article 76: The basic objectives of the environmental trusteeship system shall be:

(a) to recognise the integral and interdependent nature of the Earth and the necessity for states to cooperate in a spirit of global partnership with key sectors of societies and peoples to conserve, protect and restore the health and integrity of the Earth's ecosystem;

(b) to safeguard the global environment for present and future generations; and

(c) to ensure that international agreements protect and promote the integrity of the global environmental and developmental system and contribute to the achievement of sustainable development.[92]

Chapter XIII. The Trusteeship Council

Composition

Article 86: (1) The Trusteeship Council shall consist of the following members:

(a) Fifteen members elected by the General Assembly, based on equitable geographic representation of the five regional groups.

(b) Election shall be for a three-year term.[93] Outgoing members may be re-elected for one consecutive term. Members of the Council shall be nominated by members of the United Nations and shall serve in their personal capacity. Members shall have recognized competence relating to the environment and in related fields, such as the scientific, technical, socio-economic or legal fields.

(2) Provision shall be made for observer status for non-governmental organizations representing the interests of international civil society in the protection of the global environment and in the promotion of sustainable development. Provision shall also be made for observer status for representatives of UN agencies and specialized programmes with competence in the environment and related fields.

Functions and powers

Article 87:[94] The General Assembly and, under its authority, the Trusteeship Council, in carrying out their functions, may:

(a) consider periodic reports to be submitted by states, by the decision-making organs of relevant international environmental treaties, by UNEP and by such other relevant Specialized Agencies as may from time to time be requested to do so;

(b) accept petitions and examine them in consultation with the relevant authority;

(c) examine progress in reversing environmental deterioration in consultation with the relevant authority;

(d) review the status of each of the designated global environmental areas, keeping in view the overall interest of all the inhabitants of the planet earth, in consultation with decision-making organs of the respective regulatory regimes;

(e) adopt appropriate decisions and other action, as deemed proper, from time to time, consistent with the respective international agreements and mechanisms.

Article 88:[95] The Trusteeship Council shall prepare the form and modalities for submission of periodic reports by those entities cited in Article 87(a). Such reports shall ordinarily be made on a biennial basis to the Trusteeship Council and, through it, to the General Assembly, unless the Trusteeship Council otherwise determines.

Articles 89–91 would remain unchanged.

Conclusion

This chapter has reviewed proposals advanced for reform of the United Nations Trusteeship Council. It has sought to illustrate how such a reformed body might be deployed in improving the effective implementation of international environmental agreements reflecting the common concern of humankind. However, little progress has been made in this direction since proposals for reform were first made two decades ago. Writing late in 1991, Geoffrey Palmer observed: "my reading of the situation ... suggests that there is no political will to take decisions that will give us the tools to do the job."[96] Much the same may be said of the situation over a decade later, with the relatively modest advances at Johannesburg in 2002 suggesting a period of institutional retrenchment rather than radical reform.[97] It is salutary to note the vast representation of non-state actors at the Johannesburg summit and the explosion in public participation in diverse forums. Thus it is perhaps not wholly naïve to suggest that this participation, assuming it brings with it, amongst other things, a universal and intergenerational perspective, will exert pressure to reflect such interests institutionally. Such representation is, of course, but one feature of the universalizing, integrating and intergenerational role that an "Environmental Security Council" would perform in filling an implementation and compliance "gap" in existing environmental treaties.

Notes

1. *Report of the Secretary-General: Renewing the United Nations, A Programme for Reform*, A/51/950, 14 July 1997.

2. That such political will can be generated is evidenced by the environmental treaty regimes that employ reporting and inspection procedures and, more recently, non-compliance mechanisms; see, generally, Malgosia Fitzmaurice and Catherine Redgwell, "Environmental Non-Compliance Procedures and International Law", *Netherlands Yearbook of International Law*, Vol. 31, 2000, pp. 35–65. See further the conclusion, below.

3. For example, the Preamble of the 1992 United Nations Convention on Biological Diversity expressly states that the conservation of biological diversity both within and beyond national jurisdiction is the common concern of humankind, and that its conservation and sustainable use should be for the benefit of present and future generations (Preamble, third and final indents); the 1992 Framework Convention on Climate Change likewise acknowledges that change in the earth's climate and its adverse effects are a common concern of humankind, and that the climate system should be protected for the benefit of present and future generations of humankind (Preamble, first indent, and Article 3(1)).

4. Patricia W. Birnie and Alan E. Boyle, *International Law and the Environment*, 2nd edn, Oxford: Oxford University Press, 2002, p. 97. They continue: "Whereas the 1972 Stockholm Declaration on the Human Environment had simply distinguished between the responsibility for areas within and beyond national jurisdiction, the Rio treaties use the concept of 'common concern' to designate those issues which involve global responsibilities" (ibid., endnotes omitted).

5. Catherine Redgwell, *Intergenerational Trusts and Environmental Protection*, Manchester: Manchester University Press, 1999, p. 147.

6. Alan E. Boyle, "The Rio Convention on Biological Diversity", in Michael Bowman and Catherine Redgwell, eds, *International Law and the Conservation of Biological Diversity*, London: Kluwer Law International, 1996, p. 40; see also Alan E. Boyle, "International Law and the Protection of the Global Atmosphere: Concepts, Categories and Principles", in Robin R. Churchill and David Freestone, eds, *International Law and Global Climate Change*, London: Kluwer Law International, 1991, pp. 11–13. On the legal implications of the "common concern" concept, which remain unsettled, see Birnie and Boyle, *International Law and the Environment*, pp. 98–99.

7. See the 1979 Moon Treaty and the 1982 Law of the Sea Convention, for example.

8. Alexandre Kiss, "La Notion de patrimonie commun de l'humanité", *Recueil des Cours, Academie de Droit International*, Vol. 175, 1985.

9. Yves Berthelot suggests that enhancing the role of international institutions is one method for achieving such aims: "Are International Institutions in Favour of the Environment?", in Luigi Campiglio et al., eds, *The Environment after Rio: International Law and Economics*, London/Dordrecht/Boston: Graham & Trotman/Martinus Nijhoff, 1994, p. 275.

10. For discussion of the current status and functions of the Trusteeship Council, see further below.

11. So characterized by Birnie and Boyle, *International Law and the Environment*, p. 203.

12. See also Chapter XI, which contains the Declaration Regarding Non-Self-Governing Territories. Under Article 73, members of the United Nations recognize the principle that the interests of the inhabitants of non-self-governing territories are paramount in the administration of those territories and it makes explicit reference to "a sacred trust". The basic objectives of the trusteeship system are then set out in Article 76 (Chapter XII), which reflects the fundamental principles declared in Article 73 and constitutes the obligations of the trustee.

13. Charter of the United Nations, 26 June 1945, Article 76(b).

14. H. Duncan Hall, *Mandates, Dependencies and Trusteeship*, London: Stevens, 1948,

p. 277; Dietrich Rauschning, "United Nations Trusteeship System", in Bruno Simma, ed., *The Charter of the United Nations: A Commentary*, 2nd edn, Oxford: Oxford University Press, 2002, p. 1102.

15. All surviving League-mandated territories were placed under the UN trusteeship system, save for the territories soon to become independent, namely Iraq, Syria, Lebanon, Israel and Jordan. South West Africa eventually achieved independence as Namibia in 1990 after a lengthy dispute between South Africa and first the League and then the United Nations over its status. In 1966 the UN General Assembly terminated South Africa's mandate (UNGA Res. 2145 (XXI), which was confirmed by the International Court of Justice in its Advisory Opinion *Legal Consequences for States of the Continued Presence of South Africa in Namibia (South West Africa)*, 21 June 2001). For discussion of the special petitions system established for South West Africa after 1945, see further Carl A. Norgaard, *The Position of the Individual in International Law*, Copenhagen: Munksgaard Press, 1964, pp. 128–131.

16. See Robert Jennings and Arthur Watts, *Oppenheim's International Law*, 9th edn, London: Longman, 1992, Vol. 1, Part 1, p. 308 et seq.

17. For detailed discussion of these three categories, see C. V. Lakshminarayan, "Analysis of the Principles and System of International Trusteeship in the Charter", thesis, University of Geneva, Institut de Hautes Etudes Internationales, 1951, Chapter IV.

18. *Petitions from the International League for Peace and Freedom*, T/PET/General/15, Geneva, 4 October 1947, T/PET/General/16, Copenhagen, 4 October 1947, and T/PET/General/18, Helsinki, 9 October 1947.

19. At least one multilateral treaty has taken into account the possibility of such United Nations administration under Article 81 of the Charter: see the 1969 Convention Relating to Intervention on the High Seas in Cases of Oil Pollution Casualties (Article XIII.1).

20. Although the three governments of the United Kingdom, New Zealand and Australia formed the administering authority for Nauru, in practice it was Australia that acted in the day-to-day administration of the trusteeship; see the submissions of counsel for Nauru, Professor Crawford, at CR 91/20, 19 November 1991, pp. 75–76, quoted in the separate opinion of Judge Shahabuddeen in the *Case Concerning Certain Phosphate Lands in Nauru (Nauru v. Australia), Preliminary Objections*, [1992] ICJ Reports, p. 280. The majority of the Court in that case rejected the Australian objection to the admissibility of Nauru's claim on the basis that New Zealand and the United Kingdom were not parties to the proceedings; see ibid., p. 262, para. 57; but on this point see the dissenting opinion of Judge Schwebel, p. 329 et seq.

21. In the *Northern Cameroons Case*, [1963] ICJ Reports 15, the Court considered the legal status of the trusteeship agreement to be an international agreement with a treaty character; in the *South West Africa Cases*, [1962] ICJ Reports 330, the Court likewise viewed "the Mandate, in fact and in law, [as] an international agreement having the character of a treaty or convention" between the League Council and South Africa (*Advisory Opinion on the International Status of South West Africa*, [1950] ICJ Reports 128, p. 133).

22. Ultimately this phrase was left undefined in the Charter; for discussion of the efforts at the San Francisco Conference to define it, see Lakshminarayan, "Analysis of the Principles and System of International Trusteeship in the Charter", pp. 111–115.

23. Be they the inhabitants of the trust territory or, perhaps more generally, humankind.

24. For further discussion of the objectives of trusteeship agreements as set out in Article 76, see Rauschning, "United Nations Trusteeship System", pp. 1106–1114.

25. In addition, in 1947 the Trusteeship Council approved provisionally a questionnaire that, pursuant to Article 88 of the UN Charter, formed the basis for annual reports by the administering authorities to the General Assembly. It included questions of broad environmental concern such as housing and town planning, public health, and sanita-

tion. For further description of the trusteeship agreements and the questionnaire, see Jennings and Watts, *Oppenheim's International Law*, pp. 310–311, n4 and p. 315, n4.

26. Ramendra N. Chowdhuri, *International Mandates and Trusteeships: A Comparative Study*, The Hague: Martinus Nijhoff, 1955, p. 305.

27. *Trusteeship Agreement for the Former Japanese Mandated Islands*, No. 123, 2 April 1947, Article 6, para 2.

28. Under Article 85 of the UN Charter. On 13 December 1946 the first eight trusteeship agreements were approved by the General Assembly by Resolution 63(I).

29. UN Charter, Article 83.

30. In 1949, the United Nations General Assembly passed a resolution requiring the Trusteeship Council to recommend to all administering governments that the UN flag be flown alongside the flags of the administering authority and (if any) the trust territory; Jennings and Watts, *Oppenheim's International Law*, p. 318 (UNGA Res. 325(IV) (1949)). This was a visual representation of the relationship between the United Nations as the depositary of "residuary sovereignty" and the administering authority *qua* trustee exercising sovereignty over the territory subject to the supervision of the United Nations; ibid., p. 316.

31. UN Charter, Article 87.

32. UN Charter, Article 86(1)(b).

33. UN Charter, Article 90.

34. Chowdhuri, *International Mandates and Trusteeships*, p. 301; Rauschning, "United Nations Trusteeship System", p. 1100.

35. The Covenant of the League of Nations, Article 22, para. 9. The reporting function was preserved by Article 80 of the UN Charter, the "conservatory clause", which was relied upon by the ICJ in its *Advisory Opinion on the International Status of South West Africa*, 1950, pp. 133–134 and 136–137; for further discussion of Article 80 see Rauschning, "United Nations Trusteeship System", pp. 1121–1122.

36. UN Charter, Article 91.

37. See, further, Norgaard, *The Position of the Individual in International Law*, pp. 133–136.

38. Article 28, para. 2, of the Covenant of the League of Nations requires that the Committee be composed of "nationals of the State Parties to the present Covenant who shall be persons of high moral character and recognized competence in the field of human rights, consideration having been given to the usefulness of the participation of some persons having legal experience"; Article 28, para. 3, provides that such members "shall be elected and shall serve in their national capacity".

39. Article 71 of the UN Charter laid the groundwork in permitting ECOSOC to "make suitable arrangements for consultation with non-governmental organizations which are concerned with matters within its competence" (it may also make arrangements for representatives of Specialized Agencies and programmes – e.g. UNEP – to participate, without vote, in its deliberations (Article 70)). ECOSOC Resolution 1996/31 sets out the principles that currently govern non-governmental organization consultative status in ECOSOC; see, further, ⟨http://www.un.org/esa/coordination/ngo/⟩. In 1946 there were 41 organizations with such status, whereas today there are over 2,350.

40. See A. Gowlland, "The Environmental Accountability of the World Bank to Non-State Actors: Insights from the Inspection Panel", *British Yearbook of International Law*, Vol. 72, 2002, p. 213, and ⟨http://www.worldbank.org⟩. An eminent international environmental lawyer, Professor Edith Brown Weiss, is currently the president of the Panel.

41. Edith Brown Weiss, *In Fairness to Future Generations: International Law, Common Patrimony and Intergenerational Equity*, New York/Tokyo: UNU/Transnational Publishing, 1989, pp. 124–126. The rights of future generations may be preserved in the present through the appointment of "planetary commissioners", or trustees, to represent the

interests of future generations. See also Glen Plant, "Institutional and Legal Responses to Global Warming", in Churchill and Freestone, eds, *International Law and Global Climate Change*, p. 176 (who considers the creation of an international environmental ombudsperson to represent the interests of future generations, preferably, in his view, under UN General Assembly control).

42. Weiss, *In Fairness to Future Generations*, pp. 120–123. *Minors Oposa* v. *Secretary of the Department of Environment and Natural Resources, International Legal Materials*, Vol. 33, 1994, p. 173, might be seen as an example, although there the children acted on behalf, and as representatives, of future generations, rather than an institutional representative of future interests such as a trustee or ombudsperson performing this function. Lawrence Susskind (*Environmental Diplomacy*, Oxford: Oxford University Press, 1994) is rightly much more sceptical about the possibilities for the representation of future generations in other contexts, such as treaty negotiations.

43. Prepared by the Advisory Committee established to the United Nations University Project on "International Law, Common Patrimony and Intergenerational Equity", reproduced in Weiss, *In Fairness to Future Generations*, Appendix A. In particular, a seven-point strategy for implementing intergenerational equity is suggested, including: (a) representation by states not only of present but also of future generations; (b) designation of ombudsmen or commissioners for protecting the interests of future generations; (c) monitoring systems for cultural and natural resources; and (d) conservation assessments giving particular attention to long-term consequences. See also Edith Brown Weiss, "The Planetary Trust: Conservation and Equity Between Generations", *Ecology Law Quarterly*, Vol. 11, 1984; and "Proposals for Strengthening the Legal and Institutional Framework" recommended to the World Commission on Environment and Development by the Experts Group on Environmental Law, reproduced in R. D. Munro and Johan G. Lammers, eds, *Environmental Protection and Sustainable Development: Legal Principles and Recommendations Adopted by the Experts Group on Environmental Law of the World Commission on Environment and Development*, London: Graham & Trotman, 1986.

44. Christopher Stone, "Defending the Global Commons", in Philippe Sands, ed., *Greening International Law*, London: Earthscan, 1993, p. 40; see also Christopher Stone, *The Gnat Is Older Than Man: Global Environment and Human Agenda*, Princeton, NJ: Princeton University Press, 1993, pp. 83–88.

45. For an overview of UNEP's environmental law-making activities, see Birnie and Boyle, *International Law and the Environment*; see also Ved P. Nanda, "Environment", in Christopher C. Joyner, ed., *The United Nations and International Law*, Cambridge: Cambridge University Press, 1997.

46. Stone, "Defending the Global Commons". Stone first put forward the concept of guardians of natural objects in his seminal article "Should Trees Have Standing: Towards Legal Rights for Natural Objects", *Southern California Law Review*, Vol. 45, 1972, p. 450.

47. David Wood, "Intergenerational Equity and Climate Change", *Georgetown International Environmental Law Review*, Vol. 8, No. 2, 1996, pp. 302–303. See also David Tolbert, "Global Climate Change and the Role of International Non-Governmental Organisations", in Churchill and Freestone, eds, *International Law and Global Climate Change*, pp. 100–101 ("NGOs as Ombudsmen for, or Guardians of, the Environment"); and Philippe Sands, "The Environment, Community and International Law", *Harvard International Law Journal*, Vol. 30, 1989, p. 394 (NGOs as "guardians of the environment").

48. Steve Charnovitz, "Two Centuries of Participation: NGOs and International Governance", *Michigan Journal of International Law*, Vol. 18, 1997, p. 274; see also David

Tarlock, "The Role of Non-Governmental Organisations in the Development of International Environmental Law", *Chicago-Kent Law Review*, Vol. 68, 1993, p. 61; K. Raustiala, "The 'Participatory Revolution' in International Environmental Law", *Harvard Environmental Law Review*, Vol. 21, 1997, p. 537; United Nations Conference on Environment and Development (UNCED), *Agenda 21*, A/CONF.151/26 (vol. III), 1992, Chapters 23–32 ("Strengthening the Role of Major Groups").

49. Susskind, *Environmental Diplomacy*, pp. 54–55.

50. Commission on Global Governance, *Our Global Neighbourhood: The Report of the Commission on Global Governance*, Oxford: Oxford University Press, 1995, p. 254.

51. UNCED, *Agenda 21*. See George (Rock) Pring and Susan Noe, "The Emerging International Law of Public Participation Affecting Global Mining, Energy, and Resources Development", in *Human Rights in Natural Resource Development: Public Participation in Sustainable Development of Mining and Energy Resources*, Oxford: Oxford University Press, 2002; and, more generally, J. Ebbesson, "The Notion of Public Participation in International Environmental Law", *Yearbook of International Environmental Law*, Vol. 8, 1997, p. 51.

52. See also Richard Bilder, "The Settlement of Disputes in the Field of the International Law of the Environment", *Recueil des Cours, Academie de Droit International*, Vol. 144, No. 1, 1975, p. 231 ("perhaps international organizations, such as UNEP, acting as agents of the international community, may take measures to protect its interests").

53. The report also recommends that a special UN Commission for Environmental Protection and Sustainable Development be established under a Convention on the same; Experts Group on Environmental Law, "Proposals for Strengthening the Legal and Institutional Framework", in Munro and Lammers, eds, *Environmental Protection and Sustainable Development*, p. 15.

54. Nico Schrijver, "International Organization for Environmental Security", *Bulletin of Peace Proposals*, Vol. 20, No. 2, 1989, pp. 120–121; see also the "forms of new institutional authority" canvassed in Catherine Tinker, "Environmental Planet Management by the United Nations: An Idea Whose Time Has Not Yet Come?", *New York University Journal of International Law and Politics*, Vol. 22, 1990, pp. 821–827.

55. Geping Rao, "The United Nations as a Guardian for Future Generations", in Emmanuel Agius and Salvino Busutti, eds, *Future Generations & International Law*, London: Earthscan, 1998.

56. Weiss, *In Fairness to Future Generations*.

57. Patricia Birnie, "International Environmental Law: Its Adequacy for Present and Future Needs", in Andrew Hurrell and Benedict Kingsbury, eds, *The International Politics of the Environment: Actors, Interests, and Institutions*, Oxford: Clarendon Press, 1992, p. 79; Susskind, *Environmental Diplomacy*.

58. Birnie, "International Environmental Law", p. 79.

59. At the national level, France appointed a "Council for Future Generations" to offer advice on its own initiative, or to be consulted, where planned activities impact on the rights of future generations. See Decret No. 93-298, of 8 March 1993, *Journal Officiel de la Republique Francaise*, 10 March 1993, cited in Alexandre Kiss, "The Rights and Interests of Future Generations", in David Freestone and Ellen Hey, eds, *The Precautionary Principle and International Law: The Challenge of Implementation*, The Hague: Kluwer Law International, 1996, p. 26.

60. There are as yet only glimmerings of generational claims being recognized on the international level evident in *Case Concerning Certain Phosphate Lands in Nauru*; and the *Advisory Opinion on the Legality of the Threat or Use of Nuclear Weapons*, [1996] ICJ Reports 266. See also *LCB v UK*, 27 EHRR (1999) 212, discussed in Birnie and Boyle, *International Law and the Environment*, p. 91, n98. None constitutes express international judicial recognition of the rights of future generations.

61. UNCED, *Agenda 21*, Chapter 38, paras. 11–14. For the work of the CSD, see ⟨http:// www.un.org/esa/sustdev/csd/⟩.

62. First Report of the ILA International Committee on Legal Aspects of Sustainable Development, in *Report of the Sixty-Sixth Conference of the ILA*, London: International Law Association, 1995, p. 120.

63. David VanderZwaag, *Canada and Marine Environmental Protection: Charting a Course towards Sustainable Development*, London: Kluwer Law International, 1995, p. 34, n143, citing M. P. A. Kindall, "UNCED and the Evolution of Principles of Environmental Law", *John Marshall Law Review*, Vol. 25, 1991, p. 27. See also Birnie and Boyle, *International Law and the Environment*, p. 51; and note 70 below.

64. Also noted was the proposal to establish a non-governmental Earth Council and other initiatives taken by local government and business; UNCED, *Agenda 21*, Chapter 38, para. 45. See Nicholas Robinson, ed., *Agenda 21: Earth's Action Plan (Annotated)*, New York/London/Rome: Ocean Publications, 1993, p. 619.

65. For discussion of UNEP's role since UNCED, see Birnie and Boyle, *International Law and the Environment*, pp. 53–58; and B. H. Desai, "Revitalising International Environmental Institutions: The UN Task Force Report and Beyond", *Indian Journal of International Law*, Vol. 40, No. 3, 2000, pp. 478–481.

66. UNCED, *Agenda 21*, Chapter 38, para. 13(f); see also the mandate and functions of the CSD, agreed in 1993 and reaffirmed at Johannesburg in 2002, contained in *Institutional Arrangements to Follow up on the UN Conference on Environment and Development*, UNGA Res. A/47/719, 29 January 1993, para. 3(h) of which simply reiterates the wording of Chapter 38, para. 13(f). The language of Chapter 38, para. 13(f) is weaker than one of the proposed alternatives, which would have empowered the Commission "to consider reports presented by relevant treaty bodies on the implementation of environmental conventions"; see Robinson, *Agenda 21*, p. 610, n4. National reporting to the CSD occurs on a voluntary basis, in accordance with national reporting guidelines established by the CSD secretariat (The Eleventh Session of the Commission on Sustainable Development, 2003; see ⟨http://www.un.org/esa/sustdev/csd/⟩).

67. *Programme for the Further Implementation of Agenda 21*, A/RES/S-19/2, 28 June 1997.

68. Birnie and Boyle, *International Law and the Environment*, p. 54.

69. Concluding statement of the General Assembly President, A/45/PV.82, 1991, p. 21, cited in Carolyn L. Willson, "Changing the Charter: The United Nations Prepares for the Twenty-First Century", *American Journal of International Law*, Vol. 90, 1996, p. 122.

70. *Review of the Role of the Trusteeship Council*, 87th Plenary Meeting, A/50/142, 11 December 1995.

71. Commission on Global Governance, *Our Global Neighbourhood*, p. 216.

72. UN Press Release SG/SM/6428; see further discussion by Lee Kimball, "Institutional Developments", *Yearbook of International Environmental Law*, Vol. 8, 1997.

73. *Report of the Secretary-General: Renewing the United Nations*, para. 85 (emphasis added).

74. Note by the Secretary-General, *A New Concept of Trusteeship*, A/52/849, 31 March 1998 (emphasis added).

75. For analysis see Desai, "Revitalising International Environmental Institutions", pp. 478–481.

76. *The Report of the United Nations Task Force on Environment and Human Settlements to the Secretary-General*, 1998, annexed in the *Report of the Secretary-General: United Nations Reform – Measures and Proposals – Environment and Human Settlements*, A/53/463, 6 October 1998.

77. See, generally, Jacob Werksman, ed., *Greening International Institutions*, London: Earthscan, 1996.

78. *The Report of the United Nations Task Force on Environment and Human Settlements*,

Annex, para. 20. On "treaty congestion", see Edith Brown Weiss, "International Environmental Law: Contemporary Issues and the Emergence of a New World Order", *Georgetown University Law Journal*, Vol. 81, No. 3, 1993, p. 675.

79. This is suggested as a replacement for the Inter-Agency Environmental Coordination Group (IAECG); see *The Report of the United Nations Task Force on Environment and Human Settlements, Recommendation 1*, para. 22.

80. *The Report of the United Nations Task Force on Environment and Human Settlements*, Annex, para. 20.

81. Under Article 108 of the Charter, an amendment to the Charter will enter into force only when three conditions are met: (i) the amendment must have been adopted by a vote of two-thirds of the members of the General Assembly; (ii) two-thirds of the members of the United Nations must ratify the Charter amendment in accordance with their respective constitutional processes; and (iii) this two-thirds majority must include all the permanent members of the Security Council.

82. Paul Szasz, "Restructuring the International Organizational Framework", in Edith Brown Weiss, ed., *Environmental Change and International Law: New Challenges and Dimensions*, Tokyo: United Nations University Press, 1992, p. 362.

83. EC Treaty, Article 2. The Environmental Title was added through the first significant amendment of the EC Treaty by the 1986 Single European Act (Title VII). See, further, Joanne Scott, *EC Environmental Law*, London: Longman, 1998, Chap. 1.

84. See, for example, *Reparations for Injuries Case*, [1949] ICJ Reports 174, p. 180 (implied powers/principle of effectiveness).

85. Birnie and Boyle, *International Law and the Environment*, p. 48; see also Simma, ed., *The Charter of the United Nations: A Commentary*.

86. *Report of the Secretary-General: Renewing the United Nations*, para. 85.

87. There already exists a *general* forum for cooperation through the UN system Chief Executives Board (CEB) for Coordination. This comprises the executive heads of the UN Specialized Agencies and programmes (27 in total), who meet biannually to promote "cooperation within the UN family in the pursuit of the common goals of Member States across a range of substantive and management issues" (see ⟨http://ceb.unsystem. org/⟩). The renewed emphasis on implementation issues at the WSSD Johannesburg summit in 2002 led to the CEB being specifically charged with addressing inter-agency coordination in the area of sustainable development, although no specific measures have yet been implemented.

88. See, further, ⟨http://www.wto.org⟩ (trade policy review).

89. As Bodansky notes, comparatively few international environmental treaties have specific arrangements for *review* of reports; Daniel Bodansky, "The Role of Reporting in International Environmental Treaties: Lessons for Human Rights Supervision", in Philip Alston and James Crawford, eds, *The Future of UN Human Rights Treaty Monitoring*, Cambridge: Cambridge University Press, 2000, p. 370.

90. In addition, this mechanism could be adapted for use by environmental treaty instruments lacking an implementation committee or non-compliance procedure.

91. What follows is inspired in part by Desai's suggestions for amendment of the UN Charter, setting out the new mandate for the Trusteeship Council (and in the light of suggestions for a much-strengthened UNEP, here referred to as the United Nations Environment Protection Organization, "UNEPO"). Desai's proposed amendments are as follows ("Revitalising International Environmental Institutions", pp. 501–502):

Article 87: The General Assembly and, under its authority, the Trusteeship Council, in carrying out their functions, may:
(a) consider reports submitted by the UNEPO;

(b) examine progress in reversing environmental deterioration in consultation with UNEPO;

(c) review the status of each of the designated global commons keeping in view the overall interest of all the inhabitants of the planet earth, in consultation with decision-making organs of the respective regulatory regimes;

(d) adopt appropriate decisions and other action, as deemed proper, from time to time, consistent with the respective international agreements and mechanisms.

Article 88: The Trusteeship Council shall prepare the form and modalities for submission of periodic reports by each regulatory regime of the global commons areas. The decision-making organs of the respective regimes shall make an annual report to the Trusteeship Council and, through it, to the General Assembly.

92. It should be noted that (a) embraces current wider notions of participation by international civil society; (b) introduces an expressly intergenerational focus, and is equally attentive to intragenerational equity; and (c) emphasizes the integrative and oversight function of the Council. "International agreement" is used advisedly, to ensure that the Council is not expressly limited in its oversight to international *environmental* agreements (and the definitional/boundary difficulties to which such precision would inevitably give rise) and explicitly embraces sustainable development.

93. An additional provision should be inserted for variable periods of initial election to ensure some continuity of membership.

94. See note 91 above.

95. See note 91 above.

96. Geoffrey Palmer, "New Ways to Make Environmental Law", *American Journal of International Law*, Vol. 86, 1992, p. 259. He expressly considers the "institutional gap", observing that, whereas many of the problems resulting from the absence of a strong multilateral international environmental institution are widely recognized, "the logical inference from the facts seems politically unpalatable: the only way to cure the problem is to create a proper international environmental agency within the United Nations system that has real power and authority" (ibid., p. 262). In 1989, New Zealand proposed the establishment of an Environmental Protection Council; see, further, the discussion in Palmer, "New Ways to Make Environmental Law", p. 279.

97. For an overview of the Johannesburg summit, see Kevin R. Gray, "World Summit on Sustainable Development: Accomplishments and New Directions?", *International and Comparative Law Quarterly*, Vol. 52, 2003, pp. 256–268.

8

Expanding the mandate of the United Nations Security Council

Lorraine Elliott

Introduction

The mandate of the United Nations Security Council is the maintenance of international peace and security. The range of actions the Security Council can take in meeting this responsibility is based on Chapters VI and VII of the UN Charter, and is expanded by the normative and operational precedent established by actual Council practice on behalf of the international community of states. In determining the kinds of actions that will meet this mandate, the Council has to take into account the norms of international law, including (but not confined to) the laws of war and international humanitarian law. Both the United Nations in general and the Security Council in particular face demands for reform, on the grounds that they are undemocratic and administratively and normatively ill equipped to deal with contemporary challenges, including environmental ones.

Questions about whether the Security Council's mandate can or should be expanded to take account of environmental issues have arisen against the backdrop of a re-evaluation of what it means to be secure in a post–Cold War world and how best to achieve this. This re-evaluation has been motivated by the collapse of the familiar bipolarity of the latter half of the twentieth century and the need to understand new configurations of power and the changing nature of threats. A range of problems (or risk environments) bound up with the complex and confusing processes and consequences of globalization and fragmentation are now being defined as possible sources of violence and instability, intra- and inter-state conflict, transgression of state borders, and threats to international peace and security. This re-examination of security – for whom and from what – has also encouraged a rethinking of where the locus of security lies. Traditional approaches focus on the state, even if the threats are now understood to be non-traditional ones (that is, other than military or geopolitical challenges). At the same time, and often in tension with the traditional approaches, scholars and policy makers have paid attention to human security and the ways in which war and violence, but also economic and social threats, destabilize and make insecure the lives of people and communities. Environmental degradation is now widely accepted as one such possible threat to state security, to human security and to international peace and security.

This raises a number of important issues for the Security Council and for its prominent role in ensuring and maintaining international peace and security. There is nothing specific in the Council's mandate that directs it to address environmental insecurities and threats. The Security Council mandate can be amended through formal amendment to the UN Charter. Although Parkin argues that "environmental problems offer an impeccable motive for refreshing the United Nations Charter",[1] Charter amendment is an unusual event that is difficult to achieve and highly politicized. Expansion of the Security Council mandate to accommodate environmental security challenges is much more likely through an interpretive process that constitutes what Justice Roslyn Higgins has called "lawful, imaginative adaptations to contemporary needs".[2] This chapter examines the kinds of environmental challenges that might warrant Security Council attention and assesses how those concerns fit within the Council's mandate for maintaining international peace and security. In his *Millennium Report*, Secretary-General Kofi Annan identified a number of strategies crucial to the pursuit of peace and security in the twenty-first century.[3] These included preventing deadly conflict, strengthening the centrality of international humanitarian law, targeting sanctions and strengthening peace operations. Together these outline a useful and manageable framework for the expansion of the Security Council's mandate to address the environmental causes and consequences of conflict and to contribute to international environmental governance.

United Nations Security Council

Article 24 of the UN Charter establishes the Security Council's principal mandate for the maintenance of international peace and security on behalf of the UN members. Article 39 provides the Security Council's mandate to determine what constitutes a threat to the peace, a breach of the peace or an act of aggression. Chapters VI (on the peaceful settlement of disputes) and VII (on action with respect to threats to the peace, breaches of the peace and acts of aggression) provide the Council with its operational guidelines. Together these chapters provide the Security Council with a suite of options for action in the face of events that might endanger the maintenance of international peace and security. These range from investigation of a dispute, enjoining parties to settle their dispute peacefully, recommending the terms of a settlement, establishing compliance measures, imposing sanctions, and taking such action based on the use of force as may be necessary. In exercising its mandate, the Security Council is required to respect the fundamental international legal principle of non-interference in the internal affairs of member states. In practice, this has come to require the consent of sovereign governments before forces under UN mandate can be deployed "on the ground".

Despite the apparently broad power of Article 39, for much of the life of the United Nations the international legal norm was that threats to peace and security were to be closely defined as military aggression, armed conflict or violence between two or more states. Under the UN Charter and the laws of war, the legitimate grounds for the use of force and for UN intervention were self-defence and collective security. Since the end of the Cold War and the relaxing of the veto, the Security Council has overseen Chapter VII interventions in what would in earlier times have been determined as the internal affairs of sovereign states and therefore out of bounds. It has done so on grounds other than those of armed conflict between states or an attack against a member state and, in some cases, has acted to protect citizens and others *against* the state, sometimes without the consent of the state in question.[4] The UN Secretary-General and the Security Council have also come to place greater rhetorical emphasis at least on a culture of prevention – including early warning, preventive diplomacy, preventive deployment as well as post-conflict peace-building – as the best means for achieving and maintaining international peace and security.[5] It is within this context that this chapter examines how the Security Council mandate can or could be expanded to accommodate environmental threats.

Environmental "threats"

The relationship between environmental degradation and the maintenance of international peace and security is captured in the phrase "environmental security". The term has been part of the international policy lexicon since the late 1980s. It was first used in the UN context, expressed as "ecological security", by what were then the Soviet bloc countries. The purpose here is not to revisit the debates about the intellectual and policy usefulness of the term, but a very brief tour of the major themes is warranted. The dominant area for investigation is the extent to which environmental degradation[6] or resource scarcity – non-military threats – will generate or intensify conflict, violence and instability between and within states. Although such research draws for its initial legitimacy on historical example, investigators have come to focus on the "new" strategic and potentially scarce resources such as fresh water, arable land and environmental services, including clean air and ecosystem viability. The causal relationship is a matter of some dispute, but includes actual or potential environmental scarcity, including the loss of natural resources and environmental services; "differences in environmental endowment";[7] the disruption of social and political relations; population pressures and the involuntary movement of peoples (environmental refugees).[8] The environmental security literature also draws attention to damage to the environment in times of armed conflict through the deliberate targeting of environmental facilities or as an unintended consequence or collateral damage.

There are worries within the traditional security community and the more critical environmental community that the linking of "environment" with "security" will either make the term security "so elastic as to detract seriously from its utility as an analytical tool"[9] or lock environmental challenges into the "emotive power of nationalism".[10] Despite these concerns, there is now good evidence that environmental degradation has been accepted as a potential if not actual threat to peace and security. The 1987 report of the World Commission on Environment and Development (the Brundtland Report) argued that "the whole notion of security as traditionally understood ... must be expanded to include the growing impacts of environmental stress".[11] Principle 24 of the 1992 Rio Declaration, adopted at the United Nations Conference on Environment and Development, declares warfare to be inherently destructive of the environment. Principle 25 observes that "peace, development and environmental protection are interdependent and indivisible", and Principle 26, echoing the injunctions of the UN Charter, requires that states should solve their environmental disputes peacefully.[12]

As early as 1991, the US National Security Strategy (NSS) acknowledged that "the stress from ... environmental challenges is ... contributing to political conflict",[13] and more recent NSS reports have reconfirmed this concern.[14] In a 1994 speech, then Secretary of State Warren Christopher identified environmental security, in company with terrorism and nuclear proliferation, as key issues of strategic importance to US and international security.[15] NATO's Strategic Concept observes that "security and stability have ... environmental elements as well as the indispensable defence dimensions".[16]

The relationship between environmental degradation and security has also featured in UN documents. The UN Secretary-General's *Agenda for Peace* identified ecological damage as a new risk for stability.[17] The *Millennium Report* identified a "real risk that resource depletion, especially freshwater scarcities, as well as severe forms of environmental degradation, may increase social and political tensions in unpredictable but potentially dangerous ways".[18] The 1992 Communiqué of the Security Council Summit of Heads of State and Government declared that "non-military sources of instability in the economic, social, humanitarian and ecological fields have become threats to the peace and security".[19] This suggests that the Council anticipated some authority over environment-related threats to peace and security.

The Security Council's environmental mandate: A repertoire of options

The Security Council's mandate is *already* being reinterpreted to accommodate non-traditional threats to peace and security such as complex humanitarian emergencies and gross abuse of human rights. Further attention is required to determine which environment-related circumstances might invoke or require a response, particularly a military one, under Security Council auspices and on what basis the Council would have a mandate for such action. Such action would involve an interpretive extension of the Security Council mandate relying in part on analogy with intervention on human rights grounds. It draws our attention to what is, in effect, a normative development of the *jus ad bellum* – the reasons for which states, and by extension the international community of states, might legitimately deploy force.

An environmental mandate in times of armed conflict

Security Council resolutions have clearly come to articulate a more expansive view of what constitutes a threat to international peace and security, including the consequences of the repression of civilian populations (Resolution 688) and humanitarian emergencies and the violation of international humanitarian law (Resolution 794).[20] This reinterpretation now also accommodates environment- and resource-related concerns. The Secretary-General's 1998 report on conflict and peace in Africa identifies "competition for scarce land and water resources" as a factor in conflict in Central Africa.[21] Extensive starvation in Somalia and Liberia – in both cases having broadly environmental and resource causes – has been implicated in the conflict in those countries. The Commission on Global Governance identified environmental deterioration along with population pressures as factors in the "social breakdown and internal conflict in Somalia, Rwanda and Haiti".[22] There is also a view that environmental scarcity was implicated in the intra-state conflict and genocide in Rwanda in 1994.[23]

In the case of already existing inter-state armed conflict that arose partially or predominantly because of environmental or resource depletion, it is within the Security Council's mandate under Article 39 to determine that the conflict itself constitutes the threat to peace and security and act accordingly. A more contentious issue is whether the Security Council has or should have a mandate to act when environmental degradation or resource depletion is determined to be a key cause of or antecedent to violence *within* a state and, if it does, what kind of action would be most appropriate. The precedent for expanding a mandate for such intervention would almost certainly need to rely on analogy with humanitarian intervention. The Security Council could determine, under Article 39, that environmental degradation or resource depletion and the resulting violence or armed conflict constituted a gross abuse of human rights. However, this determination would require more certainty in international law than presently exists about whether there is a recognized human right to a clean and safe environment. At present, such claims are articulated almost entirely in soft-law declarations or in formal agreements and treaties other than human rights law.[24]

The developing norm of human security, again by analogy with humanitarian intervention, offers scope for invoking Security Council action or expanding its mandate with respect to environmental degradation. The United Nations Development Programme has clearly articulated a view that environmental degradation is a non-military threat to human well-being.[25] Threats to international peace and security, which allow for a Security Council determination under Article 39, could therefore encompass those activities that undermine human security. Through the Global Policy Forum, the Security Council has become more open to working with non-governmental organizations (NGOs) to examine ways in which human security could be made more relevant to its mandate. Nevertheless, the phrase itself does not appear in Security Council resolutions and there are strongly differing views about whether its mandate to act can accommodate such a "liberal" interpretation of security.

A much stronger basis for confirming that the Security Council has a mandate under Chapter VII to act to protect the environment or to protect states and/or individuals from environmental degradation in times of armed conflict is provided by international humanitarian law and the laws of war. The International Committee of the Red Cross (ICRC) has confirmed environmental protection in times of armed conflict to be a fundamental tenet of the laws of war and international humanitarian law.

The 1977 Convention on the Prohibition of Military or Other Hostile Use of Environmental Modification Techniques (ENMOD) is the main piece of international law that specifically covers protection of the environment during times of armed conflict. However, Article 1 places restrictions on only those military or hostile uses of environmental modification practices that have "widespread, long-lasting or severe effects" as a means of destroying, damaging or injuring any other state which is party to the Convention.[26] Optional Protocol I to the 1949 Geneva Conventions adopts similar language, requiring combatants to limit environmental destruction, language that is often described as "vague and permissive".[27] Article 35 of the Protocol prohibits methods of warfare that are "intended or may be expected to cause widespread, long-term and severe damage to the natural environment". Article 55 reinforces this injunction and further links such damage to "the health or survival of the population". Such practices are not, however, listed as grave breaches of the Protocol or the Geneva Conventions (and, thereby, a war crime) under Article 85. This has been rectified in the Rome Statute establishing the International Criminal Court. Article 8(2)(b)(iv) includes in its definition of war crimes "intentionally launching an attack in the knowledge that such attack will cause ... widespread, long-term and severe damage to the natural environment which would clearly be excessive ... to the overall military advantage anticipated".[28] The tests of what constitutes "widespread", "long-term", "severe" and "excessive" are interpretive but together these agreements confirm that "destruction of the environment not justified by military necessity violates international humanitarian law".[29] General Assembly Resolution 47/37 (1992) on the destruction of the environment in times of armed conflict employs similar terminology.[30]

Other legal statements give further strength to the view that the international community condemns damage to the environment in times of armed conflict. The Draft Articles on State Responsibility prepared by the International Law Commission, for example, included mass pollution of the biosphere in the category of international crimes.[31] Principle 26 of the 1972 Stockholm Declaration on the Human Environment avows that the environment must be protected from all means of mass destruction.[32] The 1982 World Charter for Nature states that "nature shall be secured against degradation caused by warfare and other hostile activities" (in Article 5) and that "military activities damaging to nature shall be avoided" (in Article 20).[33]

The ICRC argues that, "under certain circumstances, such [environmental] destruction is punishable as a grave breach of international humanitarian law" and that, "in the event of breaches of rules of international humanitarian law protecting the environment, measures shall be taken to stop any such violation and to prevent further breaches".[34] Although the ICRC does not specify by whom such measures should be taken, the Security Council has already claimed, by other actions, competence to prevent, halt or punish breaches of international humanitarian law. The Council has also stated quite clearly that "the perpetrators of ... serious violations of international humanitarian law should be brought to justice".[35] ENMOD specifically invokes the Security Council in cases of default on the Convention's provisions. Under Article 5, states can bring a complaint to the Security Council, which is then entitled to undertake an investigation in response to such complaints. Parties to the Convention are required to provide support or assistance to any other party requesting it, if the Security Council decides that harm has been or is likely to be caused, although the nature of that support or assistance is not specified.

The Security Council has acted specifically on concern for the environmental consequences of warfare, most notably in the case of the 1990 Gulf War and Iraq's burning of Kuwaiti oil wells and the deliberate spill of oil into the Persian Gulf. Security Council Resolution 687 confirmed, in clause 16, that Iraq was "liable under international law for any direct loss, damage – including environmental damage and depletion of natural resources – or injury to foreign governments, nationals and corporations as a result of its unlawful invasion and occupation of Kuwait".[36] The Compensation Commission, later established under Resolution 692, awarded Kuwait compensation in the sum of US$610 million. This has been defined as "the first determination under international law of a state's liability for harm to the environment itself" in the context of armed conflict.[37] It is the only example thus far of the Security Council acting to hold a state accountable for environmental destruction in times of armed conflict. It does, however, reinforce the view that "environmental destruction outside the permissible bounds of the laws of warfare constitutes an act of aggression, breach of peace or threat to international peace and security" and that the Security Council has a mandate to act in such circumstances.[38]

Environmental threats to peace and security

It is less clear, however, whether the Security Council has or should have a mandate to act against more general environmental threats to peace and security or, in an even broader context, to act against environmental pariah states or to enforce compliance with international environmental law.

The proposition that the Security Council has or should have a mandate to deploy force on environmental grounds has been explored at some length, usually by analogy with the expansion of the mandate on other grounds. Former British Admiral of the Fleet, Sir Julian Oswald, anticipated that Chapter VII powers might accommodate a traditional coercive role for militaries (individually or collectively) in the face of environmental insecurities. Oswald perceived this as an enlargement of "that laudable sense of general responsibilities expressed by the current UN actions based on human rights violations".[39] Crispin Tickell, a former UN diplomat, has also suggested that "environmental problems in one country affecting the interests of another could easily come within the purview of the Security Council". Such action, he suggests, is "no less likely than a force to rid the world of weapons which could threaten [hu]-mankind and compel respect for the rules of the international community".[40] A report for the Environmental Change and Security Project at the Woodrow Wilson Center identified the threat of force "to compel compliance ... on environmental agreements" as one of a number of ways in which military assets could be used to address environmental challenges.[41]

In the absence of actual armed conflict, the Security Council would need to determine under Article 39 that environmental degradation or some action with environmental consequences constituted a non-military threat to international peace and security. Under the Charter, the Security Council has the authority and responsibility to respond to complaints concerning a threat to the peace brought before it by a member state. Thus member states themselves can determine that environmental disputes between or among them are likely to constitute a threat to the peace, in this case because they might lead or have led to armed conflict. The Secretary-General is also able to bring to the Council's attention matters that, in his/her opinion, are a threat to international peace and security.

The grounds for a mandate for the Security Council to act in such cases have been assumed to rely on states' individual or collective right to self-defence, in this case against environmentally destructive activities that have a trans-boundary impact. Murphy argues that the right of self-defence enshrined in Article 51 of the UN Charter can be taken to include defence against environmental threats under *jus ad bellum*.[42] He suggests that "there is little doubt" that the Security Council "holds the legal authority to respond to serious environmental disasters with military force pursuant to its enforcement powers".[43] As noted earlier, there is considerable evidence that governments now view environmental degradation as crucial to their broader security interests. The International Court of Justice has also identified "ecological balance" as central to the "essential interests of all states".[44] But this is probably insufficient to establish a mandate for the Security Council to take action on the grounds of environmental collective self-defence in the absence of armed conflict.

Such a right *might* be strengthened if the Security Council were to issue a decision that environmental practices with severe consequences constitute a threat to international peace and security and are contrary to the purposes of the Charter, as it has done on terrorism for example. Under Article 25, member states agree to accept and carry out Council decisions (which are, in theory at least, made on behalf of the international community). Expansion of the Security Council mandate to take action in cases of environmental self-defence encounters the same "dilemma of intervention" that Secretary-General Annan has identified in humanitarian situations.[45] Yet "sovereignty" and "consent" are concepts and practices made fragile by the transnational and global environmental consequences of activities within states. Environmental degradation blurs the distinction between domestic and international jurisdictions. Further, the view that states, or more particularly political regimes or governments, *lose* their sovereign right to non-intervention and legitimate statehood in cases of gross human rights abuses could, in such circumstances, be extended to environmental degradation and the potentially non-derogable norm of planetary trust.

The problem here rests on whether international environmental law provides a normative or legal basis for such directives. This body of law articulates a number of principles that suggest that states are bound by a global environmental obligation. These principles include the Precautionary Principle and the requirement that states should not cause damage to the environment of other states or to areas beyond national jurisdiction. If these principles *were* determined to have achieved the status of customary international law or peremptory norms from which no derogation is permitted, this might allow the Security Council to claim that the "fundamental values of the international community" were being violated.[46]

However, this is complicated further by the fact that environmental treaties generally do not forbid practices with trans-boundary environmental consequences. Rather they seek to regulate them and to manage their impact. Nor is there anything within this legislative framework that mandates the Security Council to determine whether there has been a breach of an international environmental agreement or whether such a breach constitutes a threat to the environment in a way analogous to its Article 39 powers to determine a breach of the peace or a threat to international peace and security. There are also political dangers in expanding the Security Council mandate on what are as yet quite shaky legal and normative grounds. Tinker, for example, is concerned that such action would likely reflect the interests of the permanent members of the Security Council, or could run the risk of authorizing states to pursue unilateral and punitive military action on environmental grounds.[47] In general, commentators have been cautious about a role for the Security Council where member states are in dispute over issues related to environmental degradation but where there is no obvious threat to peace. Such issues should be dealt with under the appropriate mechanisms established by relevant multilateral agreements or under the auspices of other agencies within the United Nations.[48]

The deployment of force and military strength is itself contentious as a modality for responding to environmental scarcity and insecurity, even in the context of a response to armed conflict. Military intervention could itself result in further environmental damage. Such deployment might be able to halt any further environmentally destructive behaviour on the part of aggressors (whether states or other actors), but it has limited or no utility as a strategy for environmental repair. It also runs the risk of focusing on symptoms rather than causes. And, as the World Commission on Environment and Development observed, "there are no military solutions to environmental insecurity".[49]

Intervention of this kind, however, is not the only modality available to the Security Council. Indeed, military action and the use of force under Chapter VII are intended to be a *last* resort, in general accordance with the laws of war. The Security Council has a number of other options. The Council can investigate and mediate, appoint special representatives or request the Secretary-General to do so. It can determine the principles upon which peaceful settlement should be reached. It can employ its "good offices" in times of environmental dispute. Article 36(3) of the UN Charter allows the Security Council to encourage parties to a legal dispute, which would include those relating to treaties on the environment and resources, to seek arbitration from the International Court of Justice. Under Article 41, the Council may recommend sanctions or the severance of diplomatic relations. Sanctions in particular have been identified as a "particularly effective measure for environmental delinquencies".[50] Nevertheless, as the imposition of economic sanctions against Iraq demonstrated, sanctions tend to affect the poorest and most vulnerable in the target state and could, in fact, exacerbate environmental degradation and its impact on human security rather than mitigating it.

Rapid deployment in environmental emergencies

Malone suggests that the "legitimisation of Security Council authority in environmental management can and should begin with the relatively modest, but compelling proposal that environmental emergencies be absorbed into its sphere of activity".[51] This echoes proposals such as those of the Swiss government for the establishment of a Green Cross to parallel the Red Cross, or suggestions by the Organization for Security and Co-operation in Europe for some form of "green helmets" as a counterpart to the United Nations' peacekeeping/making "blue helmets". There is a history, although not a very well-known one, of the United Nations responding to concerns about environmental emergencies that might provide a basis for Security Council authority or action. In 1991, the United Nations Environment Programme (UNEP) established a pilot UN Centre for Urgent Environmental Assistance.[52] In general, however, the Security Council does not, and probably should not, have a role in environmental emergencies except to the extent that they can be determined to fit within its role in humanitarian intervention or as a result of conflict or extreme violence or when such emergencies are bound up in disputes. Environmental emergencies have become the responsibility of the Joint Environment Unit established and run by UNEP and the Office for the Coordination of Humanitarian Affairs, supported by the Advisory Group on Environmental Emergencies. The unit provides an "integrated United Nations emergency response capacity to activate and provide international assistance to countries facing environmental emergencies".[53] It is notable, however, that the Security Council is not represented on the Advisory Group.

A mandate for preventive environmental security

In the past decade, the United Nations in general and the Security Council in particular have paid considerably more attention to the importance to peace and security of preventive action and preventive diplomacy that address the root causes of conflict. The Secretary-General has confirmed that these deep-rooted causes of conflict include environmental ones and that conflict prevention is one of the primary obligations of member states.[54] Both the Secretary-General and the Security Council have accepted that conflict prevention and sustainable and equitable development (which includes environmental protection) are mutually reinforcing activities. The Secretary-General has challenged the Security Council to consider how prevention could be made a more tangible dimension of its day-to-day work.[55] Indeed, the Security Council has committed itself, in Resolution 1366, to "pursue the objective of prevention of armed conflict as an integral part of its primary responsibility for the maintenance of international peace and security".[56]

The Secretary-General has identified a number of strategies, especially under Chapter VI of the Charter, by which the Security Council might enhance its contribution to preventive diplomacy. These include the consideration of periodic reports from the Secretary-General on issues likely to constitute potential threats (including natural resources) and the expansion of Security Council fact-finding missions.[57] At present, a number of factors militate against the Security Council taking a more active role in preventive diplomacy. Any such role would require a strengthening of the Secretariat's early warning capacity. Greater attention would have to be given to the provision of "timely and in-depth briefings" from the Secretariat under Article 99 of the Charter. In general, the Council's role is likely to be confined primarily to operational rather than structural prevention, focusing on "measures applicable in the face of immediate crises" and those that are "implemented as a preventive or peacebuilding response to problems that could lead to the outbreak or recurrence of violent conflict".[58]

The Secretary-General has also suggested that the Security Council's role in preventive diplomacy might require the development of new mechanisms, which could include informal working groups or other forms of subsidiary organs. Article 29 allows the Security Council to establish such subsidiary organs as it deems necessary for the performance of its functions. Under this article, the Council has established two Standing Committees and three Ad Hoc Committees. Both Standing Committees focus on procedural matters and it seems unlikely that agreement would be reached to establish a Standing Committee with a focus on policy such as environment and development.[59] Two of the three Ad Hoc Committees do have a policy focus but were established in conjunction with specific Security Council resolutions.[60] The Security Council Committee on Terrorism, comprising only representatives of those UN members that are already permanently or temporarily on the Security Council, was established under paragraphs 6 and 7 of Resolution 1373.[61] It is required to monitor implementation of the resolution, which includes a requirement that member states provide reports on their actions to give effect to Resolution 1373. Beyond that, however, it is charged with delineating its own tasks and work programme. In the policy sphere of environment and sustainable development, it is important that a Security Council committee, were it to be established, not duplicate competence elsewhere. For example, the Commission on Sustainable Development is charged with monitoring implementation (with emphasis on *Agenda 21*) and calling for reports. There is also the danger that any new committee would become just one more "talking shop" (a charge levied at the Commission on Sustainable Development) or duplicate the power imbalances and political interests of the Council's members.

Post-conflict peace-building

As part of the reinvigorated focus on prevention, the Security Council has emphasized the importance of social reconstruction in post-conflict peace-building, which includes "fostering sustainable institutions and processes in areas such as sustainable development".[62] As an example, the Secretary-General has observed that "access to land-based resources by the poor" can "help to prevent conflicts that are based on or related to tensions over limited [or degraded] natural resources".[63] This is important also because the environmental as well as social consequences of armed conflict frequently act as a barrier to such social reconstruction and economic rehabilitation. For example, 80 per cent of Angola's farmland was abandoned during the civil war because of the extent of landmine infestation. During the conflict in Burundi, food production, which was already inadequate, dropped a further 17 per cent.[64]

The importance of sustainable development as a key component of Security Council mandates for peace-building and social reconstruction in disrupted states is not in doubt. A few examples will suffice. In his letter to the Security Council of June 1999 on the Council's mandate in Guinea-Bissau, the Secretary-General referred to the overall goal of "restoring peace and sustainable development" in that country.[65] Resolution 1318 on an effective role for the Security Council in maintaining international peace and security (particularly in Africa) reaffirms its "determination ... to give special attention to the promotion of durable peace and sustainable development in Africa".[66] The mandate for the United Nations Transitional Administration in East Timor (UNTAET), authorized under Chapter VII of the Charter and set out in Resolution 1272, includes assisting "in the establishment of the conditions for sustainable development".[67] Resolution 1346, which extended the life of the United Nations Mission in Sierra Leone (UNAMSIL), referred in the preamble to the importance for peace and sustainable development of the "legitimate exploitation of the natural resources ... for the benefit of its people", although it is quite likely that, in this particular context, the natural resources in question were diamonds.[68] Similarly, resolutions on Cambodia (see Resolution 792 for example[69]) included references to the importance of regulations on the use of natural resources, including support from member states for a moratorium on the export of logs. The challenge is one of expertise, an issue returned to below.

Although mandates for peacekeeping and peace-building missions, including transitional authorities, identify sustainable development as a goal, they rarely specify that the peacekeeping or intervention forces must themselves adhere to relevant environmental principles and multilateral environmental agreements. This is in contrast, for example, to the now regular injunction in Security Council resolutions that "Member States ... incorporate HIV/AIDS awareness training into their national programmes in preparation for deployment".[70] Or, as with Resolution 1270 on Sierra Leone, the requirement that the UN mission there include personnel with "appropriate training in international humanitarian, human rights and refugee law, including child and gender-related provisions, negotiation and communication skills, cultural awareness and civilian–military coordination".[71] Yet this is particularly important because, as the Secretary-General has observed, "humanitarian action can have important ... environmental repercussions".[72]

In 1994, the ICRC presented to the Secretary-General draft "Guidelines for Military Manuals and Instructions on the Protection of the Environment in Times of Armed Conflict". These were later attached to the Secretary-General's report on the UN Decade of International Law, and General Assembly Resolution 49/50[73] invited states to disseminate these guidelines widely and to give "due consideration" to incorporating them into their military manuals.[74] A study for the Millennium Project of the American Council for the United Nations University confirmed that "no mandates or instructions regarding environmental security in the theater were included in any Council resolution".[75] The only formal statement is found in the Secretary-General's Bulletin on the observance by United Nations forces of international humanitarian law, dated August 1999. Paragraph 6.3 states that "the UN force is prohibited from employing methods of warfare ... which are intended or may be expected to cause widespread, long-term and severe damage to the natural environment".[76] In general, the attention given to environmental protection by forces under a UN mandate varies depending on the extent to which such issues are accounted for in contributing countries' military manuals. Environmental protection, including clean-up on departure, seems not to have been well managed by UN forces. In some cases, "host" countries of UN missions have sought some form of financial compensation from the United Nations for environmental damage caused in the execution of a Security Council mandated mission.[77]

International environmental governance

The Security Council's likely mandate to act in response to environmental threats fits well with Secretary-General Kofi Annan's strategies for "freedom from fear" outlined in his *Millennium Report* and identified in the introduction to this chapter. The Council's environmental mandate, as it applies to peace and security, can or could best be expanded in the following areas:

- appropriate action to enforce the environmental dimensions of international humanitarian law, the laws of war and war crimes;
- the potential imposition of economic or other sanctions in response to severe "environmental delinquencies";
- a contribution to environmental conflict prevention and preventive diplomacy as part of the development of a culture of prevention within the United Nations;
- reinforcing and supporting sustainable development and environmental protection in post-conflict peace-building and social reconstruction;
- including environmental guidelines in the rules of engagement and deployment for UN-mandated forces, including transitional authorities and observer missions.

The central question is how the expansion of the Security Council's mandate in this way could contribute to the overall functioning of the system of international environmental governance.

Approaches to international environmental governance

Oran Young argues that "an effective governance system is one that channels behavior in such a way as to eliminate or substantially ameliorate the problem that led to its creation".[78] The expansion of the Security Council mandate to accommodate environmental "threats" (broadly defined) could contribute to this goal in two ways. The first is functional, particularly through a commitment to environmental protection in times of armed conflict and through the pursuit of sustainable development in post-conflict reconstruction. The second is normative. An expanded mandate for the Security Council might contribute further to dismantling the separation between so-called global "welfare" issues and global security policy and to strengthening international commitment to the Precautionary Principle and norms of global stewardship.

Under Article 24 of the UN Charter, the rationale for authority to be delegated to the Security Council is to ensure prompt and effective action. However, prompt and effective action in accordance with an expanded mandate – and thus the enhancement of international environmental governance – will be difficult absent Security Council reform. Such reform needs to take account of demands for democratization, more equitable representation, transparency and accountability.[79] There are two reasons. First, as Ambassador Hasmy Agam of Malaysia has observed, "the working method and procedure of the Council constrain innovative action".[80] Second, without Security Council reform, the risk is high that various forms of environmental intervention become caught up in the geopolitics and charges of selective intervention and "liberal western imperialism" that have been levied at humanitarian intervention.

In pursuing an environmental mandate, the Security Council will also need to develop more effective working relations with other agents of environmental governance within and outside the United Nations. This will obviously include the United Nations Environment Programme but will also likely include the Commission on Sustainable Development, relevant General Assembly committees, and a range of non-governmental actors. This will be essential to enhance the Security Council's contribution to environmental preventive security, to ensure that the appropriate expertise is available for fact-finding missions, to monitor compliance with international environmental law, and to strengthen the environmental dimensions of UN peacekeeping operations. Again, this could enhance international environmental governance by ensuring that global or international environmental decision-making is more fully integrated across a range of policy concerns and institutional actors. However, this would require better coordination across the United Nations than presently exists in the area of environment and development.

It is crucial, however, that an expanded Security Council mandate gives greater priority to preventive and reconstructive Chapter VI powers rather than to coercive Chapter VII powers. The "securitization" of environmental issues in the Security Council may help to "generate concern at the top level for the threats to the global environment".[81] However, the militarization of environmental policy, should Security Council attention come to focus primarily on coercive measures, is an inappropriate long-term methodology for responding to environmental insecurity and scarcity. Such coercive measures are not directed towards environmental repair or mitigation. They also run the risk of creating further environmental damage or exacerbating the root causes of conflict, as well as authorizing the unilateral deployment of force in response to environmental threats.

Interface between policy and science

The legitimacy of an expanded environmental mandate for the Security Council will be enhanced if its actions are based on the best scientific information available in areas in which the Council seeks to establish competence. Security Council fact-finding missions must now include scientific evaluation of environmental harm as well as a social science analysis of the likely impact of such harm on conflict and insecurity (including human insecurity). The implementation of the environmental components of international humanitarian law will require careful assessment of the environmental impact of armed conflict and the development of a body of expertise in making such assessment.[82] Security Council mandated peacekeeping missions and transitional peace-building arrangements will need to involve and coordinate expertise in environmental repair and sustainable development.

Financing

An expanded mandate for the Security Council draws attention again to the inadequacy of funding for international environmental governance and sustainable development and for peacekeeping, peace-making and peace-building. Preventive environmental diplomacy cannot be achieved without adequate and stable funds. Yet, as the Secretary-General has observed, the Secretariat has "regularly encountered difficulties in securing financial and human resources in a timely fashion" to support Security Council missions.[83] It is important to recognize again that preventive security (or what former US Secretary of Defense Perry called "preventive defense"[84]) is less costly than coercive interventions in times of armed conflict or as punitive action against environmental dispute or environmental destruction.

Participation levels

The Security Council is notoriously closed in its policy deliberations. The issue of participation challenges Security Council practice and the legitimacy of an expanded environmental mandate on two levels. The first is the extent to which the Council itself is broadly representative of the international community of states. This has become a central theme in debates about Security Council reform, as it is in demands for reform of the United Nations more generally. The second level is that of non-state stakeholder participation. Strategies for expanding the Security Council's environmental mandate will work only if the articulation and implementation of Council decisions recognize the important contribution of a range of actors, including local communities and civil society organizations, the scientific community and the private sector. Security is no longer the purview of the military and strategic community alone. This is especially important in post-conflict peace-building and a new emphasis on sustainable development and environmental protection that requires greater attention to effective civil–military relations in UN missions.

Policy influence

An expanded environmental mandate for the Security Council could have an important role to play in influencing the policy milieu and actor behaviour at the global, regional, national and local levels. The potential for Chapter VII action in times of armed conflict or threats to peace and security could provide incentives (albeit negative ones) for compliance with the environmental (as well as other) components of international humanitarian law or the laws of war. In the context of broader Security Council and UN reform, smaller states could be made to feel more secure in the knowledge that a fair and effective Security Council will act to implement collective environmental security, by which the international community condemns environmentally destructive behaviour. The more effective incorporation of environmental guidelines in Security Council rules of engagement and deployment would provide models for national defence forces to adopt such guidelines in their own military manuals. Further, Security Council decisions that reinforce the importance of sustainable development for post-conflict peace-building, if properly resourced, would enhance capacity-building and technology transfer. The Security Council also has an important role in building international norms, including those on the environment. Security Council decisions, under both Chapters VI and VII, could contribute to the strengthening of international environmental law, including compliance and enforcement strategies, and to a more effective normative commitment to the Precautionary Principle, extraterritorial stewardship and sustainable development.

Notes

1. Sara Parkin, "Environment and Security: Issues and Agenda", *Disarmament Forum*, No. 1, 1999, p. 45.
2. Bardo Fassbender, "Quis judicabit? The Security Council, Its Powers and Its Legal Control", *European Journal of International Law*, Vol. 11, No. 1, 2000, p. 219.
3. United Nations Secretary-General, *Millennium Report*, A/54/2000, 2000, pp. 44–53.
4. The UN mission in Somalia, established in 1992, was the first where the Security Council had authorized an intervention on humanitarian grounds without sovereign consent.
5. United Nations Security Council, *Statement by the President of the Security Council*, S/PRST/2000/25, 20 July 2000, p. 1.
6. Alexandre S. Timoshenko, "Ecological Security: Response to Global Challenges", in Edith Brown Weiss, ed., *Environmental Change and International Law: New Challenges and Dimensions*, Tokyo: United Nations University Press, 1992, p. 423. The idea that environmental concerns should be figured into national security calculations, particularly those of the United States, has an earlier provenance; see, for example, Lester Brown, *Redefining National Security*, Worldwatch Paper No. 14, Washington, D.C.: Worldwatch Institute, 1977; and Richard H. Ullman, "Redefining Security", *International Security*, Vol. 8, No. 1, 1983, pp. 129–153.
7. World Commission on Environment and Development (WCED), *Our Common Future*, Oxford: Oxford University Press, 1987, p. 292.
8. For more on these issues and debates surrounding them, see, *inter alia*, Geoffrey D. Dabelko and David D. Dabelko, "Environmental Security: Issues of Concept and Redefi-

nition", *Environment and Security*, Vol. 1, No. 1, 1996, pp. 23–49; Norman Myers, *Ultimate Security: The Environmental Basis of Political Stability*, Washington, D.C.: Island Press, 1996; Thomas Homer-Dixon, *Environment, Scarcity and Violence*, Princeton, NJ: Princeton University Press, 1999; Lorraine Elliott, "What Is Environmental Security: A Conceptual Overview", in Alan Dupont, ed., *The Environment and Security: What Are the Linkages?*, Canberra Papers on Strategy and Defence No. 125, Canberra: Strategic and Defence Studies Centre, Australian National University, 1998; Lorraine Elliott, "Environmental Security", in William T. Tow, Ramesh Thakur and Taek Hyun, eds, *Asia's Emerging Regional Order: Reconciling "Traditional" and "Human" Security*, Tokyo: United Nations University Press, 2000.

9. Mohammed Ayoob, "The Security Problematic of the Third World", *World Politics*, Vol. 43, No. 2, 1991, p. 259.

10. Daniel Deudney, "The Case against Linking Environmental Degradation and National Security", *Millennium*, Vol. 19, No. 1, 1990, p. 461.

11. WCED, *Our Common Future*, p. 19.

12. *Rio Declaration on Environment and Development*, Report of the United Nations Conference on Environment and Development, A/CONF.151/6 (Vol. I), Annex I, 12 August 1992.

13. Kent Hughes Butts, "Why the Military Is Good for the Environment", in Jyrki Käkönen, ed., *Green Security or Militarised Environment*, Aldershot: Dartmouth Publishing, 1994, p. 86.

14. Gregory D. Foster, "Environmental Security: The Search for Strategic Legitimacy", *Armed Forces and Society*, Vol. 27, No. 3, 2001, pp. 384–385. Foster also reports that the US Central Intelligence Agency now has an environmental centre whose responsibilities include "monitoring and assessing the role played by the environment in country and regional instability and conflict" (p. 387).

15. Christopher T. Timura, "Environmental Conflict: and the Social Life of Environmental Security Discourse", *Anthropological Quarterly*, Vol. 74, No. 3, 2001, p. 104.

16. North Atlantic Treaty Organization, *The NATO Handbook*, Brussels: NATO, 1996, available at ⟨http://www.nato.int/docu/handbook/index.htm#3⟩. NATO's Committee on the Challenges of Modern Society (CCMS), which was established in 1969 to give the Alliance a "social dimension", focuses primarily on environmental protection and quality of life, including defence-related environmental problems (see ⟨http://www.nato.int/ccms/info.htm⟩).

17. United Nations Secretary-General, *An Agenda for Peace: Preventive Diplomacy, Peacemaking and Peace-keeping*, Report of the Secretary-General Pursuant to the Statement Adopted by the Summit Meeting of the Security Council on 31 January 1992, New York: United Nations, p. 5.

18. UN Secretary-General, *Millennium Report*, p. 44.

19. United Nations Security Council, *Statement by the President*, A/47/253, 31 January 1992.

20. United Nations Security Council, Resolution 688, S/RES/688, 5 April 1991, and Resolution 794, S/RES/794, 3 December 1992.

21. United Nations Secretary-General, *Report on the Causes of Conflict and the Promotion of Durable Peace and Sustainable Development in Africa*, S/1998/318, 13 April 1998, para. 15.

22. Commission on Global Governance, *Our Global Neighbourhood*, Oxford: Oxford University Press, 1995, p. 95.

23. Nathan Ruff, Robert Chamberlain and Alexandra Cousteau, *Report on Applying Military and Security Assets to Environmental Problems*, Environmental Change and Security Project Report No. 3, Washington, D.C.: Woodrow Wilson International Center for Scholars, 1997, p. 89.

24. Foster, "Environmental Security".
25. United Nations Development Programme, *Human Development Report*, Oxford: Oxford University Press, 1994.
26. A number of Understandings adopted as part of the negotiating record set out definitions of each of these criteria: "widespread" is interpreted as encompassing an area of several hundred square kilometres; "long-lasting" means for a "period of months"; and "severe" indicates "serious or significant disruption or harm to human life, natural and economic resources or other assets"; cf. Protocol I to the 1949 Geneva Conventions, which identifies long-term as "measured in decades".
27. Merrit P. Drucker, "The Military Commander's Responsibility for the Environment", *Environmental Ethics*, Vol. 11, No. 2, 1989, p. 145.
28. *Rome Statute of the International Criminal Court*, A/CONF.183/9, 17 July 1998.
29. International Committee of the Red Cross (ICRC), "International Committee of the Red Cross Guidelines for Military Manuals and Instructions on the Protection of the Environment in Times of Armed Conflict", *Review of European Community and International Environmental Law*, Vol. 9, No. 1, 2000, p. 80.
30. United Nations General Assembly, *Protection of the Environment in Times of Armed Conflict*, A/RES/47/37, 25 November 1992.
31. Timoshenko, "Ecological Security", p. 437.
32. *Declaration of the United Nations Conference on the Human Environment*, A/CONF.48/14, 16 June 1972.
33. United Nations General Assembly, *World Charter for Nature*, A/RES/37/7, 28 October 1982.
34. ICRC, "International Committee of the Red Cross Guidelines", pp. 80–82.
35. United Nations Security Council, Resolution 1318, *Declaration on Ensuring an Effective Role for the Security Council in the Maintenance of International Peace and Security, Particularly in Africa*, S/RES/1318, 2000, p. 3.
36. United Nations Security Council, Resolution 687, S/RES/687, 3 April 1991, para. 16.
37. Catherine Tinker, "'Environmental Security' in the United Nations: Not a Matter for the Security Council", *Tennessee Law Review*, Vol. 59, No. 4, 1992, p. 789.
38. Linda A. Malone, "'Green Helmets': A Conceptual Framework for Security Council Authority in Environmental Emergencies", *Michigan Journal of International Law*, Vol. 17, No. 2, 1996, p. 523.
39. Julian Oswald, "Defence and Environmental Security", in Gwyn Prins, ed., *Threats without Enemies*, London: Earthscan, 1993, p. 118.
40. Crispin Tickell, "The Inevitability of Environmental Security", in Prins, ed., *Threats without Enemies*, p. 23.
41. Ruff et al., *Report on Applying Military and Security Assets to Environmental Problems*, p. 83.
42. Michael K. Murphy, "Achieving Economic Security with Swords as Ploughshares: The Modern Use of Force to Combat Environmental Degradation", *Virginia Journal of International Law*, Vol. 39, No. 4, 1999, pp. 1181–1219.
43. Ibid., p. 1197.
44. Ibid., p. 1192.
45. UN Secretary-General, *Millennium Report*, pp. 47–48.
46. Brendan Reilly, "'Clear and Present Danger': A Role for the United Nations Security Council in Protecting the Global Environment", *Melbourne University Law Review*, Vol. 20, No. 3, 1996, p. 767.
47. Tinker, "'Environmental Security' in the United Nations", pp. 787–801. Malone, "'Green Helmets'", p. 525. Malone also draws attention to the dangers that "ecological

self-help or ecological self-defence" will cloak "expanded assertions of state authority to engage in unilateral or collective measures" (p. 525).

48. In 1997, for example, US Ambassador John McDonald suggested that the United Nations establish an environmental mediation programme, which, as well as training environmental mediators, would set up a panel of expert mediators to help resolve trans-boundary environmental disputes (see Joe B. Sills, Jerome C. Glenn, Theodore J. Gordon and Renat Perelet, *Environmental Security: United Nations Doctrine for Managing Environmental Issues in Military Action*, report prepared for the Millennium Project of the American Council for the United Nations University, n.d.; available at ⟨http://www.acunu.org/millennium/es-un-chapt4.html⟩).

49. WCED, *Our Common Future*, p. 19.

50. Malone, "'Green Helmets'", p. 532. Szasz makes a similar point, arguing that "the use of collective economic pressures under article 41 might be more effective in respect of environmental offences" (Paul C. Szasz, "Restructuring the International Organisational Framework", in Weiss, ed., *Environmental Change and International Law*, p. 360, fn 61).

51. Malone, "'Green Helmets'", p. 532.

52. Ibid.

53. Advisory Group on Environmental Emergencies, *Note by the Secretariat: Practical Results*, EU/AG/21, 16 October 2000, para 1.

54. UN Secretary-General, *Millennium Report*, p. 2.

55. See Hasmy Agam, "The Role of the Security Council in the Prevention of Armed Conflict", 20 July 2000 (filed at Global Policy Forum: ⟨http://www.igc.apc.org/globalpolicy/security/reform/membstat/0007maly.htm⟩).

56. United Nations Security Council, Resolution 1366, S/RES/1366, 30 August 2001, clause 1. In a statement early in 2001, the President of the Security Council expressed the Council's view that "the quest for peace requires a comprehensive, concerted and determined approach that addresses the root causes of conflict" (United Nations Security Council, Statement by the President of the Security Council, *Peacebuilding: Towards a Comprehensive Approach*, S/PRST/2001/5, 20 February 2001, p. 1).

57. United Nations Secretary-General, *Prevention of Armed Conflict: Report of the Secretary General*, A/55/985; S/2001/574, New York: United Nations Security Council, 7 June 2001, p. 12.

58. Ibid., p. 7. Structural prevention, on the other hand, encompasses longer-term development and humanitarian measures that seek to prevent crises arising in the first place or to prevent them from recurring.

59. The two Standing Committees are the Committee of Experts on Rules of Procedure and the Committee on Admission of New Members.

60. The two Ad Hoc Committees with a policy focus are the Governing Council of the UN Compensation Commission established by Security Council Resolution 692 (S/RES/692, 20 May 1991) and the Committee established pursuant to Resolution 1373 (S/RES/1373, 28 September 2001) concerning counter-terrorism.

61. United Nations Security Council, Resolution 1373.

62. Statement by the President of the Security Council, *Peacebuilding*, p. 2.

63. UN Secretary-General, *Prevention of Armed Conflict*, p. 26.

64. Ibid., p. 6.

65. United Nations Secretary-General, Letter from the Secretary-General addressed to the President of the Security Council, S/1999/737, 30 June 1999.

66. United Nations Security Council, *Declaration on Ensuring an Effective Role for the Security Council in the Maintenance of International Peace and Security, Particularly in Africa*, p. 2.

67. United Nations Security Council, Resolution 1272, S/RES/1272, 25 October 1999, clause 2(f).
68. United Nations Security Council, Resolution 1346, S/RES/1346, 30 March 2001.
69. United Nations Security Council, Resolution 792, S/RES/792, 30 November 1992.
70. United Nations Security Council, Resolution 1327, *Strengthening United Nations Peace-keeping Operations*, S/RES/1327, 13 November 2000, p. 3.
71. United Nations Security Council, Resolution 1270, S/RES/1270, 22 October 1999, clause 15.
72. UN Secretary-General, *Report on the Causes of Conflict and the Promotion of Durable Peace and Sustainable Development in Africa*, para. 48; see also para. 56.
73. General Assembly Resolution 49/50, *United Nations Decade of International Law*, A/RES/49/50, 9 December 1994.
74. ICRC, "International Committee of the Red Cross Guidelines", pp. 80–82. The ICRC later produced a model draft military manual that incorporated the guidelines; see Jean-Marie Henckaerts, "Towards Better Protection for the Environment in Armed Conflict: Recent Developments in International Humanitarian Law", *Review of European Community and International Environmental Law*, Vol. 9, No. 1, 2000, pp. 13–19.
75. Sills et al., *Environmental Security*, section 1.2, available at ⟨http://www.acunu.org/millennium/es-un-chapt1.html⟩.
76. Secretary-General's Bulletin, *Observance by United Nations Forces of International Humanitarian Law*, ST/SGB/1999/13, 6 August 1999.
77. Ibid.
78. Oran Young, *International Governance: Protecting the Environment in a Stateless Society*, Ithaca, NY: Cornell University, 1994, p. 30.
79. For a brief introduction to these issues, see, *inter alia*, Michael J. Kelly, "UN Security Council Permanent Membership: A New Proposal for a Twenty-First Century Council", *Seton Hall Law Review*, Vol. 31, 2000, pp. 319–407, and James A. Paul, "Security Council Reform: Arguments about the Future of the United Nations System", Global Policy Forum, 1995, at ⟨http://www.igc.apc.org/globalpolicy/security/pubs/secref.htm⟩.
80. Agam, "The Role of the Security Council in the Prevention of Armed Conflict", para. 5.
81. Nico Schrijver, "International Organisation for Environmental Security", *Bulletin of Peace Proposals*, Vol. 20, No. 2, 1989, p. 116.
82. UNEP was closely involved in the Security Council commission established to determine compensation for Kuwait after the invasion by Iraq. The bombing campaign in Kosovo prompted UNEP and the UN Centre for Human Settlements (HABITAT) to undertake a formal assessment of the environmental consequences. The Balkans Task Force (BTF) identified a number of direct and indirect environmental and related humanitarian consequences of the Kosovo conflict. NGOs with an interest in armed conflict and environmental degradation include Green Cross International and the Institute for International Cooperative Environmental Research (IICER), which works closely with NATO on environmental protection and security.
83. UN Secretary-General, *Prevention of Armed Conflict*, p. 34.
84. Ashton B. Carter and William J. Perry, *Preventive Defense: A New Security Strategy for America*, Washington, D.C.: Brookings Institution Press, March 1999.

Index

227